Walter C. Patterson was born in Canada in 1936. He took a postgraduate degree in nuclear physics at the University of Manitoba. In 1960 he moved to Britain, where he became involved in environmental issues. He joined the staff of Friends of the Earth in London in 1972, was their energy specialist until 1978 and was their lead witness at the Windscale Inquiry. Since 1978 he has been an independent commentator and consultant, dealing with energy and nuclear policy issues. He is energy consultant to Friends of the Earth, and was a witness at the Sizewell Inquiry. He is a regular contributor to a number of publications, including *New Scientist* and *The Guardian*, and he also appears on radio and television. He is an editorial advisor to the *Bulletin of the Atomic Scientists*. Walter C. Patterson is the author of *Nuclear Power* (1976, and since updated), *The Fissile Society* (1977) and *Fluidized Bed Energy Technology: Coming to a Boil* (1978).

The Plutonium Business

and the Spread of the Bomb

Walter C. Patterson
(*for the Nuclear Control Institute*)

Sierra Club Books   San Francisco

Copyright © 1984 by Nuclear Control Institute
All rights reserved. No part of this book may be reproduced in any form or by any electronic or mechanical means, including information storage and retrieval systems, without permission in writing from the publisher. Originally published in Great Britain by Paladin Books, Granada Publishing Ltd., London.

Library of Congress Cataloging in Publication Data

Patterson, Walter C., 1936—
    The plutonium business and the spread of the bomb.

    Bibliography: p.
    Includes index.
    1. Plutonium.   2. Breeder reactors.   3. Nuclear nonproliferation.   I. Title.
TK9360.P38 1984   333.79'24   84-22181
ISBN 0-87156-837-3

Jacket design © 1984 by Lawrence Ratzkin

Printed in the United States of America

10 9 8 7 6 5 4 3 2 1

Contents

Preface

In approaching Walter C. Patterson to write *The Plutonium Business*, Nuclear Control Institute had one basic objective in mind: to simplify and de-mystify for the general public the evolution of plutonium from the rare stuff of atomic bombs to a plentiful civilian fuel that may yet be used in nuclear power plants throughout the world.

The danger is enormous – all the more so because most of the world's citizens are unaware of it. By the turn of the century, less than two decades away, there may be plutonium fuel being trafficked in commerce sufficient to build about 100,000 atomic bombs. This *will* be the situation if those who would make a business out of plutonium get their way.

Who are these people? How did the material used in the Nagasaki bomb become their fuel of the future? How did elected governments in the free world, and the centrally managed governments of the Communist world, come to embrace such a dangerous idea? What is the potential for 'civilian' plutonium being made into weapons by nations or by terrorists? Walt Patterson is ideally suited to answer these questions. He is a physicist and safe-energy specialist long associated with Friends of the Earth UK, who has written extensively on the industrial use of plutonium and has been active in public-interest efforts to block such use throughout the world. He brings to the subject a vast knowledge and first-hand experience, as well as a sense of humour and a point of view.

It will become apparent to the reader that *The Plutonium Business* is not another academic tract on plutonium and nuclear proliferation. This report is intended to engage the reader, overcome apathy and provide some practical suggestions on how to stop the global spread of plutonium before it gets out of control. At the same time, Patterson's study is well documented, including appendices with key documents on plutonium policy and an extensive bibliography for those wishing to pursue the subject.

Nuclear Control Institute is a Washington-based non-profit organization that develops studies and strategies for stopping the spread of nuclear weapons. Curbing the production and use of plutonium is essential to all meaningful nuclear non-proliferation efforts. Yet plutonium proves to be the most intractable proliferation problem, largely because of the mystique that has come to surround this man-made element, as detailed in Patterson's study.

Among the members of the Board of Directors of Nuclear Control Institute is Dr Theodore T. Taylor, once the foremost designer of nuclear fission bombs in the United States arsenal, now a developer of advance solar-energy technology and a leading advocate of stronger safeguards and controls on civilian nuclear technology to prevent misuse for nuclear weapons. Dr Taylor, in the foreword to this report, describes the 'life or death' implications of the widespread use of plutonium. Dr Taylor, who knows as well as anyone how plutonium can be used or misused, is clearly worried. The point of this report is that we all should be worried, lest we perish in our ignorance.

Paul Leventhal
President
Nuclear Control Institute
Washington, DC
May 1984

Foreword

Walt Patterson leads us through the history of mankind's efforts to develop the peaceful uses of plutonium in a world in which at least five nations have made enough nuclear weapons to destroy civilization. It is a history of intertwining boundless enthusiasm and cold fear; advanced technology and familiar human failings; visions of hope and of despair.

Plutonium has been with us since 1940. It was the first artificially produced element made in quantities big enough to be seen with the naked eye. Now there are about 400,000 kilograms worldwide. Roughly half of it has been separated from the radioactive fuel and is in the world's stockpile of nuclear weapons. Several dozen tonnes of separated plutonium are being used for Research and Development and plutonium breeder reactor fuel, or awaiting recycling in non-breeder nuclear power plants. The rest has been produced in civilian power reactors around the world and is still unseparated and stored for eventual separation or disposal.

If present plans for nuclear power are fulfilled, within fifteen years the world's rate of production of plutonium in nuclear power plants will be more than 200,000 kilograms per year. Most of this would be separated from spent fuel and then recycled or used to fuel new breeder reactors, and plutonium in forms that can be easily used for making nuclear weapons will be in hundreds of nuclear facilities and transport vehicles in dozens of countries.

It takes less than 10 kilograms of plutonium from a nuclear power plant to make an atomic bomb that is *now* old fashioned. The information and non-nuclear materials needed to make such bombs are now accessible worldwide.

This is the dual nature of plutonium: it can power cities or it can blow them up.

The record is not auspicious for peace. Many countries capable of making nuclear weapons have not subjected themselves to controls over plutonium under the Non-Proliferation Treaty. It is sometimes argued that the existence of plutonium in a country's nuclear power system has little to do with national decisions to acquire nuclear weapons. If a nation wants nuclear weapons, so the argument goes, it can get the nuclear materials directly, by building 'dedicated' facilities, perhaps secretly, to produce plutonium or highly enriched uranium, rather than diverting plutonium from 'peaceful' facilities already in operation. But this argument is made in the context of a world in which commercial plutonium separated from highly radioactive materials is not commonplace, as it would be if the planned plutonium economies become a major source of power for the world. A decision to make nuclear weapons could be acted on much more rapidly, and yield much greater numbers of nuclear weapons, in a country that is already producing large quantities of separated plutonium than in a country that is not. It has already been revealed that in the United States the use of power-reactor plutonium for increasing stockpiles of plutonium in weapons has received serious consideration. Why should not that temptation be even stronger in a nation that now has no military plutonium, but wants it desperately?

The big question is whether, in the light of the forty-four-year history of plutonium, it can be so controlled worldwide that its growing presence for peaceful uses will not greatly increase the dangers of its destructive use, whether by military forces, terrorists, or criminal blackmailers. The time to ponder this question is now, not after future history has given the answer. The answer may well be a matter of life or death.

Dr Theodore B. Taylor
Damascus, Maryland
May 1984

Introduction: the plutonium rush

The truck pulls up to your house. The driver leans down from the cab and calls to you across the lawn. 'Here's your fuel for the winter – two tons of nitroglycerine. Where do you want it?'

A bizarre scenario? Try this one. Plutonium – a potential nuclear explosive – is now being readied for use all over the world as fuel for nuclear power plants. Some is already in use. The plutonium, which originates in the used fuel from conventional nuclear plants, is separated out of this 'spent' fuel and made into new fuel. Some of this new plutonium fuel will be used in conventional nuclear plants. Most of it, however, will be used in nuclear facilities called 'fast breeder reactors', which many nuclear planners expect to become the main source of the world's electricity. If their expectations are fulfilled, our grandchildren will live in a world in which thousands of tons of plutonium will be bought and sold every year. That amount of plutonium would be enough to make hundreds of thousands of atom bombs.

The proposed use of this potential nuclear explosive as a fuel is not only dangerous but unnecessary. Nowhere in the world is plutonium fuel economic, nor will it be in the foreseeable future. The technology for separating plutonium from spent fuel has proved to be extraordinarily difficult to master, and prohibitively expensive. It aggravates the problem of radioactive waste, and poses serious health risks. Fast breeder reactors are plagued by persistent technical problems, and their capital cost is crippling. So unpromising is this technology that almost the entire cost of its pursuit to date has been borne not by the world's nuclear industry but by the world's taxpayers.

Yet, despite all, plutonium promoters have succeeded, for three decades, in exerting extraordinary influence on the energy planning and decision-making of national governments everywhere in the world. More taxpayers' money has been devoted to research and development for the use of plutonium fuel than to any other energy research. Those spending this money – mostly in government nuclear agencies and their contractors, egged on by politicians – want to go on doing so. But their efforts are helping to spread nuclear weapons all over the world. In the telling phrase of nuclear analyst Albert Wohlstetter, we and our children's children will find ourselves living in a 'nuclear-armed crowd'.

How have we come to this incredibly dangerous pass? How have those in a small scientific and political élite exercised such powerful leverage for such a long time, with so little to substantiate their claims? What was it about the international climate that served their cause and furthered their ambitions? Why is it that for many years the world's public, and its governments, have heard only what plutonium advocates have wanted them to hear? The true story is now becoming public knowledge, and citizens almost everywhere are making their opinions heard. Is there still time to change direction? Or must we face a future in which atom bombs are effectively an article of commerce?

Until 1940 plutonium was unknown, existing in nature only in the minutest traces. It was first separated and identified in 1941, at the University of California at Berkeley. The initial interest in plutonium was the pure scientific excitement of finding a new chemical element; but the discovery at once attracted official interest of another kind. The world was at war, and work was underway on a terrible new weapon – the 'atomic bomb'. The weapons scientists needed to be able to trigger a 'chain reaction' that would release a shattering burst of energy – a 'nuclear explosion', millions of times more powerful than any chemical explosion. At the time the only known nuclear explosive was a rare form of uranium, called uranium–235, extremely difficult and costly to extract.

Then came word that plutonium, newly created, might also be a nuclear explosive; and so it proved. Experiments showed that plutonium, like uranium–235, would undergo a chain reaction. Furthermore, plutonium could be produced from ordinary uranium, and then separated from it chemically.

Suddenly there was a second route to the atom bomb. Both routes reached their destinations, uranium-235 over Hiroshima on 6 August 1945, and plutonium over Nagasaki three days later.

For nearly a decade after World War II nuclear efforts were dedicated almost exclusively to military objectives. One main focus was the production and separation of plutonium for weapons. Some scientists, however, were also looking toward civilian applications of nuclear materials and technologies. Here, too, they saw a key role for plutonium. The obvious civilian application was to generate electricity; but there was one serious uncertainty. In the late 1940s and early 1950s uranium, the essential nuclear material, was rare and costly; and only about one per cent of it, the uranium–235, could be 'burnt' in a reactor. There was, however, an elegant solution. As uranium is burnt in a reactor, some of the unused uranium is turned into plutonium. Once extracted from the spent fuel, the plutonium can be mixed with ordinary uranium to make new fuel. Such 'mixed oxide' fuel can be used in conventional nuclear power plants. It would be even better, however, to use the plutonium in a different kind of reactor, called a 'fast breeder'. The fast breeder would burn plutonium more efficiently, while at the same time actually producing more plutonium than it burned – hence the term 'breeder'. Using plutonium in fast breeders would multiply manyfold the energy that could be obtained from a given amount of raw uranium.

The concept had an exquisite symmetry. Electricity use was bound to increase; more and larger power plants would be needed. Some would be conventional nuclear plants burning uranium. In order not to waste this rare and precious material, the used 'spent' fuel from these plants would be collected and 'reprocessed' to recover the unburnt uranium and freshly created plutonium. The plutonium would be made into fuel for fast breeders, which in turn would produce more electricity and more plutonium. The plutonium and residual uranium in the spent fast breeder fuel could then be recovered by reprocessing, and made into yet more fast breeder fuel, for more fast breeders – and so on, for ever and ever. In essence, modern alchemy could transform the otherwise useless rock of uranium ore into an effectively limitless supply of high-quality energy.

It was an engineer's dream. Nuclear planners accordingly viewed plutonium and the fast breeder as cornerstones for the long-term future of civil nuclear power. Their view did, to be sure, incorporate certain unstated assumptions:

- Electricity demand would have to increase fast enough to necessitate new power plants.
- Nuclear electricity would have to be economically competitive with that from other sources, despite the presumed rarity of uranium.
- Nuclear technologies themselves, some no more than a gleam in the planners' eyes, would have to perform as anticipated.
- Any side-effects, such as nuclear waste, would have to be manageable.

One serious question remained. Was it possible to develop civil nuclear technology without at the same time spreading nuclear weapons? A top-level report to the American government in 1946 expressed grave doubt: 'The development of atomic energy for peaceful purposes and the development of atomic energy for bombs are in much of their course interchangeable and interdependent.' But even this uncompromising declaration did not unduly trouble the planners. They were certain that the public would be cheering them on toward a brighter nuclear future.

Plutonium advocates have pursued this vision for more than thirty years. The fast breeder reactor has been their Holy Grail. In the United States, the United Kingdom, the Soviet Union, France, Federal Germany, Italy, Japan, India and elsewhere the quest for the fast breeder has absorbed the energies of the nuclear faithful and the finances of their governments, with vociferous jockeying for leadership. Part I of this book describes how the concept of plutonium as a civil fuel established itself in the minds and budgets of nuclear planners around the world. It also describes how the technical and economic reality of reprocessing and the fast breeder stubbornly refused to correspond to the concept. Part II describes the dilemma created when an ostensibly civil plutonium programme in India culminated in a nuclear explosion. It then recounts the sorry history of the only serious governmental attempt to get a grip on the problem. Part III describes the most recent stages of the controversy.

In the 1980s, the belief of the plutonium advocates burns on undimmed; their influence on policy persists. Of their original vision, however, little has been realized. The articles of their faith stand revealed as illusory:

– Electricity demand has all but ceased to grow. Even after a quarter-century of coddling, nuclear electricity is hard put to compete economically with coal and other supply technologies.

– Of uranium, once rare and cherished, there is now an embarrassing glut.

– Reprocessing, the technology for separating plutonium from civil reactor fuel, has proved to be technically acutely difficult, and dauntingly expensive.

– Fast breeders have an abysmal track record for cost and performance, inspiring little confidence and even less commitment from electrical suppliers. Even their most fervent advocates now concede that fast breeders cannot compete commercially with conventional nuclear plants, for many decades to come.

– Worst of all, the airy certainties about 'safeguards' on the civil use of plutonium have evaporated. It is flatly impossible, technically or diplomatically, to guarantee that ostensibly peaceful plutonium will stay that way, and not suddenly reappear in a bomb.

In 1984, plutonium still makes at best a negligible contribution to world energy supplies. Its future prospects are equally meagre. Yet the most influential energy planners in many countries continue to presume the validity of historical assumptions about it. Swallowing more government money than any other energy research activity, the plutonium business rolls on. Potential atom bomb material is now being produced at a rate of over forty tonnes per year – thus far, to be sure, mostly as unreprocessed spent fuel. It is being stockpiled around the world, with no idea of what is to become of it or how to keep it from undergoing the grim metamorphosis into bombs.

The final section of this book discusses what might be done by an informed public to bring about government action while there is still time. Before we are locked irretrievably into a global plutonium economy, we must surely look again at the prospects for success – and the implications of failure – in this numbingly expensive, precariously dangerous undertaking. Instead of financing it lavishly from public funds, should not the world be trying to get out of the plutonium business? Or shall we turn our entire planet into a nuclear time-bomb?

PART ONE

Plutonium dreams

1946–74

1 The plutonium people

The world's first specimen of plutonium was invisible. An almost indetectably minute quantity of it was produced in February 1941, at the Radiation Laboratory of the University of California at Berkeley, by bombarding a metal target in a machine called a cyclotron. Glenn Seaborg and his colleagues carried out the subtle chemical analysis that identified element 94 – the first 'artificial' element ever created. Uranium, element 92, was the heaviest element found in significant quantity in nature. It was named after the planet Uranus; and Seaborg's group decided to follow the solar system farther out. Element 93, identified soon after, would be named 'neptunium', after Neptune. Element 94 would be named 'plutonium', after Pluto. Seaborg and his colleagues apparently did not recall that Pluto had been named after the Greek god of the underworld. The infernal association thus inadvertently attached to their new element was to become all too appropriate.

The existence and the characteristics of plutonium had been predicted before its discovery. Tests rapidly verified the key prediction. Plutonium was indeed 'fissile': it would undergo a nuclear chain reaction, and could therefore be used in an atomic bomb. Production and fabrication of a sufficient quantity of plutonium at once became one of the main objectives of the Manhattan Project, the top-secret bomb-development programme of the early 1940s. Plutonium therefore arrived in secret; and secrecy has continued to envelop it.

Since 1942, Seaborg's minuscule sample of plutonium has been followed by hundreds of tonnes more; but it is still invisible, literally and figuratively, to all but a tiny minority. Because it is both radioactive and fissile, physical access to it has always been tightly restricted, for reasons of both safety and security. The public never sees it, and has had very little say in what becomes of it. Nobody knows the total amount of plutonium produced to date, since much has been produced explicitly for use in nuclear weapons, and these quantities are still a closely guarded official secret everywhere.

Only a very select group of people has been directly involved with plutonium, in practice or policy-making or both. Seaborg himself was one of the first of these 'plutonium people', as were his senior colleagues on the Manhattan Project. The Project's atmosphere of unparalleled secrecy continued after the end of World War II, cloaking nuclear activities everywhere in mystery. Although the United States, Britain, the Soviet Union and France had been wartime allies, nuclear fission divided them at once into hostile camps. The United States Atomic Energy Act 1946 summarily cut off British and French access to American nuclear data, although both countries had helped to launch the Manhattan Project. This American slap in the face made both the West European countries more determined to embark on their own independent programmes. It also left a legacy of deep bitterness.

On a government level each country distrusted the nuclear motives of the other three, a distrust that rapidly evolved into intense nuclear nationalism. This deep-seated nationalism in due course gave the plutonium people in the various countries powerful leverage over their governments. The possession of plutonium and plutonium technology, with its military implications, became a mark of international standing and international pride. Those responsible were accorded appropriate élite status, at least within the upper echelons of government privy to policy.

The United States, Britain, the Soviet Union and France each established a national nuclear organization, financed by the central government and responsible to it: the United States Atomic Energy Commission; the British Division of Atomic Energy Production, Ministry of Supply; the Soviet State Committee on Atomic Energy; and the French Commissariat à l'Energie Atomique. Each had superficially different structures and responsibilities. But each embarked forthwith on establishing plutonium technology. Each built plants

4

to produce and separate plutonium – either explicitly or implicitly for use in weapons. Each also began to pursue programmes for the use of plutonium as civilian power plant fuel.

Among the many pioneer plutonium people involved in these programmes were Walter Zinn and Hans Bethe in the United States, Sir John Cockcroft and Sir Christopher (later Lord) Hinton in Britain, Igor Kurchatov in the Soviet Union, and Bertrand Goldschmidt in France – each one a leader of his nation's nuclear activities, and a key contributor to policy. Since 1942 the number of plutonium people has grown, from hundreds to hundreds of thousands. Some are in universities. Some are in electricity supply industries. Some are in design, engineering and manufacturing firms, on the shop-floor and in the boardroom. Some are in government departments dealing with energy policy and planning, export trade, foreign affairs and – of course – defence. Because decisions about plutonium are of such importance, the most senior plutonium people are now, as they have been since the early 1940s, heads of state: presidents, prime ministers and their ilk. Their advisors tend to come from the main stronghold of the plutonium people – the national nuclear organizations.

To be sure, not all nuclear people are plutonium people. On the contrary, there have been from the outset some nuclear scientists, engineers and administrators who are acutely wary of the material. In the world's electronuclear industries, for instance, planners and decision-makers over the years have been less than wholehearted about using plutonium as fuel for civil power plants. Nevertheless, the interests and beliefs of the plutonium people have exercised a profound influence on governmental nuclear and energy policy in many countries for four decades – despite the opposition of some of their own nuclear colleagues, and despite some remarkably prescient forebodings at the outset.

The Acheson-Lilienthal report
The most ominous cloud to cast its shadow over the hopes for civil use of nuclear energy and plutonium fuel appeared as early as 1946. A committee chaired by American Under

Secretary of State Dean Acheson published 'A Report on the International Control of Atomic Energy'. The main body of the report was written by a five-man group chaired by David Lilienthal, chairman of the Tennessee Valley Authority and soon to become first chairman of the United States Atomic Energy Commission. The report was an incisive analysis of the implications of nuclear fission for the world. At its heart was a sombre warning that ostensibly civil applications of nuclear technology might nevertheless provide access to nuclear weapons.

The report declared flatly that:

> The development of atomic energy for peaceful purposes and the development of atomic energy for weapons are in much of their course interchangeable and interdependent ... there is no prospect of security against atomic warfare in a system of international agreements to outlaw such weapons controlled only by a system which relies on inspection and such police-like methods. The reasons supporting this conclusion are not merely technical, but primarily the inseparable political, social and organizational problems involved in enforcing agreements between nations each free to develop atomic energy but only pledged not to use it for bombs. National rivalries in the development of atomic energy readily convertible to destructive purposes are the heart of the difficulty.

In particular, the report noted:

> Take the case of a controlled reactor, a power pile, producing plutonium. Assume an international agreement barring the use of the plutonium in a bomb, but permitting the use of the pile for heat or power. No system of inspection ... could afford any reasonable security against the diversion of such materials to the purposes of war.

Later in the report the authors added:

> Among the activities which we would at the present time classify as those dangerous for national exploitation are the following: ... the operation of the various types of reactors for making plutonium, and of separation plants for extracting the plutonium.

6

It was an uncompromising, unambiguous view, amply supported by scientific evidence. Unfortunately, it ran directly counter to the thinking already under way as to the future development of civil nuclear power, about which the plutonium people had very definite ideas.

2 Separating plutonium: the origins of reprocessing

The first full-scale nuclear programme in the world was the Manhattan Project in the United States. It was an exclusively military programme, directed toward the production of an atomic bomb. However, the technical ground-rules it laid down were to shape nuclear thinking for many years to come, not only in the United States but in many other countries.

Once Seaborg had identified plutonium, and it had proved to be fissile, the next requirement was to produce it in quantity. The cyclotron at Berkeley could produce it only in minute amounts. The following year, however, a far more effective production method emerged. On 2 December 1942 a team under the direction of the immigrant Italian physicist Enrico Fermi started up the world's first 'nuclear reactor'. Called 'Chicago Pile No. 1', it was built in a disused squash court under the grandstand of the football stadium at the University of Chicago. Fermi's reactor demonstrated that uranium could be turned into plutonium, in whatever quantity desired. Ever since that day, every reactor burning uranium for whatever reason has produced plutonium.

The process works like this. Ordinary uranium as found in nature consists of two kinds of atom, called uranium-238 and uranium-235: two 'isotopes' of uranium. Only seven out of a thousand atoms of natural uranium are uranium-235. When the innermost core or 'nucleus' of an atom of this rare form of uranium is struck by a bullet-like particle called a neutron, the nucleus may split in two. This 'nuclear fission' will release two or three more neutrons. Some of these neutrons in turn may strike other nuclei and split them, releasing still more neutrons, in what is called a chain reaction. Such a chain reaction will occur only if sufficient uranium is brought together in a suitable arrangement. One such arrangement is called a nuclear bomb. Another arrangement is called a nuclear reactor.

In a nuclear reactor some of the neutrons from fission strike other nuclei of uranium–235 and keep the chain reaction going. Others leak out of the system and are lost. Sometimes, however, a neutron strikes a nucleus of a uranium–238 atom, which 'swallows' it and turns into plutonium–239. Some of the newly formed plutonium–239 nuclei are subsequently struck by neutrons. Those nuclei may in turn split, joining in the chain reaction. On the other hand the plutonium–239 nuclei may swallow further neutrons, turning successively into plutonium–240, –241 and –242. Plutonium that is not split continues to accumulate within the uranium in the reactor until the chain reaction is shut down and the uranium is taken out of the reactor.

To produce plutonium for the Manhattan Project, a series of enormous reactors were built along the Columbia River in the northwestern state of Washington, at a site called Hanford, between 1943 and 1945. The Hanford reactors did not work very well; but the fact that they worked at all was a considerable feat of engineering.

The Hanford reactors were built explicitly to produce plutonium for the atomic bomb. However, the plutonium produced in a reactor is intimately intermingled with the remaining uranium and the broken fragments of split nuclei, called fission products, also present within the uranium. To recover the plutonium for use, it must be separated chemically from the uranium and the fission products. The fission products are 'radioactive' – sometimes intensely so. Accordingly, after undergoing a chain reaction, the 'irradiated' uranium must be handled remotely. The radiation from the fission products also poses difficulties for chemical processing. The entire processing plant has to operate without direct human intervention. Moreover, the radiation also attacks the solvents and seals and other materials and equipment used in the processes.

Separating plutonium and unused uranium from the waste fission products – 'reprocessing' of the irradiated uranium – is thus technically very demanding. Nevertheless, reprocessing has been undertaken in a growing number of countries since

THE PUREX PROCESS

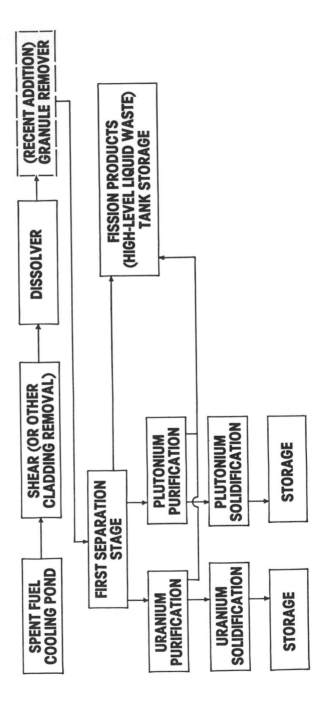

the 1940s. The earliest reprocessors – the first nations to separate plutonium in quantity – were the United States, Britain, the Soviet Union and France.

The United States
The world's first chemical separation of plutonium in kilogram quantities took place in 1944–5 at Hanford. The technology employed at the time was primitive. By the early 1950s, however, it had evolved into a much more sophisticated process. It could separate irradiated uranium almost completely into plutonium, unused uranium and fission products. This 'plutonium-uranium extraction' technology was dubbed the Purex process. It came into its own with the construction of the vast Purex reprocessing plant at the United States Atomic Energy Commission installation at Savannah River, Georgia.

The Savannah River plant was authorized by President Harry Truman in 1950, and started up in 1954. Its capacity of 15 tonnes of uranium per day far exceeded that of any other reprocessing plant before or since. However, the uranium reprocessed at Savannah River had been left in reactors for at most a few months. The Atomic Energy Commission wanted plutonium–239 for weapons; it did not want to leave the plutonium in the reactors long enough to be turned into plutonium–240 and higher isotopes, which made the plutonium – although still usable – less satisfactory for bomb-making. The brief sojourn in a reactor was referred to as a 'low burnup'. Low-burnup uranium had undergone a chain reaction only briefly, contained only a modest amount of fission products, and was therefore not very radioactive. It was thus comparatively easy to reprocess. Spent fuel from a power-plant reactor, with a burnup of three or four years, and tens of times more radioactive, was to prove quite another matter.

Purex technology fulfilled all the relevant criteria for the weapons programme. It recovered the plutonium for making the bombs; and it recovered the unused uranium, to be reused in reactors to make more plutonium. This latter attribute was almost equally important. When the Purex process was being developed, uranium was a strategic material, rare and costly, and available from only a very few sources, all of them outside the United States. The recovery of the unused uranium was at the time a key feature of the process.

The Purex process did, to be sure, have drawbacks. It used large quantities of liquids, including water, acid and organic solvents, all of which became contaminated with radioactivity. These liquid wastes required some form of treatment before disposal. The fission products emerged as a concentrated, fiercely radioactive acid solution that could not be disposed of safely, and had to be stored in tanks. Many millions of gallons of this 'high-level waste' accumulated at Hanford and Savannah River, with no clear idea of what might eventually be done with it.

Britain

Britain, as noted earlier, had played a crucial early role in the Manhattan Project. British scientists, and their expatriate colleagues who had fled to Britain to escape the Nazis, wrote some of the crucial early analyses that suggested the possibility of an atomic bomb, and alerted the British government at a time when the American government was still unconcerned about the possibility. The danger of invasion of Britain prompted the British government to agree to move bomb-development activities to the United States; and many British scientists made the long journey to the weapons-laboratory at Los Alamos, New Mexico.

In 1946, however, the United States summarily denied Britain any further access to American nuclear data or co-operation. Britain at once embarked on its own top-secret nuclear weapons programme, culminating in a nuclear explosion on 3 October 1952, off the coast of Western Australia. The explosive in the bomb was plutonium. It had been created in plutonium production reactors at a site in northwestern England called Windscale, and separated in a reprocessing plant called B204, also at Windscale. B204 had started up earlier in 1952; despite the American ban on access to detailed engineering data, some early design work had been done by British scientists; and the B204 plant used process technology broadly similar to the Purex technology at Savannah River.

Like Savannah River, B204 separated out plutonium, unused uranium and fission products from uranium which had undergone only a brief irradiation – that is, low burn-up. The fission products, in the form of acidic liquid high-level waste, were stored in tanks on the Windscale site. The two plutonium-production reactors at Windscale were followed by four dual-purpose reactors at a site called Calder Hall, immediately next door. The Calder Hall reactors were built to produce weapons-plutonium while generating electricity as a by-product. The spent fuel from these reactors was likewise reprocessed in B204. Reprocessing spent fuel from power reactors was thus taken for granted from the outset.

In Britain the separation and recovery of the unused uranium were even more important than they were in the United States. In the early 1950s the US discovered a series of deposits of its own indigenous uranium in Colorado and elsewhere. Britain, however, was still dependent on imports, and the uranium import market was still acutely sensitive politically. In the early 1950s Britain even built a uranium isotope separation plant at Capenhurst, Cheshire, whose purpose, unlike that of the uranium enrichment plants built in the United States, was not to produce nearly pure weapons-grade uranium–235. Instead it was to enrich the uranium recovered from the B204 reprocessing plant.

This uranium contained even less than seven atoms of uranium–235 per thousand; the rest had been split in the chain reaction. The Capenhurst 'Low Separation Plant' restored the proportion of 235 back to seven atoms per thousand, so that the uranium could be returned for further use in the Windscale plutonium production reactors. The Plant cost some £14 million, at 1953 British prices, equivalent to more than twenty times that amount in 1984. It illustrates how deeply the need to economize on uranium, and to recover both uranium and plutonium, were ingrained in the minds of British nuclear planners such as Sir John Cockcroft, Sir Christopher (later Lord) Hinton and Sir William Penney.

The Soviet Union
The Soviet Union had begun nuclear research well before the end of World War II. The growing hostility between the

Western allies and the Stalin régime, and the rapid diplomatic chill which set in after 1945, left no doubt that the Soviet Union would develop nuclear weapons. Information about the Soviet weapons programme remains sketchy to this day. But it is believed that the Soviet Union built plutonium production reactors and reprocessing facilities in the South Ural mountains near the city of Sverdlovsk. The first Soviet nuclear explosion, in August 1949, was a plutonium bomb; and plutonium continued to figure prominently in the Soviet programme when it expanded into civil activities in the mid-1950s.

France
Like Britain, France had played a part in the Manhattan Project; several leading scientists had come from France. After the end of World War II, France too was subject to the American ban on access to nuclear data; nevertheless, France also embarked on a nuclear programme – albeit one not at first explicitly directed towards production of a bomb. The French G–1 reactor at Marcoule was a dual-purpose power-plus-plutonium reactor, like the British gas-graphite reactors at Calder Hall, next door to Windscale. Unlike Calder Hall, the G–1 reactor's primary purpose was, at the outset, electricity generation. But the French also built a reprocessing plant at Marcoule, to take the spent fuel from the G–1 and subsequent reactors. The Marcoule reprocessing plant started up in 1958. When, in that same year, de Gaulle decided that France should have its own nuclear weapons, the necessary plutonium facilities were ready to hand.

The thinking of the French nuclear planners thus paralleled that of their American and British counterparts. Irradiated uranium, whether from a dedicated plutonium production reactor or in the form of spent fuel from a power reactor, had to be reprocessed to recover uranium and plutonium. That was understood without question as the appropriate way to proceed. Once they had the separated plutonium, the next step was to plan to use it – not only for bombs but also for electricity.

14

3 Burning plutonium: the origins of the fast breeder reactor

After Enrico Fermi and his team had demonstrated that a nuclear reactor would work, nuclear designers had a field day thinking up possible reactor concepts. There were in the early days literally dozens. Most never left the drawing boards; and most of those which were actually built proved unsafe or uneconomic or just uninteresting. One concept in particular, however, struck sparks from nuclear imaginations.

The first reactors, for production of weapons-plutonium, incorporated material like carbon graphite or a rare form of water called 'heavy water' in the core of the reactor. This 'moderator' slowed down the neutrons released by splitting nuclei; otherwise these high-energy 'fast' neutrons tended to go right through nuclei without splitting them. Subsequent reactor designs, for power production, like the so-called 'light-water reactors', used ordinary water in the core for the same purpose. However, if a fast neutron did split a nucleus, it produced on average a higher number of new neutrons to add to the chain reaction. A nucleus of plutonium–239 split by a fast neutron produced much the largest harvest of fresh neutrons – on average nearly three per fission.

Accordingly, designers envisaged a compact reactor core containing as little other material as possible, in order to keep the neutrons fast and their rate of reproduction high. The core could be made of uranium–235; but plutonium–239 would give much the best rate of reproduction. If the core were surrounded by a 'blanket' of the common isotope uranium–238, the neutrons which emerged from the core would turn some of this useless uranium into more plutonium. (Another heavy metal, 'thorium', could also be used as blanket material, and turned into uranium–233, another isotope which would sustain a chain reaction.) If the core and

15

blanket were packed so tightly together that comparatively few neutrons were lost or wasted, the amount of plutonium produced during a given time would be greater than the amount burned. The reactor would 'breed' plutonium. Such a design would be a fast-neutron plutonium-breeding reactor: a 'fast breeder reactor'.

Unlike most of the other reactor concepts dreamed up in the 1940s, the fast breeder offered something startling and distinctive. While generating electricity from its heat output it would at the same time, in effect, make its own fuel out of otherwise useless material. Since uranium was itself so scarce, expensive and politically sensitive, planners were delighted at the prospect of turning the uranium–238 (99.3 per cent of the total) into plutonium and burning it, too.

Some analysts anticipated that the fast breeder, producing many times as much useful energy from the same initial amount of uranium, would lower dramatically the average fuel cost per unit of electricity. However, by focusing on the putative improvement in the economical use of uranium, the planners overlooked a crucial corollary. The whole process would require not just a fast breeder itself but a special ancillary assemblage of other capital plant:

– not one but two reprocessing plants, one to recover plutonium from the spent uranium fuel of conventional nuclear plants and one to reprocess spent plutonium fuel from the fast breeder itself

– a plant to purify the recovered plutonium

– a plant to convert it into the right chemical form for use in new fuel

– a plutonium fuel manufacturing plant

Plutonium is a profoundly unpleasant industrial material. Its radioactivity makes it fiercely toxic in minute quantities. Moreover, it is nearly pure fissile material; plant designers and operators have to guard against an accidental chain reaction that would produce lethal penetrating radiation. Industrial plutonium plant would therefore be exceedingly complex and costly.

Nevertheless, these considerations did not deter the plutonium people. They were convinced that nuclear power plants of whatever kind would be economically competitive with other forms of electricity generation, and that nuclear electricity from a plutonium-fuelled fast breeder would be more or less competitive in due course. The capital cost of the fast breeder would probably be somewhat higher than that of a conventional nuclear plant. But this higher capital cost would be offset by lower fuel costs, occasioned by the fast breeder's improved uranium economy.

The cost of capital was of only secondary importance in any case – the prevailing interest rates were below five per cent. No one, however, had any practical experience of estimating nuclear costs of any kind in a commercial context. Furthermore, those making the estimates were to be found not in commercial finance and industry but in the United States Atomic Energy Commission and its sister organizations in other countries. The Commission's early espousal of the fast breeder was quickly emulated by the United Kingdom Atomic Energy Authority, established in 1954, and by the Soviet State Committee on Atomic Energy.

The United States
In the United States, in the dawn of the civil nuclear programme at the beginning of the 1950s, the attitude of Commission insiders to plutonium fuel and the fast breeder was summed up by physicist-author Samuel Glasstone. In the first edition of his classic *Sourcebook on Atomic Energy*, prepared for the Commission and published in 1952, Glasstone put it like this:

> It is evident, therefore, that the general usefulness of nuclear fission energy, apart from special cases, will depend to a great extent on the possibility of breeding, to convert all the non-fissionable uranium and thorium into fissionable material ... Until success in this connection is achieved, the future of nuclear energy is somewhat in doubt. 'Unless the problem of breeding is solved,' says a US Atomic Energy Commission report, 'there is a question as to the ultimate contribution of nuclear fission to the world's supply of energy ... Even the specialized uses of an atomic reactor ... such as for the propulsion of a naval vessel, will be limited if breeding does not succeed ... [But] if we get

17

breeders we are sure to get power.' The situation, however, is not desperate, for even if breeding, in the sense of increasing the stockpile of fissionable material, is difficult, regeneration, namely partial or complete replacement of uranium–235 by plutonium–239, or by uranium–233, will still be possible.

In later years this latter concept – the manufacture of fuel for conventional nuclear plants not by enriching uranium to 3 or 4 per cent uranium–235, but by adding a suitable amount of plutonium to ordinary uranium – would come to be called 'recycling'.

Glasstone described a possible nuclear future:

> If the accumulation of fissionable material proves feasible, the nuclear power industry may perhaps develop along the following lines. At a few central stations there would be located large breeder-reactors with their associated chemical extraction plants. The chief function of these reactors would be to convert uranium–238 and thorium–232 into the respective fuels, with energy production as an incidental objective. The concentrated fissionable materials would then be distributed in the form of assembled cores for use in smaller reactors in remote areas, or mobile power plants in ships, including submarines and possibly for aircraft engines and railroad locomotives. After a certain period of use the fuel core of the reactor would be removed and replaced by a new one; the spent core would be sent to a central station for reprocessing.

All the omens for fast breeders seemed propitious. The first electricity generated by a nuclear source came from a fast breeder: the 200–kilowatt Experimental Breeder Reactor (EBR–1) at the National Reactor Testing Station in Idaho on 20 December 1951.

Nevertheless, in 1953, shortly before completing his term as chairman of the Atomic Energy Commission, Gordon Dean, in his *Report on the Atom*, offered a cautious and sceptical view about the role of breeding and plutonium fuel. He noted that Walter Zinn and his colleagues had succeeded in demonstrating that the Experimental Breeder Reactor would indeed breed.

> The reactor is operating in such a way that it is burning up uranium–235 and, in the process, it is changing non-fissionable uranium into fissionable plutonium at a rate that is at least equal

to the rate at which the uranium–235 is being consumed. Breeding has been achieved . . .

I think, however, that we must take care to see that this encouraging development is kept in its proper perspective. This news does not mean that economic power from atomic fuels is here. It does not mean that overnight we have suddenly obtained all the fissionable material we want or need. It does not mean that uranium can now be regarded as a virtually costless fuel. It is quite possible that the breeding principle will not even be incorporated in the first atomic power plants. It may be that some other type will be more feasible from the economic point of view, at least at first and possibly for some time. A large-scale breeder reactor can be a costly proposition. It requires a very large initial investment of scarce fissionable fuel. In addition, before the newly created fuel can be extracted and put to use, it must go through a chemical separation process which is currently one of the most expensive aspects of the atomic energy business.

The achievement of breeding also does not mean that we are suddenly independent of raw uranium ore. Far from it. Breeding is a slow process, and a reactor may have to operate for five years or longer before it succeeds in yielding as much new fuel as was initially invested in it. Our great current demand for uranium–235 and plutonium for weapons, and our equally great need for raw uranium ore to meet this demand, will not be lessened one iota.

The real significance of breeding is that it is now possible for mankind ultimately to utilize all of the uranium that can be extracted from the earth's surface for atomic fuel, whether it is fissionable or not in its natural state . . .

In summary, I should like to emphasize that the achievement of breeding with uranium is an important event, but it is not one that is likely to cause any immediate, or even imminent, revolutionary change in the economics of atomic power production. What it constitutes, mainly, is another encouraging and important factor which can be introduced into the many calculations being made to determine the best technical and economic approach to real, competitive atomic power.

It was, on balance, a more guarded assessment than those which would later emanate from the precincts of the Atomic Energy Commission – especially after 1961, when the chair once held by Dean was taken over by Glenn Seaborg, the father of plutonium.

Britain
In Britain the fast breeder occupied a central position in nuclear planning virtually from the outset. British fast breeder

development had to begin with fuel made from uranium–235; there would not be a plutonium fuel fabrication facility, nor any plutonium to spare from the weapons programme, for many years to come. Nevertheless, by 1950 – five years before the first nuclear power programme was even announced – British nuclear people had already assumed that the plutonium-fuelled fast breeder was the key to any long-term civil nuclear programme. In her official history of British nuclear affairs, *Independence and Deterrence*, Margaret Gowing noted that the committee on power reactors could not concur on the reactor design to be adopted: 'The only point on which there was general agreement throughout all these years was on the long-term future – on the ultimate and overriding importance of breeder reactors, which would produce more secondary fuel than they consumed.'

Their reasoning was akin to that in the United States; but British nuclear planners felt its force even more keenly. As noted earlier, Britain had no significant indigenous uranium, and had already encountered troublesome obstacles to reliable access to imports. A power reactor which could create its own fuel was almost too good to be true. In 1950 Sir John Cockcroft, head of the Atomic Energy Research Establishment at Harwell, gave a lecture entitled 'The Development and Future of Nuclear Energy'. In it he described the long-term objective:

> to build nuclear power stations which will produce power at a cost not very different from a coal-fired station. For this to be worthwhile we must have adequate uranium–ore reserves in sight to fuel our nuclear power stations for many centuries . . . For this we have to develop a new type of atomic pile known as the 'breeder pile', because it breeds secondary fuel [plutonium] as fast or faster than it burns the primary fuel uranium–235. . . . These piles present difficult technical problems, and may take a considerable time to develop into reliable power units. Their operation also involves difficult chemical engineering operations in the separation of the secondary fuel from the primary fuel.

Fast breeder research got under way at Harwell in the late 1940s, even before the birth of the United Kingdom Atomic Energy Authority. The Authority, created by the Atomic Energy Act of 1954, was, like the United States Atomic

Energy Commission, a unique agency. It was funded by the national government, and charged with devising and executing the nation's nuclear policy, both military and civil, subject only to nominal overseeing by the government itself. The Authority's first major civil undertaking was the design and construction of the Dounreay Fast Reactor, fuelled with uranium–235, at the Dounreay Experimental Reactor Establishment on the north coast of Scotland. The remote location was chosen explicitly because of uncertainties about the possible behaviour of the reactor, which also prompted its enclosure in a steel dome some 43m in diameter. Dounreay became the home of the British fast breeder community – and also the only major employer in the entire northeast corner of the Scottish Highlands, a factor which was later to loom large in political terms. The Dounreay Fast Reactor started up in November 1959; but it was to experience protracted teething troubles.

The Soviet Union
In the Soviet Union scientific interest in the fast breeder dated from 1949 – more or less the same time· as it first attracted serious practical attention in the United States and Britain, albeit, so far as is known, independently of them. The first Soviet fast breeder was the BR–5. Only the second power reactor in the country, it was built at the nuclear research centre at Obninsk, south of Moscow. The BR–5 started up in 1958 and first delivered power in 1959. As was also the case in the United States and Britain, this was well before the first conventional civil nuclear power plant began operation.

In the three original nuclear weapons states, therefore, the fast breeder had acquired a substantial momentum even before the balance of nuclear development in general had shifted from weapons to electricity. The momentum came almost entirely from within the national nuclear organizations, backed by their governments. Manufacturing industry and electricity suppliers were reluctant to get involved, except as government contractors. They were prepared to participate, but only provided someone else – to wit taxpayers – paid most of the bills. In any case, these original fast breeders were power plants only incidentally. Their primary role was as test facilities for the design of components and systems for the larger plutonium-fuelled fast breeders already foreseen by the nuclear planners in the three countries.

4 Plutonium international

'Atoms for Peace'

For most of the decade after Hiroshima, virtually the entire emphasis of government nuclear activities was military. By 1952 the production and stockpiling of nuclear weapons by both the United States and the Soviet Union had created an unparalleled arms race. Dean Acheson's 1946 report on the dangers of nuclear technology and the need for its international control had fallen on stony ground. Six years later, in 1952, as Secretary of State, he set up a Panel of Consultants on Disarmament, headed by Robert Oppenheimer, former director of the Los Alamos weapons laboratory, and with a young Harvard academic called McGeorge Bundy as secretary. The Panel's findings were bleak. Never again would it be possible to guarantee that all the world's fissile material was accounted for and unavailable for use in weapons. There was already too much of it, in too many places. The Panel's study warned that 'the present danger is not one of hysteria but of complacency'. Its main recommendation was that the United States government come clean with the public and reveal the full extent of the desperate dilemma created by international nuclear developments.

The study, which eventually became known as the 'Candor report', was greeted with consternation in early 1953 by the incoming Eisenhower administration and its military advisors. Aides attempted to draft a presidential statement conveying the daunting dimensions of the problem; but they met with failure. The facts were just too frightening. 'We don't want to scare the country to death,' commented Eisenhower. Rejecting a further draft he asked, 'Can't we find some hope?' Eisenhower pleaded for an approach that offered a brighter side. He suggested that the United States propose an 'atomic pool', to which the Soviet Union might be invited to contribute – fissile material to be distributed for peaceful uses, as a step toward disarmament. On 8 December 1953, Eisenhower, addressing the General Assembly of the United Nations, declared that the United States was to embark on a programme to be called 'Atoms for Peace'. He invited the other nations of the world to join in pursuit of the 'peaceful atom', and underwrote his appeal by offering generous technical and economic assistance toward the establishment of nuclear programmes around the world.

As a quid pro quo for its nuclear assistance the United States would require a pledge from recipient countries that they refrain from acquiring nuclear weapons. In this way Eisenhower and his government were attempting to lay the foundations for international agreement on the control of nuclear energy. But they were also turning their backs completely on the findings of the 1946 Acheson-Lilienthal report. That report had dismissed out of hand the feasibility of an international control régime based only on pledges of good faith and some form of inspection. As a response to the Candor Report, Atoms for Peace had the flavour of desperate wishful thinking – especially since the 'atomic pool' disarmament notion sank instantly without trace.

Nevertheless, Atoms for Peace ushered in a new era of cooperation and growth in nuclear activities, nationally and internationally. Eisenhower's announcement was followed by the United States Atomic Energy Act of 1954, in accordance with which a staggering amount of data on nuclear materials and technology was soon declassified. With vigorous support from the United States, the first United Nations Conference on the Peaceful Uses of Atomic Energy took place in Geneva in 1955. It was the first major international convocation of nuclear people since Atoms for Peace had begun to lower the barriers of secrecy and multilateral nuclear hostility. National nuclear organizations which had hitherto kept warily to themselves in a climate of Cold War distrust, even between allies, found themselves invited to meet and compete on an incipient commercial basis with their opposite numbers in other countries.

Among these national nuclear organizations were the

United States Atomic Energy Commission, the daddy of them all and at the height of its power; the United Kingdom Atomic Energy Authority; the French Commissariat à l'Energie Atomique; the Soviet State Committee on Atomic Energy; the Indian Department of Atomic Energy; the Argentine Atomic Energy Commission; and many other similar organizations with broadly similar names and powers. It was clear to the delegates at the Geneva Conference that they had a great deal in common. They were in the main highly trained scientists and engineers, privy to esoteric information pertaining to the most powerful weapons ever produced. They belonged to organizations entrusted by governments not only to produce the weapons but also to advise on their development and deployment, almost always under conditions of top-level secrecy and confidentiality, from which the vast majority of their fellow citizens were excluded.

This nuclear secrecy was a drastic departure from the traditional openness of international scientific endeavour. The nuclear people had created an inner sanctum of science, whose ground-rules differed diametrically from those hitherto common to all of science. The Geneva Conference did indeed lower barriers between the nuclear people in different countries; but the barriers between nuclear people and the rest of the public remained substantially intact everywhere.

The nuclear people were accorded status on a plane above even their scientific colleagues in less exotic disciplines. In each of their countries they constituted an influential, privileged élite – although they might not have put it in quite those terms. Their initiation into the nuclear mysteries meant that lay politicians and the public held them in awe and deferred to their judgement. Such was the power and influence of the nuclear people that they could dip freely into the public purse in pursuit of their objectives.

The Geneva Conference heralded a new chapter in international nuclear relations. For the first time nuclear people could meet their fellows from other countries in an atmosphere of free discussion about matters which had hitherto been tightly restricted. It was an occasion for mutual congratulation, reciprocal encouragement and the reinforcement of shared enthusiasms – not least about the peaceful potential of plutonium and the fast breeder. Many senior people in the national nuclear organizations had already had significant involvement with plutonium work, either theoretical or practical. Once it became diplomatically permissible they quickly shared their enthusiasm with like-minded colleagues in other countries.

Enrico Fermi's widow Laura published a memoir of the conference whose title captured with telling aptness the evangelical fervour of the gathering. It was called *Atoms for the World*. This first Geneva Conference, and its successor in 1958, saw the coalescence of an international nuclear priesthood, whose common purpose and common interests from then on regularly transcended national boundaries and sectional concerns.

The national nuclear organizations
By the late 1950s a rapidly increasing number of countries – including many in what would come to be called the Third World – had government-financed nuclear organizations, inspired by and often modelled on the United States Atomic Energy Commission, and with a similar brief. They were empowered:

– to gather and generate nuclear know-how

– to design, build and operate a variety of nuclear installations

– to stimulate and service nuclear activities by other industries in their countries, especially the electricity supply industries

– to promulgate a view of the future development and role of nuclear technology in their countries

– by no means least, even in non-weapons countries, and even when explicitly disavowed – to achieve a stance of readiness should the national government decide that it must for whatever reason acquire nuclear weapons

In Sweden, for instance, the question of whether the country should produce nuclear weapons raged for several years. In the early 1960s the country eventually decided 'No'. Had it however decided 'Yes', there was never any doubt that the Swedish nuclear establishment could forthwith oblige.

By the late 1950s there were nuclear research programmes underway not only in the original nuclear countries – the United States, the United Kingdom, the Soviet Union, France, and Canada – but also in Scandinavia, the six members of the European Community, Japan, China, India, Pakistan, Argentina, Brazil, South Africa, Israel, South Korea, Taiwan and a lengthening roster of other Third World countries. Many already had operating research reactors and research laboratories, often provided by the original nuclear countries as a new form of bilateral aid and co-operation. One of the earliest examples of such bilateral nuclear activity was that between Canada and India, which got underway in the early 1950s, subsequently involving also the United States. It was to have unforeseen and unwelcome consequences.

By that time nuclear activities had expanded beyond pure research and weapons development, into the area long anticipated by nuclear thinkers: the use of nuclear energy to generate electricity. In the late 1950s, however, the abundance of cheap oil, natural gas and coal made electricity suppliers unenthusiastic about committing themselves to an unfamiliar and novel technology that seemed likely to be significantly more expensive. Nevertheless, the United States Atomic Energy Commission had launched its Cooperative Power Reactor Demonstration Program, funded from the Commission's budget, with the reluctant consent of some electrical suppliers. The United Kingdom Atomic Energy Authority had persuaded the British government to proceed with A Programme of Nuclear Power, as the official White Paper of February 1955 had been entitled. The programme had been drawn up without the Central Electricity Authority, who were merely given a month to comment on it before its publication. In each country the manufacturing industry was happy to participate, since it was taking little if any risk on government contracts. Executives of the major boiler and turbo-plant firms foresaw a lucrative future once nuclear power technology had become established – as all agreed it would. Similar views and circumstances were reflected in

THE NUCLEAR FUEL CYCLE

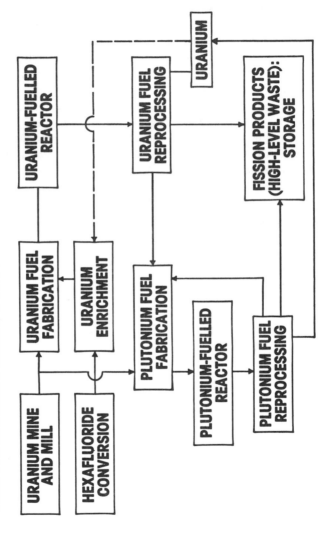

many other industrial countries; and the public was carried along by the glowing propaganda of the national nuclear organizations.

By the late 1950s the five original nuclear countries already had operating prototype power plants. A number of other countries – among them the Federal Republic of Germany, Italy, Spain, the Netherlands, Belgium, and Japan – would soon join them. Full-fledged commercial nuclear plants were just over the horizon – although the enthusiasm for them continued to be more pronounced among the national nuclear organizations than within the electricity supply industry.

Such nuclear power plants would require a variety of specialized services if they were to become a successful addition to the world's energy technologies. Accordingly, many national nuclear organizations were already studying the future requirements of what would eventually be labelled a nuclear fuel cycle. It might entail:

– uranium mining and extraction
– fuel fabrication
– uranium enrichment, for some types of power reactor
– heavy water manufacture, for other types
– reactor design, construction and operation
– spent fuel reprocessing
– radioactive waste management and disposal
– plutonium fuel fabrication
– recycling of plutonium fuel in conventional nuclear power plants
– use of plutonium fuel in fast breeder reactors
– reprocessing of fast breeder fuel and blanket
– refabrication of recovered plutonium into fresh fast breeder fuel

Ordinary uranium–238 would go around and around this fuel cycle, being gradually converted into plutonium and burned to generate electricity. Establishment of such a nuclear fuel cycle, by the design, construction and operation of the various support facilities, became a central objective of almost all the national nuclear organizations.

From the first Geneva Conference onwards, the national nuclear organizations were no longer strictly in international competition. On the contrary: each had an interest in encouraging the others, in order that each might return to its government and point to progress being made elsewhere, as an argument for more funds and support. The great majority of the professional nuclear community appeared to subscribe to a common set of convictions and priorities. Nuclear generation of electricity must be fostered, as a fundamental raison d'être of the national nuclear organizations; it was of course in poor taste to mention any possible weapons connection. Electricity suppliers must be persuaded to invest in nuclear power plants. One way to do so was to call attention to other countries in which such investment was taking place; national nuclear organizations were therefore likely to be eager to see nuclear activities accelerating elsewhere.

Even the long-term policies of the various national organizations showed a strong family resemblance. With the virtually unique exception of Canada, all the countries with nuclear programmes were proceeding on a common assumption about the fate of spent fuel from civil power reactors. Canada, with ample supplies of indigenous uranium, no historical involvement with plutonium separation or reprocessing, and no ambitions toward acquisition of nuclear weapons, had decided that spent fuel should be consigned to indefinite storage, awaiting research into final disposal. But every other country with an identifiable viewpoint assumed that civil spent fuel, like irradiated uranium from plutonium production reactors, would be taken to a reprocessing plant somewhere and there reprocessed to recover the unused uranium and the plutonium. What would become of the high-level liquid waste thus created was never clearly stated; it would be stored – somehow – pending an unspecified final disposal.

The technical premises that shaped the civil nuclear power programmes getting under way all over the world were therefore more or less identical to the technical premises underlying the military weapons-plutonium programmes which had gone before. The same assumptions and considerations about the key role of plutonium governed the thinking of planners, even though the objectives of the civil programmes were nominally entirely different, and even though the technical and economic context of nuclear activities in general was undergoing a rapid and dramatic change away from that which had shaped the weapons programmes.

The same organizations – indeed often the same people – who had been used to maintaining stringent security about their military plutonium facilities and stocks as a matter of the highest national priority were seemingly unconcerned about encouraging other countries to establish similar plutonium facilities and stocks. All would be well if the facilities and stocks were 'peaceful'. Peaceful plutonium would be, they were certain, an unparalleled boon. Keeping it peaceful, even with reprocessing plants and fast breeder reactors, they considered to be no problem.

The International Atomic Energy Agency

The casual official adoption of this attitude ran counter, not only to the seminal findings of the Acheson-Lilienthal report a decade earlier, but also to the outcome of the first attempt, shortly thereafter, to mount an international control régime. The very first resolution which had been passed by the General Assembly of the newly chartered United Nations in 1946 had set up the United Nations Atomic Energy Commission. It was a short-lived entity, which failed utterly to acquire any authority or power over the national nuclear programmes of member nations.

Be that as it may, Atoms for Peace brought with it a renewed enthusiasm for some form of supranational agency to oversee the dissemination of nuclear information and keep the results within the desired bounds. A key feature of Atoms for Peace had been that the provision of nuclear assistance would be administered through an international organization, to ensure that nuclear activities in client countries were not directed toward military ends. The outcome was the creation of a unique offshoot of the United Nations: the International Atomic Energy Agency. The Agency came into being in the aftermath of the Atoms for Peace programme and the first Geneva Conference. After prolonged international deliberations it was formally established by United Nations statute in 1957. It was to exercise a two-fold function: to encourage civil nuclear programmes while discouraging governments from pursuing military nuclear programmes.

A certain amount of international nuclear co-operation, like that between Canada and India, including the provision of financial and technical support, had already begun earlier in the 1950s. It was based on bilateral agreements between the governments of the donor and recipient countries, in which the recipient accepted that the assistance would foster the 'peaceful use' of nuclear energy. The advent of the International Atomic Energy Agency provided a diplomatically convenient way to supervise such undertakings. The dual function of the Agency was formalized in the concept of 'safeguards'. In return for the provision of a nuclear facility, the recipient would accept safeguards on it. The very word itself was reassuring: to guard something and keep it safe ought to mean that nothing could go wrong. The term was to prove better as a public-relations slogan than as a description of what actually took place.

Even after the establishment of the Agency, safeguards continued for some years to be based on bilateral agreements between donors and recipients. In 1962, however, the United States and Japan concluded a nuclear agreement which assigned to the Agency the responsibility for administering the relevant safeguards. From that time onward safeguards agreements became gradually trilateral, with the Agency as the third party.

A safeguards agreement, however, said nothing about 'guards' or indeed about safety. Instead, it specified the means by which the supervising authority – eventually the Agency – could seek to establish that all activity at a nuclear facility was within permitted limits. For instance an agreement might state:

– that seals could be put on sensitive features of the facility – doors, valves and the like – and removed only by a visiting safeguards inspector

– that surveillance cameras could be set up to take pictures of sensitive areas automatically

– that visiting inspectors could study the books, and cross-check the accounts recording the presence and movements of sensitive materials like fuel elements

Safeguards were thus a way of detecting whether anything illicit had occurred – but not of preventing its occurrence. The premise was that the threat of detection would serve as a deterrent to discourage the misuse of safeguarded materials or installations. Nevertheless even this deterrent effect left something to be desired. What would happen in the event that a safeguards inspector discovered evidence of a discrepancy or a transgression was by no means clear. In principle, a safeguards inspector discovering evidence of a transgression would report the discovery to Agency headquarters in Vienna. The Agency staff would weigh the evidence; if it appeared sufficiently substantive, the staff would report the discovery to the Agency's Board of Governors. The Board might then announce publicly that the Agency had evidence that a country appeared to be in breach of its international under-takings not to misuse nuclear assistance.

No one could say, however, what might then ensue. Presumably the donor country, and possibly others, would take diplomatic measures to prevent the explosion of a nuclear device, and apply pressure to the offending country to comply with its previous nuclear commitments. However, the whole process, from the initial detection of a suspected 'diversion' of civil activities into military, would undoubtedly take weeks, if not months. Whether such safeguards could indeed give adequate warning of diversion and incipient misuse was all too debatable. The practical effectiveness of the measures could not be tested, even for the most basic of nuclear facilities like small research reactors. Questions arose not only about the reliability of safeguards hardware such as cameras, but also about the institutional response to a genuine suspected diversion. The texts of safeguards agreements were always secret, making the effectiveness of safeguards yet more difficult to ascertain.

Despite the vagueness surrounding the functional worth of

safeguards, the national nuclear organizations and their corporate contractors in the industrial countries, especially the United States, pressed ahead with plans to disseminate the technology internationally. The policy package they offered embodied all their assumptions about the eventual shape of their own domestic nuclear power programmes – including, of course, the separation and use of plutonium as fuel. Well into the 1960s no serious attention had been paid to what safeguards might mean or how they might work when applied to a reprocessing plant or a fast breeder reactor. It was simply taken for granted that there would be acceptable and effective safeguards for such facilities.

From 1962 onwards the member countries of the United Nations gradually evinced markedly different attitudes about the appropriate balance between the promotional and safeguarding efforts of the International Atomic Energy Agency. Those countries which already possessed nuclear weapons and those with otherwise well-established nuclear programmes looked upon the Agency first and foremost as a way to constrain weapons development by non-weapons countries. On the other hand many non-weapons countries, notably in what came to be called the Third World, looked upon the Agency as the fountainhead of nuclear riches, in the form of knowhow, materials and hardware. These countries acknowledged the strings attached to such benefits; but they found the strings irksome, and lamented that the Agency was too concerned with limiting the nuclear activities of its members and not enough with fostering them. This dichotomy was to become progressively more conspicuous and divisive.

The Non-Proliferation Treaty

When, in 1960, France set off its first nuclear explosion, the development was unwelcome internationally but not really unexpected. When, however, four years later, in 1964, the People's Republic of China exploded a nuclear bomb the rest of the world sat up in sudden alarm – not least the original nuclear powers, the United States and the Soviet Union. The two countries had been making desultory moves toward some form of international agreement designed to reduce the likelihood that other nations would join the 'nuclear club' of weapons-powers. After the Chinese explosion these moves acquired a fresh urgency. In 1968, after lengthy and delicate diplomatic negotiations between the sponsor governments, the United Nations General Assembly agreed to open for signature a treaty drawn up and co-sponsored by the United States, the Soviet Union and Britain. Known as the Non-Proliferation Treaty, it came into force on 5 May 1970, already ratified by the United States, Britain, the Soviet Union and forty other nations.

Article I of the Treaty says that nuclear weapons states will not transfer nuclear weapons to non-weapons states, or in any way assist such states to acquire nuclear weapons. Article II says that non-weapons states will not accept or otherwise acquire nuclear weapons. Article III says that each non-weapons state will accept safeguards on all its nuclear activities; and that no state will provide nuclear material or technology to any other state unless that state accepts safeguards on all its nuclear activities. Article IV says that all parties 'undertake to facilitate, and have the right to participate in, the fullest possible exchange' of knowhow and technology 'for the peaceful uses of nuclear energy', 'without discrimination'. The correct interpretation of this Article was to become acutely contentious. Article V says that 'potential benefits from any peaceful applications of nuclear explosions will be made available to non-nuclear weapons states party to the Treaty'. Article VI says that all parties undertake 'to pursue negotiations in good faith on effective measures relating to cessation of the nuclear arms race at an early date and to nuclear disarmament'. This Article applied to the existing weapons states in particular, to complement the undertaking of non-weapons states that had agreed to forgo nuclear arms. It proved to be a hollow commitment.

Until the Treaty came into force, safeguards had been applied only to individual facilities or consignments of material, as and when they were provided. The Treaty requirement was much more stringent. It stipulated that a non-weapons country party to the Treaty would not be eligible to receive any nuclear technology or material from a foreign supplier party to the Treaty unless safeguards were applied even to those facilities and materials manufactured or produced within the country. This Treaty requirement was in due course to lead to some strange inconsistencies in international nuclear commerce. By no means every nation subscribed to the Treaty; and those that did not came to find themselves, ironically, in an unexpectedly advantageous position – scarcely the intention of those who had drafted the Treaty. Despite the plainly unambiguous import of Article III, nuclear exporters came to have no compunction about supplying non–NPT parties, with no insistence that customers accept full-scope safeguards. Exporters party to the Treaty were unwilling to give France a major advantage in international nuclear commerce. France is not a party to the Treaty and does not require that its foreign clients accept full-scope safeguards. The consequent free-for-all was to undermine drastically the credibility of the Treaty.

Nevertheless, the Non-Proliferation Treaty defined the formal ground-rules for the future evolution of civil nuclear programmes worldwide, just as such programmes were at last beginning to take off. That there could be such an entity as a purely 'civil' nuclear programme, when that programme was expected to include the separation and use of plutonium, was regarded as axiomatic, and went essentially unquestioned. As axioms go, this one was singularly ill-founded.

5 Reprocessing for peace

Nuclear power programmes, as it happened, were taking considerably longer to get off the ground than their more vociferous cheerleaders desired. Not until the early 1960s did the first nuclear power plants that could reasonably be called 'commercial' start up, in Britain and the United States. More rapid ordering got underway in 1964 and 1965, but these plants would not be expected to start up until the end of the decade. Nevertheless, while the nuclear diplomats and bureaucrats busied themselves with high-level policy, the planners in the national nuclear organizations pursued their long-term vision of a complete power package. It would include not only reactors but appropriate fuel supplies: both uranium and plutonium.

By this time, too, major manufacturing companies in the United States, the United Kingdom, continental Europe and Japan had decided that the commercial potential of civil nuclear power would soon be realized. They had at last begun to put significant amounts of their own capital into the establishment of nuclear manufacturing facilities. Uranium mining had long been a prominent nuclear activity in the private sector. By the early 1960s private industry had also begun to investigate the commercial prospects of other high-technology constituents of the nuclear fuel cycle.

At the beginning of the 1960s, there was no civil source of enriched uranium for fuel. The only plants in service which could produce the type of uranium required for the new civilian power reactors were the enrichment plants operated for weapons purposes by the United States Atomic Energy Commission. Nor was there any civil facility available to deal with civil spent fuel. It was politically acceptable for a military facility to supply enriched uranium to a civil reactor: uranium used in a civil power reactor could not be used in a bomb, and was therefore being removed from the weapons programme. However, returning civil spent fuel to a military reprocessing plant would invite awkward questions about the eventual destination of the plutonium. Was this plutonium from a civilian power reactor in fact going to be used in bombs? Such a question would draw unwelcome attention to the difficulty of separating civil nuclear activities from military. Nevertheless, something had to be done about civil spent fuel.

Accordingly, by the early 1960s, planners in national nuclear organizations in the United States, Britain, France, and a number of other European countries had set about the establishment of quasi-commercial civil reprocessing enterprises. The results they achieved in the ensuing decade were scarcely encouraging. The technology of reprocessing civilian spent fuel proved to be much trickier than anticipated. It grew rapidly more difficult the longer the fuel had stayed in the reactor, and the more radioactive it was. The more durable ceramic oxide fuel used in the new generation of power reactors was intended to remain in a reactor for up to four years. When it emerged it was some ten times more radioactive, and gave rise to handling problems much more challenging than those presented by the uranium metal fuel from plutonium production reactors.

Moreover, reprocessing plants which had to pay their way commercially turned out to be quite a different proposition from those paid for by military budgets. Would-be reprocessors found the technology a good way to lose large sums of money in a remarkably short time. The early experience of the first four civilian reprocessing plants – at Mol, Belgium; West Valley, New York; Morris, Illinois; and Windscale, England – would have given any but the most dogged planners pause.

Europe: Mol

The first purely civilian reprocessing plant was built at Mol, Belgium, under the auspices of the European Nuclear Energy Agency. The Agency had been created in 1957 by the international body which was soon to become the Organization for Economic Cooperation and Development. The Agency undertook three multinational nuclear projects; one was the construction and operation of the Mol facility. Twelve European countries joined forces for the purpose, under the rubric of European Company for the Chemical Processing of Irradiated Fuels – Eurochemic.

Given its multinational nature, the plant was of course to be a civil facility. The original intention in the late 1950s was to build a fully commercial plant with a capacity of up to 1000 tonnes of spent fuel per year – enough to service thirty or more full-scale nuclear power plants. However, the anticipated rapid growth of nuclear capacity did not materialize. The Eurochemic planners therefore scaled down their aspirations, in favour of a plant with a capacity of 70–100 tonnes per year, an experimental 'pilot production plant'. A plant of this size could not be a commercial success; its unit capital cost per tonne reprocessed would be far too high. The operators accordingly decided to dedicate the plant to reprocessing different types of fuel and fuel elements, to provide the participating countries with experience of reprocessing technology. That such experience would have an appropriate civil application appears to have been taken for granted.

At the 1955 Geneva Conference France had made public for the first time information about reprocessing technology, by describing its reprocessing plant at Marcoule. The French firm of St Gobain, which had built the Marcoule plant, supplied the technology for Mol. The Mol plant, however, incorporated important modifications, to make it possible to handle different fuels and fuel elements. Construction of the plant began in 1962; it started up in 1966 and received an operating licence in 1968. (See Table 1.)

The plant worked well enough technically; but frequent changes of fuel type and fuel elements meant that much time was taken up flushing out the plant between 'campaigns' of reprocessing. For this and other reasons the total amount of fuel reprocessed during the plant's operating life was no more than about thirty per cent of its nominal design capacity. To cope with the variety of fuels, the plant was designed to dissolve spent fuel cladding and all. This produced a substantial extra amount of liquid waste per tonne reprocessed, of widely differing chemical composition, which had to be stored in tanks on the Mol site. The process was thus ill-suited to

Table 1: Reprocessing Plants

Country	Location	Name	Owner	Fuel input	Original design capacity	Start-up	Status 1984	Throughput (tonnes)
United States	West Valley, New York	Nuclear Fuel Services	Nuclear Fuel Services	various – mostly low burnup	300 tonnes/ year	1966	permanent shutdown 1972	625 tonnes in all
United States	Morris, Illinois	Midwest Fuel Recovery Plant	General Electric (US)	(none)	—	did not start up	—	—
Britain	Windscale	B205	British Nuclear Fuels Ltd	metal	1500 tonnes/ year*	1964	operational	20000 tonnes (including weapons material)
Britain	Windscale	B204	British Nuclear Fuels Ltd	oxide	300 tonnes/ year*	1969	permanent shutdown 1973	100 tonnes in all
Britain	Windscale	Thermal Oxide Reprocessing Plant	British Nuclear Fuels Ltd	oxide	1000 tonnes/ year*	construction not commenced early 1984	?	—

Country	Location	Name	Owner	Fuel input	Original design capacity	Start-up	Status 1984	Throughput (tonnes)
France	Marcoule	Usine Plutonium-1	Cogema	metal	250 tonnes/year	1958	operational	not known (includes weapons material)
France	Cap la Hague	Usine Plutonium-2	Cogema	metal	800 tonnes/year	1966	operational	not known (includes weapons material)
France	Cap la Hague	Haute Activité Oxide	Cogema	oxide	400 tonnes/year*	1976	operational	510 tonnes to end June 1982
France	Cap la Hague	Usine Plutonium-3	Cogema	oxide	800 tonnes/year*	under construction	?	—
Belgium	Mol	Eurochemic	Eurochemic	various – mostly low burnup	70–100 tonnes/year*	1966	shutdown 1974; possible restart	180 tonnes in all
Federal Germany	Karlsruhe	Wiederaufarbeitungs-anlage Karlsruhe	Karlsruhe Nuclear Research Centre/DWK	various	40 tonnes/year	1969	operational after shutdown	(experimental)

41

Country	Location	Name	Owner	Fuel input	Original design capacity	Start-up	Status 1984	Throughput (tonnes)
Federal Germany	Dragahn	not known	DWK	oxide	350 tonnes/year	in planning stage	—	—
Japan	Tokai Mura	Tokai Mura	Power Reactor and Nuclear Fuel Corp	oxide	210 tonnes/year	1978	shutdown after leaks	less than 150
India	Trombay	Trombay	Department of Atomic Energy	oxide	50 tonnes/year	1964–65	shutdown 1974	not known
India	Tarapur	Tarapur	Department of Atomic Energy	oxide	100 tonnes/year	1978 (tests); 1981	operational	not known
Argentina	Ezeiza	Ezeiza	Comisión Nacional de Energía Atómica	oxide	25? tonnes/year	1984?	under construction	—
Pakistan	Chashma	not known	Atomic Energy Commission	oxide	not known	not known	not known	—

Country	Location	Name	Owner	Fuel input	Original design capacity	Start-up	Status 1984	Throughput (tonnes)
Brazil	Resende	not known	Institute de Pesquisas Energeticas de Nucleares	oxide	2–3 tonnes/year	1990?	under construction	—

(Data from references, notes p. 64; p. 67; p. 71; p. 73; p. 75; p. 78; p. 79; and p. 230; and Bibliography, (45). Note that data starred (*) appears in different values in different official sources at different times.)

adoption for a genuine commercial reprocessing plant for civil fuel. The relevance of experience at Mol soon proved to be marginal at best.

As an experimental facility the Mol plant could not hope to meet commercial economic criteria. Nevertheless, its cumulative losses became hard to ignore. Despite Eurochemic's reduced expectations it sought business eagerly. By the end of the 1960s, however, it was facing mounting competition from Britain and France. In 1971 Britain joined with two of the countries participating in Eurochemic, France and the Federal Republic of Germany, to set up a tripartite company called United Reprocessors, registered in Germany. The intention was to pool their expertise and pursue a monopoly of commercial reprocessing business that would have nothing to do with Eurochemic. As the losses at Mol continued to mount, the remaining Eurochemic partners threw in the towel. Before the end of 1971 they had agreed to run down operations at Mol. In July 1974 the Eurochemic plant was shut down and mothballed. But it did not go away.

United States: West Valley

A yet bleaker fate befell the first civil reprocessing plant in the United States. The Atomic Energy Commission, egged on by the Joint Committee on Atomic Energy, was eager to establish a civil nuclear power industry. In keeping with the American tradition of free enterprise, it wanted private companies not only to build and operate power reactors but also to provide all the necessary ancillary services, with the exception of uranium enrichment. One of the services assumed necessary was reprocessing of spent fuel. The Commission's first attempt to interest industry in civil reprocessing, in 1957, drew a blank. There would be no commercial spent fuel available for some years, making the prospect for profitable contracts unexciting. Furthermore, the eventual fate of high-level waste was deeply uncertain. Private companies did not fancy finding themselves responsible for long-term management of materials which would remain dangerous much longer than companies could foresee their own corporate existence.

In 1959, the State of New York, keen to attract advanced

technology, created an agency to encourage nuclear industry in the state. In 1961 the agency acquired a site about thirty miles from Buffalo, called West Valley. Shortly thereafter the Davison Chemical Company entered negotiations with the agency and the Atomic Energy Commission, leading to the plan to construct a commercial reprocessing plant at West Valley. The Commission agreed to make available the Purex technology in use at its military reprocessing plants. It also agreed to deliver spent fuel from its dual-purpose plutonium-production N-reactor at Hanford, to keep the West Valley plant busy until it could contract for enough civilian spent fuel. The plutonium separated from Hanford fuel was presumably to be returned to the Commission, for uses unspecified; coming from a weapons-production reactor it would have been pure enough for weapons-use. Were that the case it would have raised some doubt about the purely civilian nature of the West Valley plant. To get around the waste-management problem it was agreed that the West Valley plant would be owned by the New York state agency, and operated by the chemical company, now called Nuclear Fuel Services. The company was to provide a fund of $4 million, interest on which was considered sufficient to cover the cost of 'perpetual care' of the wastes, including maintenance and replacement of storage tanks. It was not, as it proved, an adequate sum.

Construction of the West Valley plant began in 1963; it started up in 1966. (See Table 1.) In order to keep down the capital cost of the plant, the designers cut a good many corners – too many, as it proved. They opted for 'contact maintenance', requiring workers to enter radioactive areas, rather than the more expensive 'remote maintenance' carried out by remote-controlled equipment. Unfortunately, the plant leaked like a sieve, exposing both its workers and the surrounding environment to embarrassing levels of radiation. By 1972 the average annual exposure of plant staff had reached 7 rem, compared to the 5 rem maximum permitted by the official regulations. This average did not include the army of transient workers brought in to clean up the worst messes; and of course the average figure disguised the fact that some plant staff received much higher exposures.

Despite this corner-cutting on safety the plant lost money

for every one of its six short years of operation. Its original owners had invested some $32 million, and had anticipated a return of 3.6 per cent per year on the basis of a fee of $23 500 per tonne of fuel reprocessed. By 1972 the fee had reached $35 000 per tonne, but even that was insufficient to show a profit. In all, the plant reprocessed only 625 tonnes of spent fuel, 380 of them from Hanford. Given a stated design capacity of 300 tonnes per year, this represented at best less than 40 per cent of capacity. At that, the Hanford fuel had little in common with fuel from the new civilian power reactors, differing both in composition and in burnup; it thus provided little in the way of relevant technical experience. It was supplied not under a commercial contract, but rather as a Commission subsidy. Even after the first commercial nuclear power plants began coming into service, Nuclear Fuel Services found commercial reprocessing contracts hard to come by. By the end of the 1960s electrical suppliers were being offered much better terms by two other entrants in the reprocessing field, General Electric and Allied Chemical, on behalf of the larger plants they were planning.

By 1972 Nuclear Fuel Services was facing mounting criticism about the operating conditions at West Valley. The Atomic Energy Commission was progressively tightening constraints on discharges of radioactivity, and local environmental groups were demanding that the plant reduce its outpourings into the adjoining waterways. In October 1972 the company shut the plant down, ostensibly for upgrading and expansion. It never reopened; but its story was far from over.

United States: Morris

General Electric had a clearcut aim when, in the mid-1960s, it undertook design and construction of a civil reprocessing plant at Morris, Illinois. General Electric was unhappy about the flood of liquid high-level waste poured out by the conventional Purex process. Instead, it came up with a radically different technology, which it called Aquafluor: a 'dry' process using the chemistry of volatile solids. The company was so confident that it foresaw the day when each nuclear power plant would have its own individual Aquafluor reprocessing plant right on site, to deal with its own spent fuel.

By 1972, however, the Morris plant, nearing completion, was eliciting more hand-wringing than plaudits. The original estimated cost of the plant had been $36 million; General Electric kept pumping in money, but by 1974, after an expenditure of some $64 million, it had to admit defeat. In two years of 'cold tests' with dummy fuel the equipment kept breaking down, and pipes and valves clogged repeatedly. Worse still, the company found that the plant, once contaminated with radioactivity, would be impossible to maintain; in industrial terms the plant simply did not work. In July 1974 General Electric notified the Atomic Energy Commission that it had had enough: 'even with long design and development programs, it is difficult to see solutions for many of these problems.' The plant never started up. By mid-1974, however, 60 tonnes of spent fuel had already arrived in the cooling ponds at Morris according to contracts already signed; much more was on the way. Even without operating, the Midwest Fuel Recovery Plant was to be a continuing focus of controversy.

The Morris fiasco seems to have summarily terminated any interest in developing more advanced process technologies for civil reprocessing. Purex technology, only slightly modified, was subsequently adopted for every other civil reprocessing plant built after Morris.

Britain: Windscale

Apart from the question about plutonium from Hanford fuel reprocessed by Nuclear Fuel Services, the plants at Mol, West Valley and Morris were all in their various ways unambiguously 'civil'. All were done in by the twofold civil consideration which military technology seems able to bypass: the need to make a plant pay its way and yet function as intended. Only two reprocessing plants built in the 1960s achieved any measure of success. They were the B205 chemical separation plant at Windscale in Britain, and the UP–2 plant at Cap la Hague in France. Both of these plants, unlike the three mentioned above, were designed initially to reprocess metal fuel of fairly modest burnup and low radioactivity. Both were also more than somewhat ambiguous in provenance, since they serviced not only civil electricity supply industries but also the military establishments in their two countries.

The B205 plant at Windscale was built by the United Kingdom Atomic Energy Authority as a successor to the purely military B204 plant. B205 started up in 1964, to handle the spent fuel from the first-generation gas-graphite 'Magnox' reactors. However, the first eight of these, at Calder Hall and Chapelcross, were dual-purpose reactors, military plutonium-production facilities generating electricity as a by-product. The plutonium recovered from the spent fuel was earmarked for British nuclear weapons.

According to the British government, the plutonium recovered in B205 from spent fuel from the nine civil Magnox stations built after Calder Hall and Chapelcross was not to be used in weapons. Plutonium from these civil stations would be stockpiled at Windscale for eventual use in fast breeder reactors. Be that as it may, the existence of B205 for weapons purposes made it natural and easy to assume that civil spent fuel ought likewise to be reprocessed. Fuel from the civil Magnox reactors was made of uranium metal, just like the military fuel from Calder Hall and Chapelcross, and the facility was already there and in operation. In any case, British nuclear planners were looking toward an early and large-scale introduction of fast breeder reactors, which would require all the plutonium that could be harvested.

However, the second programme of nuclear power plants in Britain, announced in 1965, was to be based on 'advanced gas-cooled reactors'. Such reactors used not uranium metal fuel but much more durable ceramic uranium oxide fuel, similar to the fuel used in American light-water power reactors. For technical reasons oxide fuel could not be fed directly into the B205 reprocessing plant. Accordingly, once B205 was operating satisfactorily on metal Magnox fuel, the Authority planners turned again to the original military reprocessing plant, B204, next door to B205 on the Windscale site. They decided to convert B204 into a 'Head End Plant', to chop up oxide fuel and dissolve it in acid, so that it could be fed into the B205 chemical separation plant.

The B204 Head End Plant started up in 1969, and the Authority was delighted with it. However, the advanced gas-cooled reactors, expected to supply spent oxide fuel to the Head End Plant, were already on their way to becoming an industrial disaster area. They were so far behind schedule that not one started up until seven years later. Accordingly, the Authority contracted with foreign customers, including electricity suppliers in Federal Germany, the Netherlands, Spain and Sweden, to reprocess oxide fuel from their light-water reactors, using the B204 Head End Plant feeding into B205.

Although the Head End Plant had a capacity variously stated as 100 or 300 tonnes of fuel per year, it averaged a throughput of only about 25 tonnes per year for four years of operation. This was partly because the B205 separation plant was also being used for metal fuel, and partly because, throughout much of the period, the inventory of spent oxide fuel available on site was not large enough.

Nevertheless, by 1973 the operators of Windscale had big plans for B204. The government had decided to split up the Atomic Energy Authority into separate bodies according to areas of responsibility. Windscale had become part of British Nuclear Fuels Ltd, a 'commercial' company separated from the Authority by an Act of Parliament in 1971, although the Authority owned all the shares. By this time British Nuclear Fuels had contracts to reprocess some 1150 tonnes of foreign oxide fuel; consignments were arriving steadily and being stored in the cooling ponds at Windscale. The company had announced plans to upgrade the Head End Plant, and increase its throughput capacity to more than 400 tonnes per year. The delays to Britain's own advanced gas-cooled reactors did not matter to the fuel company. Windscale would lead the world in the reprocessing of civil oxide fuel from all comers.

The company had failed to reckon with the unfamiliar characteristics of such civil fuel, and one characteristic in particular. Reprocessors knew that fuel which had spent two years or more in a power reactor was much more radioactive than weapons-production fuel. The radiation damaged the solvents, and made it much more difficult to dissolve and process power reactor fuel. But the higher burnup of power reactor fuel also caused a more subtle change in the fuel.

Some of the fission products created by the chain reaction were rare metals like rhodium, which are virtually chemically inert. If enough of them accumulated in the fuel, they coalesced into tiny granules of solid metal alloy, fiercely radioactive and almost insoluble, even in hot nitric acid.

British Nuclear Fuels found out the hard way just how serious this granule problem might be. On 26 September 1973, after the Head End Plant had been flushed out, workers began to feed in a fresh batch of fuel. They did not know that previous batches had left a thin layer of radioactive granules in the bottom of a process vessel. The heat from the granules had boiled off all the residual fluid and left the vessel scorching hot. When the fresh batch of process solution reached the hot vessel there was a violent reaction. The consequent pressure pulse spurted radioactivity past a shaft seal and into the air of the plant, contaminating 35 workers.

The plant was shut down while the Nuclear Installations Inspectorate carried out a painstaking investigation. The company declared repeatedly in public during the next two years that the Head End Plant would be restored to service when repairs were complete. Not until four years after the accident did it finally concede that the plant was a write-off. The subtle complexities of reprocessing high-burnup oxide fuel had claimed yet another victim. The Eurochemic and Nuclear Fuel Services plants had each lasted just six years from start-up to shutdown; the Head End Plant at Windscale lasted only four, and reprocessed only 100 tonnes of fuel. That did not, to be sure, discourage British Nuclear Fuels. On the contrary: it was determined to press on to greater things.

France: Cap la Hague

Like the United Kingdom Atomic Energy Authority, the French Commissariat à l'Energie Atomique built a second reprocessing plant to take over from its purely military plant at Marcoule. Like the B205 plant at Windscale, the new French plant, at Cap la Hague on the Cherbourg peninsula on the north coast of France, was designed to reprocess low-burnup metal fuel from the first generation of French power reactors, which were gas-graphite reactors akin to those in Britain. The

Marcoule military plant had been called UP–1, for 'usine plutonium' – plutonium factory. The Cap la Hague plant was called UP–2.

UP–2, like the British B205, was ambiguous. The only reactors the French officially acknowledged as military were the G–2 and G–3 dual-purpose units at Marcoule. However, the French were much less concerned than the British about distinguishing between military plutonium and civil plutonium, such as that extracted at UP–2. All the plutonium separated from spent fuel from French gas-graphite reactors has always been understood to belong to the Commissariat, and is potentially strategic military material.

Be that as it may, the designation of Cap la Hague as 'usine plutonium–2' or UP–2 left no doubt that the plant was viewed first and foremost as a plutonium extraction facility; uranium recovery and radioactive waste conditioning were less important. Like the British, and for similar reasons, the French nuclear planners were looking toward rapid introduction and expansion of a programme of fast breeders. The UP–2 plant, to supply the plutonium for fast breeder fuel, was an essential precursor of such a programme. In 1969, however, the French government decreed that henceforth new French nuclear power plants would no longer use the indigenous gas-graphite design of reactor. Instead, France would build light-water reactors like those in the United States. Like their American cousins these reactors would use durable ceramic uranium oxide fuel.

Once again it was assumed without question that since they reprocessed metal fuel, they should likewise reprocess oxide fuel. In a move paralleling that in Britain, the nuclear fuel activities of the national Commissariat were transferred to a 'commercial' organization called Compagnie Générale des Matières Nucléaires (Cogema). In another parallel move, Cogema decided in the early 1970s to add to UP–2 a head end plant, called HAO for 'haute-activité oxide', to handle oxide fuel. The arrangement was to be closely akin to that of the B204 Head End Plant feeding into the B205 chemical separation plant at Windscale. The capacity of the HAO at Cap la Hague was to be 400 tonnes per year – far more spent fuel than would be produced by the number of light-water reactors then contemplated in France. Cogema, like British Nuclear Fuels, would be seeking foreign customers. French nuclear planners, like their colleagues across the Channel, had taken for granted the universal need to separate plutonium from oxide as from metal fuel, in preparation for the dawning age of the fast breeder reactor.

6 Breeding dismay and enthusiasm

While the reprocessors were struggling with their technology, what was in fact becoming of the fast breeders on whose behalf the plutonium was to be harvested? As far back as the early 1950s several designs of breeder had been suggested. One concept had emerged as the strong favourite. It was to use fast neutrons in a compact core of plutonium fuel; the heat from the chain reaction was to be carried out of the core not by water or gas but by molten sodium metal. The design was called the 'liquid metal fast breeder reactor'.

The United States: Enrico Fermi

As mentioned earlier, this design got a head start in the United States, in the form of the Experimental Breeder Reactor–1, which produced the first-ever nuclear electricity in 1951. At the time the reactor had to use highly enriched uranium rather than plutonium in its core. Plutonium was scarce and costly, and earmarked almost exclusively for nuclear weapons. Furthermore, the technology for the fabrication of plutonium fuel was still embryonic. It involved combining uranium and plutonium oxides into 'mixed oxide', a process which was technically very demanding and accompanied by unfamiliar hazards.

Almost exactly four years after generating the first nuclear electricity, the Experimental Breeder Reactor achieved a distinctly more dubious first. On 29 November 1955, during testing, a technician inadvertently allowed the Mark II fuel charge of the reactor to overheat, leading to the first ever 'meltdown': the fuel rods in the reactor core melted like overheated candles, slumping into an intensely radioactive puddle in the bottom of the reactor vessel. Fortunately, the accident was contained, and no injuries resulted. Indeed, it

Table 2: Fast Breeder Reactors

Country	Location	Name or designation	Power (MW thermal)	Power (MW electric)	Owner	Operator	Year ordered	Start of construction	Initial Start-up	Status in 1984
USA	Arco, Idaho	Experimental Breeder Reactor-1	1	0.02	US Atomic Energy Commission	US Atomic Energy Commission	1949	1949	1951	shut down since 1963
Soviet Union	Obninsk	BR-5/10	initially 5; 10 since 1973	nil	State Committee for the Use of Atomic Energy	State Committee for the Use of Atomic Energy	not known	not known	1958	operational
USA	Idaho Falls, Idaho	Experimental Breeder Reactor-2	62.5	18.5	US Department of Energy	Argonne National Laboratory	1956	1957	1963	operational
USA	Monroe, Michigan	Enrico Fermi-1	200	60	Power Reactor Development Corporation	PRDC/ Detroit Edison	1955	1956	1963	fuel meltdown 5 October 1966; permanent shutdown in 1972; now being decommissioned

Country	Location	Name or designation	Power (MW thermal)	Power (MW electric)	Owner	Operator	Year ordered	Start of construction	Initial Start-up	Status in 1984
Britain	Dounreay	Dounreay Fast Reactor	60	14	UK Atomic Energy Authority	UK Atomic Energy Authority	1955	1955	1959	shut down in 1977
France	Cadarache	Rhapsodie	20 increased to 40 with new core	nil	Commissariat à l'Energie Atomique	Commissariat à l'Energie Atomique	1960	1963	1967	sodium leak in 1983 led to permanent shutdown
Soviet Union	Dimitrograd	Melekess BOR-60	60	12	not known	not known	1963	1965	1969	operational
Soviet Union	Shevchenko	BN-350	1000	150 plus 200 equivalent for desalination			1963	1964	1972	operational; known to have suffered serious steam generator problems; current output of electricity and desalinated water unknown

Country	Location	Name or designation	Power (MW thermal)	Power (MW electric)	Owner	Operator	Year ordered	Start of construction	Initial Start-up	Status in 1984
France	Marcoule	Phénix	563	250 gross, 233 net	CEA/EdF	CEA/EdF	1967	1968	1973	operational; recurring problems with sodium leaks; cumulative load factor to late 1983 54.8 per cent
Britain	Dounreay	Prototype Fast Reactor	600	250	UK Atomic Energy Authority	UK Atomic Energy Authority	1966	1967	1974	operational; cumulative load factor to late 1983 10.6 per cent; original steam generators to be replaced with new set
Japan	Oarai, Ibarakiken	Joyo	50/100	nil	Power Reactor and Nuclear Fuel Development Corporation	Power Reactor and Nuclear Fuel Development Corporation	1966	1970	1977; new core critical 1982	operational

Country	Location	Name or designation	Power (MW thermal)	Power (MW electric)	Owner	Operator	Year ordered	Start of construction	Initial Start-up	Status in 1984
Federal Germany	Leopolds-hafen	KNK-II	58	20	Gesellschaft für Kernforschung/Versuchsanlage	Gesellschaft für Kernforschung/Versuchsanlage	1965	1966	1971/4; operated initially as thermal reactor; fast core 1974	operational; see Bibliography, (21)
USA	Richland, Washington	Fast Flux Test Facility	400	nil	US Department of Energy	Westinghouse Hanford	1968	1970	1980	operational; see Bibliography, (53), January 1984, p. 46
Soviet Union	Beloyarsk	BN-600	1470	600	not known	not known	1967	1969	1979	operational
Italy	Brasimone	Prova Elementi di Combustibile	135/120 (sources differ)	nil	Comitato Nazionale per l'Energia Nucleare	Comitato Nazionale per l'Energia Nucleare	1969	1974	1988?	under review; facing possible cancellation

Country	Location	Name or designation	Power (MW thermal)	Power (MW electric)	Owner	Operator	Year ordered	Start of construction	Initial Start-up	Status in 1984
Federal Germany	Kalkar	SNR-300	762	327 gross, 295 net	Schnell-Bruter-Kern-kraftwerks-Gesellschaft	Schnell-Bruter-Kern-kraftwerks-Gesellschaft	1969	1973	1986?	under construction; financing of completion in dispute
France	Creys-Malville	Super-Phénix	3000	1240 gross, 1200 net	Groupement Centrale Nucléaire Européenne à Neutrons Rapides	Groupement Centrale Nucléaire Européenne à Neutrons Rapides	1972	1977	1984?	under construction; was to have been prototype for series of seven further replica plants, but design now undergoing extensive revision in attempt to reduce high capital cost; no further order expected until at least 1986

Country	Location	Name or designation	Power (MW thermal)	Power (MW electric)	Owner	Year ordered	Start of construction	Initial Start-up	Status in 1984
India	Kalpakkam	Fast Breeder Test Reactor	42	17	Department of Atomic Energy	Department of Atomic Energy	not known	not known	1984?	under construction
Japan	Tsuruga	Monju	714	280 net	Power Reactor and Nuclear Fuel Development Corporation	Power Reactor and Nuclear Fuel Development Corporation	1983	1983	1990?	ground broken for plant; details of finances still in dispute
USA	Oak Ridge, Tennessee	Clinch River Breeder Reactor	975	350	Department of Energy/ Tennessee Valley Authority	Tennessee Valley Authority	1972	1983	none	ground broken, much hardware ordered and manufactured; but cancelled by vote of Congress, 1983

(Data from 'Power Reactors 1983', August 1983 Supplement to (53); from 'Nuclear Station Achievement' by L. R. Howles, (53), January 1984, pp. 44–5; and from Draft Supplement to 1977 Final Environmental Impact Statement, Clinch River Breeder Reactor, Nuclear Regulatory Commission, July 1982. Certain small and short-lived fast neutron reactors omitted.)

was so well contained that four months passed before news of it leaked out. For some people this was just as well. With Atomic Energy Commission backing, Detroit Edison, Dow Chemical and a consortium of fifteen other suppliers were already preparing to build the world's first full-scale fast breeder power plant, on a site about fifteen miles from Detroit. In honour of the physicist who had first demonstrated a nuclear chain reaction, the fast breeder was to be named the Enrico Fermi Power Plant.

It was an ill-starred tribute. The plant excited controversy virtually from its inception, with both its design and its location attracting opposition. The Fermi plant was to have an electrical output of 60 megawatts. For a novel technology this was an enormous scale-up from the Experimental Breeder Reactor–1, whose maximum output was a mere 0.2 megawatts. The Atomic Energy Commission was by this time also building its own Experimental Breeder Reactor–2; but even this reactor was intended to have an output of only 16.5 megawatts. (See Table 2.) The dramatic scale-up in size of the Fermi plant posed a formidable engineering challenge.

The Commission's own Advisory Committee on Reactor Safeguards – 'safeguards' here means 'safety' – stated in a June 1956 report that it was unhappy about certain safety implications of the Fermi design, and could not endorse siting it so close to a major population centre. But the Advisory Committee report was suppressed by the Commission. The powerful United Auto Workers union led a bitter campaign against the plant, eventually all the way to the Supreme Court. In 1961, however, the Court decided 7–2 in favour of licensing the Fermi plant, although Justices William O. Douglas and Hugo Black registered a vehement dissent.

The Fermi plant was duly built. (See Table 2.) It started up in 1963; but one problem after another, with sodium pumps and steam generators in particular, kept it at low power when not completely shut down. Then, on 5 October 1966, a fragment of metal – that was, ironically, part of a safety device fitted belatedly at the insistence of the Advisory Committee on Reactor Safeguards – came adrift inside the reactor and jammed in the core. The consequent blockage of coolant flow led to overheating that melted two fuel elements and spread radioactivity all through the reactor.

Dealing with the accident was delicate and nerve-racking, and decontamination took many months. The Fermi reactor never fully recovered. At the end of 1971 it was shut down, never to start up again. The reactor had operated so sporadically that its spent fuel proved a peculiar nuisance. It did, of course, contain plutonium – but so little that it was impossible to reprocess. The fuel elements were eventually to be shipped to the Atomic Energy Commission facility at Savannah River, as was the radioactive sodium coolant, in shielded drums. The first full-scale demonstration fast breeder power plant had demonstrated just how far the concept was from commercial realization.

No sooner had the Fermi plant come to its ignominious end than everybody involved – the Atomic Energy Commission, the nuclear industry and even the electrical suppliers – at once seemed to set about expunging all trace of it from their collective memory. The Fermi plant quickly became a non-reactor, while the American plutonium people, in the Atomic Energy Commission and its corporate contractors and clients, busied themselves with a bigger and better idea. By the late 1960s there were fast breeder programmes underway in Britain, France, the Soviet Union, Japan and the Federal Republic of Germany. Pointing to this upsurge of overseas activity, American fast breeder people, led by the Atomic Energy Commission, proudly announced in July 1972 that they were now ready to build the nation's 'first fast breeder demonstration plant' – again.

Britain: Prototype Fast Reactor
By this time the fast breeders had already begun to spring up outside the United States. In Britain, the United Kingdom Atomic Energy Authority made no effort to involve electricity suppliers in its immediate plans. Funds for the 250-megawatt Prototype Fast Reactor, ordered in 1966, came directly from the British government. It was to be built for the Authority at its Dounreay site, next door to the existing Dounreay Fast Reactor. (See Table 2.) However, like the advanced gas-

61

cooled reactors, the Prototype Fast Reactor ran into one technical hitch after another, and slid steadily behind schedule.

Originally expected to start up in 1971, it was delayed by a multitude of minor problems and one major one, with the intricate rotating 'roof' of the reactor from which key internal parts were suspended. The reactor did start up, at last, in February 1974: just before the opening of an international conference in London, sponsored by the British Nuclear Energy Society, on Fast Reactor Power Stations. British fast breeder people, in the Atomic Energy Authority and its contractors, were profoundly relieved to see their new plant operational in time for the conference. But the operating history of the plant was to continue the pattern ominously perceptible while it was under construction.

France: Phénix
Unlike the British and Americans, the French did not at the outset regard the fast breeder as an immediate priority. Not until the early 1960s did the Commissariat à l'Energie Atomique undertake construction of their first fast breeder pilot plant, at the Cadarache Research Centre. With the usual French poetic flair, the sodium-cooled plant was called Rapsodie. When it started up in 1967, Rapsodie so stirred French souls that Commissariat planners that same year ordered a plant of prototype size – 250 megawatts. (See Table 2.) The French nuclear poets, drawing inspiration from the mythical creature that rose again from its own ashes, called the new plant Phénix.

Phénix was built at Marcoule, site of the French plutonium production reactors and the UP–1 military reprocessing plant. Although Phénix was intended to generate electricity for Electricité de France, the national government-owned utility, locating the plant on a military site was later to prove more than coincidental. Phénix started up in August 1973. British fast breeder people, as noted, had announced the start-up of their Prototype Fast Reactor just before the opening of the London conference in February 1974. Their French colleagues forthwith announced, on the last day of the conference, that Phénix had just reached full power. It was a vivid illustration of the politics of nuclear prestige, which was to be crucial for the international evolution of the plutonium dream.

Soviet Union: BN–350

The Soviet Union moved steadily along a parallel track. Their pioneer BOR–5 was followed by a larger experimental unit, the BOR–60 at Dimitrograd, which started up in 1969. (See Table 2.) Meanwhile, the Soviet nuclear planners had come up with an idea for a different kind of dual-purpose – indeed triple-purpose – plant, to be built at Shevchenko on the Caspian Sea. Called BN–350, it would be based on the sodium-cooled, plutonium-fuelled fast breeder. While breeding plutonium, it would supply 150 megawatts of electricity to the city; but the majority of its output, equivalent to another 200 megawatts of electricity, would be used for desalination.

The BN–350 was the first of the new wave of prototype fast breeder power plants to start up – on 29 November 1972. Little was heard about it in the West until November 1973, when American intelligence sources revealed that a spy satellite had photographed what appeared to be an explosion or a fire at the plant. True to form, the Soviet authorities maintained a stubborn silence about the event. Even after presenting a paper on the BN–350 at the London conference in 1974, Soviet participants would say only that there had been 'no explosion' at the site. They did admit that there had been serious sodium leaks in two of the BN–350's three steam generators. Western experts concluded that the spy satellite had seen the flare of hydrogen being burned, intentionally or otherwise, after a sodium-water reaction at the plant. News about the BN–350 continued to be difficult to come by – and in the Soviet context no news was by no means always good news.

Federal Germany: SNR–300

Other Western European countries also had a stake in what was rapidly becoming a breeder race. The fast breeder prototypes in Britain, France and the Soviet Union were all constructed as purely national projects, under the aegis of the national nuclear organization in each country. In 1972, urged on by their national nuclear laboratories, Federal Germany, Belgium and the Netherlands joined forces to construct a multinational prototype fast breeder power station akin to the British Prototype Fast Reactor, the French Phénix and the Soviet BN–350. The plant, called the SNR–300, was to be built near the village of Kalkar in Germany, not far from the Dutch border. (See Table 2.)

Electricity supply companies in the three participating countries set up a separate company, whose German acronym was SBK, with the fast breeder as its one power plant. Shares in SBK were held by the German utility RWE, with 68 per cent, the Belgian Synatom and the Dutch SEP, each with 14.5 per cent, and Britain's Central Electricity Generating Board with a nominal 3 per cent. Nuclear manufacturers in the three main participating countries similarly set up a joint company whose German acronym was INB, 70 per cent owned by the German Interatom, and 30 per cent by the Belgian Belgonucléaire and the Dutch Neratoom. The estimated cost of the Kalkar plant in 1972 was DM1535 million, the greater part of which was to come from the Bonn government with a modest contribution – DM84 million – from the German electricity suppliers. The Belgian and Dutch governments provided 15 per cent each.

Although the SNR–300 was a comparatively late entry in the fast breeder race it swiftly overtook its precursors in one unfortunate respect. The three earlier plants, in Britain, France and the Soviet Union, had all experienced delays and cost escalation during construction. However, on this score the SNR–300 quickly proved to be in a class by itself. By 1975 its estimated cost had climbed to DM2300 million – with the escalation to be borne entirely by the governments involved. Worse was to follow.

Japan: Monju

On the other side of the hemisphere, Japan had been looking at the fast breeder since 1960. By 1962 several Japanese nuclear organizations were already drafting preliminary designs. In 1968 the Power Reactor and Nuclear Fuel Development Corporation, a joint government-industry agency, took over the second stage of design work for a pilot-scale fast breeder that would burn mixed oxide fuel. The Corporation, with five other Japanese companies, laid plans to build a unit that would produce 50 megawatts of heat. The plan got the go-ahead in February 1970. (See Table 2.)

Japanese fast breeder people shared with their French colleagues a penchant for the poetic. They called their new pilot plant Joyo, meaning 'eternal light'. The light in question was purely metaphorical, since the unit did not in fact incorporate any electricity generating stage. Nevertheless, even while Joyo was still only a gleam in the designers' eyes, they were already making sketches for a much larger fast breeder, a power plant able to generate 280 megawatts of electricity. It was to be called Monju, after the sage who sat at the Buddha's right hand – symbolizing the combination of knowledge and wisdom. Even this powerful name was to be of little avail. The Monju concept, already on paper by 1965, was destined to stay there much longer than its originators anticipated or desired.

The SNR–300 in concrete and the Monju on paper both brought one significant feature of fast breeder programmes into stark relief. The moving force behind each programme was invariably one or more government-funded national nuclear organizations. Apart from the discouraging early exception of the Fermi project, manufacturing industry was prepared to participate only through government contracts; private risk capital was scarcely to be seen. Even the electricity suppliers, presumed to be the eventual beneficiaries of the fast breeder, were at best cautious and tentative participants in the prototype projects. Year by year the costs of the projects climbed, and original budget estimates sank without trace. This cost escalation was invariably borne by governments – not by electricity suppliers – even when the electricity suppliers were themselves government-owned. The lack of enthusiasm for the fast breeder on the part of the electricity supply industry was ere long to become frankly embarrassing.

The United States again

In the United States, throughout the 1960s and into the 1970s, even despite the Fermi fiasco, the fast breeder beacon burned as bright as ever. As early as 1962, even before the

Fermi plant had started up, Atomic Energy Commission Chairman Glenn Seaborg, the father of plutonium, invited by President John Kennedy to take 'a new and hard look at the role of nuclear power in our economy', submitted a report to the President entitled 'Civilian Nuclear Power', that painted the rosiest imaginable future for nuclear electricity, and for plutonium fuel. The fast breeder was 'essential to long-range major use of nuclear energy'. Seaborg reiterated the Commission's commitment to a major programme of fast breeder research, which would ensure 'the maintenance of US technological leadership in the world'.

The Experimental Breeder Reactor–1 had been shut down permanently in 1963, but not before its 18.5–megawatt successor had started up nearby. The Commission used this second Experimental Breeder Reactor for design studies. However, they soon concluded that it was not sufficiently large or powerful to carry out realistic tests rapidly enough. Accordingly, in 1965 the Commission announced that it wanted to build a 'Fast Flux Test Facility' at Hanford. It would produce 400 megawatts of heat, and would be used to test fuel and components. The Commission's Director of Reactor Development and Technology, Milton Shaw, describing these plans at a conference in London in May 1965, added that the next plant in the programme would be a 'demonstration plant'. In due course the Commission took to calling this next plant 'the nation's first demonstration fast breeder power plant' – presumably in the hope that the public would overlook the Power Reactor Demonstration Program of the 1950s, which had demonstrated, among other unwelcome results, that the Fermi fast breeder was a premature and dangerous adventure.

On 4 June 1971 President Richard Nixon delivered the first-ever Message on Energy to Congress. It included '. . . a commitment to complete the successful demonstration of the liquid metal fast breeder reactor by 1980'. He called it '. . . our best hope today for meeting the nation's demand for economical clean energy'. The passage was quoted in the Preamble to the Atomic Energy Commission's *Draft Environmental Statement for the Liquid Metal Fast Breeder Reactor Demonstration Plant*, published in 1971. Thus, even as the

Fermi plant was messily breathing its last, American fast breeder people were erecting a gleaming new billboard in front of its hulk.

On 7 August 1972 James Schlesinger, successor to Seaborg as Chairman of the Commission, was pictured with executives from nuclear manufacturers and electricity suppliers, signing agreements to set up the new project. With Westinghouse as lead contractor, the Breeder Development Corporation and the Project Management Corporation were given the go-ahead to design and construct 'the nation's first demonstration fast breeder power plant', a 350–megawatt unit on a site near Oak Ridge, Tennessee, called Clinch River. The agreements spelled out the financial details of the project. A consortium of 340 suppliers would contribute $257 million of the estimated $400 million cost of the plant, with the rest to come from the Commission. However, almost before the ink was dry on the agreements the estimated $400 million for the cost of the Clinch River Breeder Reactor had begun to look more like petty cash.

7 Reprocessors, civil and otherwise

Barnwell

As the fast breeders broke ground, the reprocessors laid plans to ensure them plenty of plutonium to burn. The most ambitious plan of all took shape not far from Clinch River. General Atomic, a nuclear offshoot of two major oil multinationals, Shell and Gulf, joined forces with Allied Chemical to form a company called Allied General Nuclear Services – AGNS, inevitably pronounced 'Agnes'. In 1968 Allied General applied for a construction permit to build yet another civil reprocessing plant. At the time it was expected that the northeastern United States would be served by Nuclear Fuel Services at West Valley, and the midwest by General Electric at Morris. Accordingly, Allied General selected a site just east of the Savannah River reservation of the Atomic Energy Commission – much of it, indeed, an offcut from Savannah River – near the village of Barnwell, South Carolina. The Barnwell plant was to be much larger than those at West Valley and Morris. Its planned annual capacity was to be 1500 tonnes of high-burnup oxide fuel; it would thus be able to deal with the spent fuel from some sixty 1000–megawatt conventional nuclear power plants. From that amount of fuel it would produce some 15 tonnes of separated plutonium per year.

The Atomic Energy Commission issued a construction permit for the Barnwell plant on 18 December 1970. However, even as the site was being cleared and the first concrete poured, the very concept of civil reprocessing was beginning – belatedly – to undergo a searching and agitated examination in the United States. Elsewhere, on the other hand – in the Federal Republic of Germany, Italy, Argentina and India, with Japan and Pakistan not far behind – the reprocessors were just getting into their stride. None of these countries possessed nuclear weapons. None of them was at the time a party to the Non-Proliferation Treaty.

Federal Germany

In Federal Germany, in the late 1960s, the Bonn government's nuclear research centre at Karlsruhe had built a small pilot reprocessing plant called the Wiederaufarbeitungsanlage Karlsruhe – mercifully abbreviated to WAK. (See Table 1.) WAK had a rated annual throughput of 40 tonnes per year; in industrial terms it was therefore only a modest step up from a bench-scale operation, one fuel pin at a time – what nuclear people refer to as the 'knife and fork' method. Be that as it may, the German nuclear planners were already aspiring to much greater things.

As early as 1969, even before the start-up of WAK, the Federal Ministry of Research and Technology had come up with a scheme for a vast installation to cope with the spent fuel from the entire Federal German civil nuclear programme. It would incorporate cooling ponds for spent fuel, a reprocessing plant on a heroic scale, plants to purify recovered uranium and plutonium, storage tanks for high-level liquid waste and a facility to immobilize this waste in glass, a 'vitrification plant'. The whole sprawling aggregation was to be sited directly over an underground geological formation called a salt dome, which would serve as a repository for the final disposal of the vitrified high-level waste. The concept was labelled with another jaw-breaking polysyllable: 'Entsorgungszentrum' – literally, a centre for removing worries. As a public relations slogan the idea caught on immediately. As a practical reality it was to have a rough ride.

In 1970 four major German chemical companies formed a consortium to build the large-scale reprocessing plant in the Ministry scheme. By 1974, however, after detailed paper studies, the four partners – none of which had any long-standing commitment to the civil use of plutonium – concluded that the plan was commercially a non-starter. They forthwith shelved the idea. Their withdrawal from the field stunned both the Bonn government and the privately owned German electricity suppliers, which had been counting on the services of the consortium to relieve them of their spent fuel.

The German 'Atomgesetz', or atomic law, required that electricity suppliers provide for management and disposal of spent fuel before a power reactor could be licensed to operate. The German courts were showing an alarming tendency to take the law at its face value. They also took the nuclear people at their word, and assumed that civil spent fuel had of necessity to be reprocessed. If there were no reprocessing available, the civil nuclear industry would soon be in serious trouble. If a supplier could not contract to have its spent fuel reprocessed, it would no longer be able to get licences for future nuclear plants. Worse still, the law might compel it to shut down plants already operating. As nuclear plant cooling ponds in the Federal Republic began to fill up with spent fuel, the suppliers were to be forced to take matters into their own hands.

More reprocessors

Other countries, too, had by the mid-1970s ventured into reprocessing; some ventures were more unambiguously civil than others. Italy constructed a small experimental reprocessing plant at Saluggia, with an annual capacity of 10 tonnes of spent fuel per year. Argentina did likewise. With assistance from Federal Germany, it built a pilot reprocessing plant at its nuclear research centre at Ezeiza near Buenos Aires. The plant operated from 1969 to 1972. Strange discrepancies emerged – and lingered – about its capacity. In later years the Bonn government was to claim that the plant could handle only 1 kilogram of spent fuel per year. However, the independent and authoritative Stockholm International Peace Research Institute put the figure at 200 kilograms per year.

It was also later reported that the spent fuel reprocessed in this pilot plant was supplied by Federal Germany for the Argentines to practise on. Why they should have wanted to practise reprocessing at all, then or subsequently, was either unclear or all too clear. Argentina stoutly insisted that its reprocessing was a purely civil exercise. However, Argentina's first power reactor, at Atucha, was of a type which does not require enriched fuel, a 'heavy-water natural uranium reactor'. So, subsequently, were its second and third. There was therefore no prospect of recycling the recovered plutonium, by using it to increase the fissile content of natural uranium for use in these reactors. The recovered uranium would be of very low quality, severely depleted in fissile uranium–235. Nevertheless, Argentina insisted that it had long-term plans for fast breeders, for which reprocessing would be essential as the technology to supply plutonium for fuel. It also declared an interest in becoming a nuclear exporter – even to the extent of exporting plutonium. Argentina refused point-blank to become a party to the Non-Proliferation Treaty. In so doing it hinted obliquely that it reserved the right to acquire nuclear weapons if it saw fit. Observers wondered aloud just how civil Argentina's interest in reprocessing might actually be.

They wondered likewise about India. India had built a 50-tonne-per-year reprocessing plant at its nuclear research centre at Trombay, near Bombay. It started up as early as 1964 – well before India's first power reactor was even under construction. Furthermore, the power plant programme upon which India thereafter embarked concentrated, like that of Argentina, on heavy-water natural uranium reactors. Only one Indian nuclear power plant used enriched fuel: the plant at Tarapur, which had two reactors supplied by the United States under an agreement signed in 1963. Nevertheless, the grandiose vision of the founding father of the Indian nuclear programme, Homi Bhabha, foresaw moving on from conventional reactors to breeders that would burn not only plutonium but also thorium fuel. Before long there would be, he declared, hundreds of indigenous Indian nuclear stations springing up all over the country.

India, too, declined to become a party to the Non-Proliferation Treaty. In the view of the Indians the Treaty was discriminatory, favouring those states already possessing nuclear weapons and creating a category of subordinate states that could not be trusted to decide their own nuclear destiny. This viewpoint was shared by other countries that also declined to become parties to the Treaty. It was all too readily defensible, and was to become more so. In any case, the sweep of Indian nuclear aspirations was so grandiloquent that foreign observers were prepared, despite reservations, to take the Indians at their word: the Trombay reprocessing plant was indeed a purely civil facility, however premature it might appear in the Indian nuclear scheme of things.

Be that as it might, as the roster of reprocessors lengthened, some worrying questions were beginning to surface. Were all these countries really interested in separating plutonium only in order to use it as fuel, in plants as yet unbuilt, at some date far in the future? Or might their interest in separated plutonium have a more obvious – and ominous – goal?

8 Explosion of concern

By the beginning of the 1970s a further complication was affecting nuclear plans in many countries. Local opposition to particular nuclear projects had started to coalesce into national opposition. There were even the first signs of co-operation on international opposition. 'The environment' had become a major public issue. In the United States, Britain and elsewhere environmental groups sprang up, dedicated to rectifying existing abuses and pressing for sounder long-term planning. At the time the interests of such groups included wildlife and nature, urban and rural development, transport, consumer protection, and many aspects of what was soon to be called 'energy policy', including civil nuclear power.

Nuclear power attracted the attention of environmental activists initially because of concern about pollutants from power plants, and then because of questions about reactor safety. At the outset, in the late 1960s and early 1970s, opponents focused on nuclear power plants themselves. In the United States they intervened in licensing hearings; in Europe and Japan they took their cases to the courts and to the streets. Then, gradually, other nuclear activities came under fire from opponents, among them reprocessing. The main concerns were much the same as those then arising about nuclear power plants. Were reprocessing plants burdening the environment with dangerous radioactive pollution? What might be the consequences of an accident at a reprocessing plant?

In the United States the West Valley debacle, especially the generous helpings of radioactivity the plant had been discharging into its neighbourhood, attracted a certain amount of public attention. The exposure of workers to radiation drew fire from the trade unions. Nuclear opponents in the United

States and elsewhere were beginning to ask what was to be done with the mounting inventory of high-level liquid waste produced by reprocessing. Their concern was heightened by news of a leak of 435 000 litres of such waste from a storage tank at the Hanford reservation between April and June 1972 – military waste, to be sure, but reprocessing waste nevertheless. However, such popular concern about reprocessing did not extend to the possible misuse of the separated plutonium, nor would it for some time to come.

The fast breeder, too, was receiving unfriendly attention from environmental groups, especially in the United States. The Atomic Energy Commission had made the fast breeder its top priority since 1967. By 1972 the Commission was spending $260 million a year – more than 40 per cent of the total Federal budget for all energy research and development – on the fast breeder alone; this expenditure was expected to leap to $323 million in 1973, and continue to increase in subsequent years. The Commission's long-term programme for fast breeders anticipated expenditures exceeding the entire remaining Federal budget for energy research and development. In response to these grandiose visions American environmental organizations took the Commission to court. They declared that the National Environmental Policy Act of 1970 required that the Commission file an environmental impact statement, not merely for the first demonstration plant at Clinch River, but for the whole programme – an anticipated 400 fast breeder power plants by the year 2000. The courts agreed with the environmentalists. The Commission duly set about preparing an environmental impact statement for its fast breeder programme, presenting all the technical, economic and environmental arguments it could marshal on the fast breeder's behalf. But it did not apparently feel any need to consider deeply the possible impact of plutonium fuel on weapons proliferation.

In the early 1970s the United States Congress likewise concentrated its attentions on nuclear issues which concerned health and safety and the environment, narrowly construed. Outside the United States a similar pattern arose. Governments and legislators responded in various ways to public pressure about nuclear issues; but the issues of public

74

concern did not appear to include the link between civil and military nuclear activities, nor how to keep separated plutonium 'peaceful'. Behind the scenes, however, expert concern was starting to become manifest, and to mount. At high-level conferences and seminars weapons specialists discussed the implications of separated plutonium falling into the wrong hands; and they grew more and more uneasy.

The issue exploded into the open, and full public view, in December 1973, when the *New Yorker* magazine published a three-part profile of a physicist named Theodore Taylor. Nuclear opponents in the United States and Europe seized on the articles and circulated them well beyond the usual limits of *New Yorker* readership. In the 1950s, Taylor had been the star fission-bomb designer for the Atomic Energy Commission. In the profile, Taylor gave popular currency to a concept that soon became a lurid cliché: the do-it-yourself atom bomb. But Taylor was not talking pulp fiction; his conclusions were based on all too solid facts.

Taylor and a law professor named Mason Willrich had been commissioned to prepare a report for the Ford Foundation Energy Policy Project. Published in April 1974, it bore the uncompromising title *Nuclear Theft: Risks and Safeguards*. It was a matter-of-fact, authoritative analysis of a blood-chilling and real possibility: that someone might steal fissile material – especially plutonium – from a civil nuclear installation and use it to make a bomb. According to Willrich and Taylor, the potential nuclear thieves and bomb-makers included not only unscrupulous governments but also criminals, terrorists and lunatics. All were judged capable of obtaining bomb material, fabricating a bomb and detonating it. *Nuclear Theft* was in no way a sensational document. It was written in low-key academic language; but it was lucid and unambiguous. Its meticulous thoroughness and bleak conclusions left many a reader pale and shaking.

Nor was it the only high-level warning. Within a month of its publication, on 30 April 1974, Senator Abraham Ribicoff, powerful chairman of the Senate Committee on Government Operations, revealed that the Atomic Energy Commission had attempted to suppress an internal report on the same subject. Entitled 'Special Safeguards Study', it had been written by a group headed by a Commission consultant named David Rosenbaum; and it had reached similar dismaying conclusions. According to the Rosenbaum report:

> The potential harm to the public from the explosion of an illicitly made nuclear weapon is greater than that from any plausible power plant accident, including one which involves a core meltdown and subsequent breach of containment. Acquisition of special nuclear material remains the only substantial problem facing groups which desire to have such weapons. . . . The factors involved in preventing the illegal acquisition of special nuclear material and the subsequent manufacture of nuclear weapons have received a great deal less attention than those associated with power plant accidents. The relevant regulations are far less stringent and we feel they are entirely inadequate to meet the threat.

The Commission, as was its wont when faced with embarrassing findings, had sat on the Rosenbaum report. However, a copy fell into the hands of Ribicoff. When he announced a press conference about it, the Commission slipped a copy to the Joint Committee on Atomic Energy, which hastily published a sanitized version.

Behind the scenes, the General Accounting Office had also been weighing in, with an on-the-spot investigation that gave the matter a feel of alarming immediacy. The gist of its findings was apparent in the title of a report published in November 1973: *Some Improvements Needed in the Program for the Protection of Special Nuclear Material.* The Office had inspected just three out of 95 American installations licensed to hold significant quantities of fissile material; and two out of these first three had already failed abysmally to meet even the most rudimentary standards for security:

> GAO noted such conditions as weak physical security barriers, ineffective guard patrols, ineffective alarm systems, lack of automatic-detection devices, and lack of an action plan in the event of a diversion of material. . . . Guards did not vary times or routes when touring the plant. . . . Fencing around the plant had broken locks on gates, holes large enough for a person to gain access to the plant, and several other weaknesses. . . . Material was stored in a prefabricated steel structure which could be breached easily.

Other disconcerting problems were coming into focus. In a power reactor, the fissile material was in the form of individual fuel elements, which could be numbered and counted. An element was either there or not. In a reprocessing plant, on the other hand, the fissile material was in a liquid solution, flowing continuously through a complex array of pipes and vessels. Neither its volume nor its concentration could be determined precisely; indeed except at the input and output ends of the plant they could not readily be determined at all. A 'material balance', to assess the agreement between the amount of fissile material entering the plant and the amount leaving, could only be made batch by batch.

Even then there were limits on the accuracy of measurement possible. Safeguards experts conceded that it was technically acutely difficult to keep track of what was going through a large reprocessing plant to any closer than about 1 per cent. A plant the size of Barnwell, for example, with a planned annual throughput of 1500 tonnes of spent fuel, would be expected to produce perhaps 15 tonnes of plutonium per year. One per cent of this would be 150 kilograms: enough for at least 15 atom bombs.

A safeguards inspector visiting a reprocessing plant was supposed to examine the records and assure himself that all the plutonium fed into the plant had come out again, still 'peaceful'. Any discrepancy between the input and the output was called 'material unaccounted for' – in the nuclear vernacular, MUF. However, the inherent limitation on the measurement of the throughput meant that there was likewise an inherent limitation on the accuracy of the records. Thus a certain amount of apparent MUF might just be the result of random variations in the measurement process. This 'limit of error on MUF' was called LEMUF.

This jargon acronym tended to obscure a fundamental weakness of the safeguards process. This weakness made it not just technically difficult but literally impossible to apply effective safeguards to a large reprocessing plant. The irreducible margin of error in measurements opened the possibility that management or staff could manipulate the plant and extract enough plutonium to manufacture several bombs per year, without serious risk of detection. This was particularly true if very small amounts of plutonium were extracted over time. In such a case the missing plutonium would be such a minute fraction of the total throughput that it would be below the limit of detectability. Safeguards inspectors would have no way to satisfy themselves that plutonium was not being diverted from the plant unseen. Such diversion might take place either by a covert decision by top management – possibly even by government – or by a shop-floor employee or group of employees bent on theft of plutonium, either for sale or for some more immediately nefarious purpose, like nuclear blackmail or terrorism.

In the eyes of many observers, there could no longer be any evading the fact: a reprocessing plant represented a severe challenge to the conventional concept of safeguards – a challenge that might completely invalidate the concept. If safeguards alone stood between civil and military applications of reprocessing technology, nuclear decision-makers were relying on a barrier that seemed all too permeable. Reprocessing, however civil in appearance and intent, opened the door to nuclear weapons, and left it open thenceforth.

None of these considerations, however, in any way dampened the ardour of the plutonium people in the United States, Britain, France or elsewhere. Within the international nuclear community, reprocessing, plutonium and the fast breeder retained their pivotal position in planning. Indeed, the oil shock of October 1973 had released a flood of fresh enthusiasm for nuclear power. Orders piled up in the reactor vendors' in-trays. At this rate, said the pundits, the world's uranium would quickly be devoured. Only a rapid move into large-scale reprocessing and a major commitment to fast breeders, to burn the recovered plutonium and produce more, would keep the lights from going out.

Such, at least, was the virtually unanimous opinion among those working on nuclear research and development in the national nuclear organizations – the United States Atomic Energy Commission, the United Kingdom Atomic Energy Authority, and their confrères in other countries. All these organizations were financed by governments – that is, by taxpayers; and most were pursuing major research and development programmes centred on the use of plutonium fuel. Their view was epitomized in the opening lines of a paper presented to the World Energy Conference in September 1974, co-authored by senior executives of the French Commissariat à l'Energie Atomique, British Nuclear Fuels and the German-based United Reprocessors:

> Nuclear energy is indispensable to meet the economic and environmental challenges of future energy requirements. Reprocessing of spent fuel, which constitutes the final step of the nuclear fuel cycle, is an indispensable part of nuclear power generation. It consists of the separation and purification of uranium and plutonium from the highly radioactive fission products in the spent fuel. Uranium and plutonium will be re-used for fabrication of new nuclear fuel . . .

The enthusiasm for reprocessing, plutonium and the fast breeder was distinctly more muted on the part of the electricity suppliers themselves, even during the frenzy of nuclear ordering in early 1974. The Kalkar and Clinch River prototypes were at the time the only fast breeders in which the suppliers had a substantial financial interest; and their costs had already begun to mount at a disconcerting rate, leaving the original estimates far behind. Despite these cost increases the suppliers did not manifest any eagerness to top up their financial contributions.

Be that as it may, the plutonium-fuelled fast breeder dominated official energy planning as it attempted to come to grips with the dramatic change in the world energy scene wrought by the Organization of Petroleum Exporting Countries. More than ever, it was asserted, plutonium and the fast breeder were needed to play the roles envisaged for them since the 1940s: they would provide the key to national 'energy security', by eliminating dependence on either imported oil or imported uranium. Official analyses in the United States and Europe did not state how long it would take the fast breeder to bring about this emancipation. Nor did they acknowledge the undertone of agitation over the problem of safeguarding the separated plutonium required for fast breeders, and the reprocessing plants that would be required to supply their fuel. The plutonium people simply did not like to talk about nuclear weapons proliferation as a corollary of their policy. They did not even like to hear about it. But they heard about it, on 18 May 1974, when India set off a bang that echoed around the world.

PART TWO

Plutonium diplomacy

1974–9

9 Pokharan and after

'The Buddha is smiling.' With this singularly inappropriate coded message, Indian scientists sent word of their achievement to India's Foreign Minister Swaran Singh and thence to Prime Minister Indira Gandhi: on 18 May 1974 an underground nuclear explosion of some 15 kilotonnes had bulged the floor of the Rajasthan desert near Pokharan. Whether the Buddha would have looked upon the explosion as a suitable sequel to his 'flower sermon' is to say the least debatable; but all India – at any rate all public India – rejoiced.

Ever since the Chinese-Indian war of 1962, India had become more and more apprehensive about its larger neighbour to the north. The Chinese nuclear tests which first burst upon the world in 1964 drastically heightened this apprehension. The day after the Indian test *The Guardian* in Britain noted bleakly the arrival of a new category of nuclear weapon: one that did not depend on sophisticated rocketry, but could be delivered by oxcart. After a lull of a decade, in which the number of nuclear weapons states had remained static at five, a sixth candidate had signalled its accession. The Third World was joining the nuclear club.

The Indians, to be sure, parried all suggestions that they had become a sixth weapons state. The Pokharan device, they insisted, was a 'peaceful nuclear explosive'. It had been manufactured using plutonium produced in the CIRUS research reactor at Trombay, and separated in the reprocessing plant at the same site. The CIRUS reactor was a heavy water reactor with a heat output of 40 megawatts. It had been provided to India in the mid-1950s by Canada, as the centrepiece of a wide-ranging programme of Canadian nuclear assistance to India. It had started up in July 1960, well before the safeguards régime of the International Atomic

Energy Agency had come into being. But the Canadians had provided the reactor under a bilateral agreement which stipulated, among other things, that no Canadian nuclear aid would be used to develop nuclear weapons.

When the furious Canadians demanded an explanation of the Pokharan explosion, the Indians merely shrugged and declared that the device had not been a bomb; the plutonium in it had exploded 'peacefully'. In justification they pointed, ironically, to the Non-Proliferation Treaty. India had always vehemently refused to become a party to the Treaty; they declared it to be discriminatory, because it permitted existing weapons states to maintain their weapons programmes while denying nuclear weapons to other parties. Nevertheless, the Indians noted that Article V of the Treaty decreed that parties to the Treaty were free, if they so wished, to detonate 'peaceful nuclear explosions', with weapons states providing the service for non-weapons states. If even parties to the Treaty could detonate such explosions, so without question could India. In one of many official Indian statements that followed the explosion, India's representative told the Board of Governors of the International Atomic Energy Agency that:

> India has always reserved its right to pursue its own independent policy of using nuclear energy for peaceful purposes, and of carrying out research and development into all meaningful applications of nuclear energy for economic development. The use of the nuclear explosion technology underground is an integral part of the Indian government's policy of using nuclear energy for peaceful purposes.

This response did not mollify the Canadians. In their fury and embarrassment they forthwith severed all further nuclear co-operation with India, including continuing work on India's CANDU nuclear plants at Rajasthan and Kalpakkam. The Canadians' fury was further inflamed by heavy-handed attacks from across their southern border. Several American politicians spoke out, deploring the sloppy, ineffectual safeguards that had allowed India thus to misuse Canadian nuclear assistance. No one in the United States appeared to notice or was willing to acknowledge that the reactor which had created the Pokharan plutonium might have been called CIRUS for good reason.

CIR stood for Canada-India-Reactor, US for United States: the initial supply of heavy water for the reactor came from the Atomic Energy Commission plant at Savannah River, and was covered by a 'peaceful use' agreement between India and the United States. Any shortcomings in the CIRUS safeguards should not, therefore, have been laid at the doorstep of Canada alone. Nevertheless, the official American government response to the Pokharan test was at first both oblique and muted. Not for two years did the Americans react officially in practical terms. When at length they did, they were to make a spectacular botch of it.

The Indian explosion was all too vivid proof that the earlier fears about the ambiguity of 'civil' nuclear programmes were fully justified. It was the first nuclear explosion produced within a programme expressly called 'civil'; and it gave a multi-kilotonne boost to the chorus of criticism of ostensibly civil plutonium technologies. Within less than five years, such criticism was to help bring about a dramatic shift in the international nuclear scene. Concern about 'civil' plutonium had been registered most intensely in the United States. However, as the plutonium bandwagon began to lose its original American momentum, it was given new impetus by the faithful in Europe, Japan and elsewhere. Foreign nuclear programmes patterned on that of the United States had by this time advanced to the stage at which separated plutonium was becoming available in quantity. India, whatever her original intentions many years earlier, could not resist – indeed, did not apparently try to resist – the temptation to find out what an Indian atom bomb would sound like. Outside India it sounded to many people like the first ominous creak of an international structure about to collapse.

The Nuclear Suppliers' Group

Be that as it may, international nuclear behaviour after the Pokharan explosion seemed to be more of an endorsement of India's action than a condemnation; indeed the chairman of the French Commissariat sent his Indian opposite number a note of congratulation. Within the following twelve months

85

international nuclear commerce moved into territory hitherto tacitly considered taboo. In 1971, nuclear exporting countries – with the notable exception of France – had set up an expert committee chaired by a Swiss scientist named Claude Zangger, to decide how to interpret the safeguards requirements of the Non-Proliferation Treaty. In the autumn of 1974 the International Atomic Energy Agency published an information circular that included a 'trigger list' recommended by the Zangger committee – those items of technology and hardware with potential nuclear weapons applications, whose export would 'trigger' the requirement of safeguards on the export. The very existence of such a list sounded a new note of caution about the nuclear export business. However, it was also a curious response to the Non-Proliferation Treaty, which explicitly required safeguards on all nuclear activities in non-weapons states party to the Treaty.

Within fourteen months of the Pokharan explosion, France agreed to supply Pakistan with a reprocessing plant. Federal Germany and Brazil concluded a nuclear co-operation agreement on an unprecedented scale. It involved a commitment to supply Brazil with not only eight power reactors but also a uranium enrichment plant and a reprocessing plant. Neither Pakistan nor Brazil was a party to the Non-Proliferation Treaty; nor did they accept full-scope safeguards as a condition of the contracts. France also agreed to supply a reprocessing plant to South Korea – a party to the Treaty but interested in nuclear weapons nonetheless. The exporting countries, France and Federal Germany, were delighted with these contracts. They seemed to signal the opening of a new era in international nuclear trade, the long-awaited breakup of the near-monopoly of the world nuclear market long held by the United States. However, the contracts also signalled the arrival of a form of competition which made some people very uneasy indeed.

France was not a party to the Non-Proliferation Treaty. Nevertheless, since the Treaty had come into force, no nuclear exporter had been prepared to supply a technology like enrichment or reprocessing to a non-weapons country: not, at any rate, as a full-scale quasi-commercial plant. The French and German contracts to supply plants capable of producing nuclear weapons material – and to non-Treaty countries like Brazil and Pakistan, at that – raised a disturbing prospect. As the international competition for nuclear export orders grew ever more heated, would the provision of 'sensitive technologies' with direct weapons applications become a commercial bargaining counter? Would safeguards themselves become ever more negotiable? Would exporters vie with one another to offer the most lenient constraints on the nuclear wares they were displaying in the global marketplace?

Even as the exporting countries took their first steps along this precarious pathway, they could not but be aware of the pitfalls gaping ahead of them. In 1975 the exporters took the work of the Zangger committee a step farther, at the instigation of the original nuclear weapons countries – the United States, Britain and the Soviet Union. These three countries convened in London with Canada, France, the Federal Republic of Germany and Japan for top-secret consultations. France's participation was significant, as the maverick among the exporters, neither a party to the Non-Proliferation Treaty nor a participant in the Zangger committee deliberations. The consultations were aimed at devising ground-rules for the international nuclear business, to prevent a free-wheeling nuclear auction, with safeguards at a premium and nuclear weapons capability an implicit sweetener of every bargain. When word of the secret meetings leaked out, the participating countries were labelled the Nuclear Suppliers' Group, the London Suppliers' Group, or just the London Club. Within a matter of months the Club expanded to fifteen members, adding Belgium, Czechoslovakia, the German Democratic Republic, Italy, the Netherlands, Poland, Sweden and Switzerland.

The details of the negotiations remained secret at the time; but reliable reports declared that the discussions centred on sensitive technologies – their identification and description and the establishment of generally applicable controls on their transfer to foreign customers. It appeared that the Club was building on the Zangger trigger list, and seeking agreement among its members that all would require safeguards on any export itemized in the Club's guidelines. A bulletin issued in 1976 described the arrangements agreed. They were, however, noticeably less restrictive than those required under the Non-Proliferation Treaty. It required each non-weapons state party to the Treaty to accept safeguards on all nuclear activities in that state. The London Club guidelines stipulated only that safeguards be applied to imported items from the trigger list.

The refusal of the exporters to adopt the Treaty requirement as the basis of their Club guidelines suggested that some members at least reserved the right to offer less stringent safeguards in the interest of winning orders. It also left the door open for exports to non-Treaty countries, under safeguards conditions less onerous than those applied to Treaty countries. Nuclear exporters were clearly reluctant to jeopardize their commercial prospects in the interest of inhibiting proliferation.

10 Proliferation comes to Washington

In nuclear affairs the secret deliberations of the Nuclear
Suppliers' Group were nothing out of the ordinary. Manipu-
lation of the nuclear marketplace by devious means was by the
mid-1970s long since standard operating procedure. In Britain and France, for instance, the choice of reactor design,
supplier and size of programme was decreed by government
after closed discussions. In the United States the Atomic
Energy Commission played a fundamental part in establishing
civil nuclear power, with subsidies of every kind. Special
legislation provided for government-backed insurance against
potential nuclear accidents, giving nuclear plants an obvious
advantage over competing technologies; and so on. The
United States was the champion of free enterprise; but even
there this ideal clashed repeatedly with nuclear reality, both
economic and diplomatic; and free enterprise lost the day.
That did not mean, to be sure, that the manipulations always
achieved their objectives: far from it.

Since 1945 successive United States administrations and
Congress had tended to leave American nuclear policy largely
in the hands of the nuclear insiders: the Atomic Energy
Commission and its ever more complaisant watchdog, the
Congressional Joint Committee on Atomic Energy. This
hands-off policy had extended not only to domestic nuclear
policy but also to nuclear foreign affairs. It was an approach
with serious limitations. The division of responsibility too
often amounted to an abdication of responsibility, especially
concerning the effect of domestic nuclear decisions on the
international nuclear scene.

In the early 1970s the Nixon administration decided that
uranium enrichment, hitherto the exclusive province of the
Commission, ought to be taken over by the private sector.

The private sector, however, did not want it. Uranium enrichment plants required a stupefying amount of capital; estimates ranged as high as $8 billion. They took many years to build, and might not eventually find enough customers. Accordingly, in a series of remarkably heavy-handed and ill-conceived moves, the Nixon administration tried to browbeat domestic and foreign customers into brutally one-sided long-term contracts for enriched uranium. The intention was to commit existing capacity and guarantee a market for new plants. When this did not have the desired effect, the Commission announced abruptly that it was closing its order books. After June 1974 it would accept no further orders for enrichment.

The thinking behind this move appears to have been to persuade electricity suppliers to line up with prospective private enrichers in the United States. If so it miscarried drastically. It drove foreign customers away from the United States entirely, and into the arms of the new commercial enrichers in Europe – the tripartite British-Dutch-German consortium URENCO, the French Eurodif, and even the Soviet Union, all of which were spurred on by the American policy. In less than three years, between 1971 and 1974, the United States, by its own maladroit machinations, had broken up what had hitherto been its own virtual monopoly on the supply of nuclear power-plant fuel. In so doing it not only threw away a key lever that had helped it not merely to sell reactors but to exercise forceful influence on the shape and direction of worldwide nuclear activities. It also severely damaged its credibility as a reliable nuclear supplier, prompting foreign clients to seek other ways of assuring their future stocks of nuclear power-plant fuel. Inevitably, spurred by their own nuclear establishments, most of these foreign clients began to look with fresh enthusiasm at plutonium.

Within the United States this development was viewed with increasing unhappiness by some influential policy-makers. Even before the Indian explosion the problem of safeguarding fissile material had permeated the consciousness of certain important politicians, among them Senators Abraham Ribicoff and Charles Percy. Under their leadership the Senate Committee on Government Operations had long been preoccupied with nuclear matters. It had just finished hammering through the Energy Reorganization Act of 1974 that split up the Atomic Energy Commission and created the Energy Research and Development Administration – soon to become the Department of Energy – and the Nuclear Regulatory Commission. Even before the dust of this dramatic change in the nuclear power structure had settled, the Committee had begun to buzz with concern about nuclear weapons proliferation. The reorganized agencies themselves were also starting to take the safeguards issue more seriously.

In two days of hearings, 12–13 March 1974, the Committee under Ribicoff had had a preview of the findings of the Taylor-Willrich study *Nuclear Theft: Risks and Safeguards* three weeks before its formal publication, when Theodore Taylor appeared as a witness. Thus alerted to the problem of safeguards and security for fissile materials, the Committee thereafter embarked on a legislative marathon that would come to fruition only four years later.

The legislation began life as the Export Reorganization Act of 1975; hearings got underway immediately. The Committee requested that the Congressional Research Service of the Library of Congress prepare the first of what was to become an impressive series of data books on the issue. *Peaceful Nuclear Exports and Weapons Proliferation*, a thick dossier including the views of many recognized authorities and experts on every aspect of the problem, appeared in April 1975.

The Committee's concern was further heightened by the Brazilian-German contract, announced in July 1975, and the French agreements to sell reprocessing plants to South Korea and Pakistan. In August 1975, in response to a lawsuit by concerned environmentalists, the Energy Research and Development Administration published a draft environmental impact statement on United States nuclear power export activities. Prompted by the Committee, the Office of Technology Assessment embarked on a study called *Nuclear Power and Safeguards*. The Senate Committee on Foreign Relations also put down a marker, with the enactment of the Symington Amendment to the International Security Assistance Act of 1976. With an eye to the French and German nuclear deals, the Amendment prohibited American economic and military assistance to any government providing or receiving sensitive nuclear technology or material, unless the recipient country accepted International Atomic Energy Agency safeguards on it. The prohibition could only be overridden by a Presidential declaration that to withhold the aid would damage America's national interest, and that 'the country in question will not develop nuclear weapons or assist another country to do so'.

The Symington Amendment was a foretaste of what was to come. Hearings in January and March 1976 before the Government Operations Committee elicited the opinions of many leading nuclear policy officials, analysts and commentators. They made vividly clear the link between civil and military nuclear activities, both inside and outside the United States – and made equally clear the urgent need to rethink American nuclear export policy in this light. Prominent on the agenda were reprocessing and the use of plutonium as powerplant fuel, not only overseas but also in the United States itself. In the words of Nuclear Regulatory Commissioner Victor Gilinsky, testifying to the Committee on 26 January 1976:

Up to this point I have talked about plutonium as an explosive material. But plutonium is also a potential fuel source suitable for use in the light water reactors found throughout the world today. As this committee is aware, the question of whether to license the use of plutonium for wide-scale use in existing US power reactors is now before the Nuclear Regulatory Commission, and it is one of sufficient complexity that a decision is not expected for at least another year.

While plutonium recycle remains an open question in this country, and while even a favorable decision here may have little relevance for nations with smaller nuclear programs, the interest in this alternative on the part of advanced nuclear nations has conveyed to other countries of the world, both large and small, the notion that plutonium recycle is an essential feature of any economically viable nuclear program. The prospects for effective coordinated international action on secure disposition of plutonium will therefore be strongly influenced by the apparent value of plutonium for recycle . . .

Mixed oxide – that is, uranium-plus-plutonium – fuel for conventional reactors was intended to be at the outset the main use of the plutonium from the Barnwell reprocessing plant, pending the arrival of fast breeders. The final environmental statement for Barnwell had been published in January 1974. But as the months passed it became clear that the plant was in trouble. It was falling more and more behind schedule. Its costs, originally estimated at $70 million, had increased by a factor of nearly ten; the original estimate, based on an almost total lack of relevant experience, had been wildly over-optimistic. It was also facing a regulatory challenge. A lawsuit by objectors had compelled the Nuclear Regulatory Commission to prepare, as Gilinsky had indicated, a 'Generic Environmental Statement on the Use of Mixed Oxide Fuel in Light Water Reactors' – known as GESMO by all but the long-winded. Given the intended use of the plutonium from Barnwell, the environmental statement had a direct bearing on the future of the plant; and the draft statement had attracted much critical comment.

To make matters worse, a lawsuit filed by the Natural Resources Defense Council had compelled the Commission to include in the statement consideration of safeguards and physical security for separated plutonium – with troubling implications for Barnwell. The plutonium people sensed that the Commission, especially Commissioner Gilinsky, was turning a distinctly jaundiced eye on Barnwell, and sensed also that Capitol Hill was having second thoughts about the key role traditionally assigned to plutonium fuel.

In April 1976 yet another government body received yet another report: the Arms Control and Disarmament Agency received the final draft of a study of the weapons-proliferation implications of the worldwide plans for plutonium fuel. The senior author was a respected strategic analyst, Professor Albert Wohlstetter of the University of Chicago. The title of the study asked a single grim question: are we *Moving Toward Life in a Nuclear-Armed Crowd?* The conclusions were similarly disturbing, especially concerning a serious difficulty associated with separated plutonium. Once separated, it could be fashioned into a weapon within weeks, or even days. Accordingly, no safeguards of the kind currently accepted could give a warning in sufficient time to permit effective international response to a suspected 'diversion' of separated plutonium. The problem of 'timely warning' rapidly assumed urgent prominence in the proliferation issue.

The diehard defenders of Barnwell were casting about for a way to rescue the plant and the classic concept of the nuclear fuel cycle – reprocessing spent uranium fuel and reusing the plutonium as fuel. It had also become clear that there was little if any coherence between American domestic and foreign nuclear policy, which all too often appeared to be working at cross-purposes: witness the enrichment-contract fiasco and its consequences. In April 1976 the Administrator of the Energy Research and Development Administration, Dr Robert Seamans, wrote to the White House drawing attention to this lack of congruence and asking that something be done.

The underlying hope at the Administration was that a policy study on the issue might define a new role for Barnwell, as an international facility. Barnwell would become yet another demonstration plant – that is, yet another plant whose costs would be picked up by taxpayers, possibly even foreign ones, relieving Allied General of a financial burden that was becoming steadily more onerous. Unfortunately for the Administration's hopes, the policy study which duly took place, far from giving Barnwell a new lease on life, was to give it virtually the kiss of death.

11 Thy neighbour's plutonium

Outside the United States the outlook for plutonium appeared to be as bright as ever, through official eyes at least. Only one small shadow was looming. In Europe as in the United States public discontent with official nuclear policies was spreading, to encompass not only nuclear power plants but also other facilities like reprocessing plants. The official reaction to this concern in Britain and in France was markedly different, but the outcome was similar.

Despite the mounting problems already encountered, Britain and France had been giving a lead to other European countries, pressing resolutely on with reprocessing, fast breeders and plans for the plutonium economy. Indeed, at the outset of the 1970s there had appeared to be in Europe, if anything, too much reprocessing available for the existing nuclear programmes. Both Britain and France had large reprocessing plants in operation, at Windscale and Cap la Hague respectively, and were proposing to expand these facilities. The possibility of overdoing it prompted the national nuclear organizations of the two countries to join with the West Germans in 1971 to form a tripartite consortium called United Reprocessors, as noted earlier. It was incorporated in the Federal Republic 'for the purpose of marketing and providing services for reprocessing of irradiated fuel from nuclear power stations using uranium oxide fuel, including the transport of irradiated fuel and recovered products and the conversion of recovered products'. United Reprocessors would serve to synchronize the expansion plans of the three partners, and keep them from accumulating an embarrassing excess of plant capacity.

As it turned out, however, the excess of plant capacity was a chimera. The B204 Head End Plant of British Nuclear Fuels at Windscale was put out of action for good by the accident of September 1973; the 'haute activité oxide' HAO unit of Cogema at Cap la Hague took longer than expected to come into service; the chemical consortium which had been the original German partners in United Reprocessors dropped out of the reprocessing business in 1974, seeing no commercial future in it. But both British Nuclear Fuels and Cogema pressed on with their separate plans. Cogema planned initially to expand the UP–2 plant at Cap la Hague. British Nuclear Fuels, however, had much bigger ideas.

Britain: THORP and PFR

In 1974 British Nuclear Fuels announced that it was planning to build a new reprocessing plant at Windscale – indeed possibly two. The proposed new plant would be a large-scale facility specifically designed to reprocess high-burnup oxide fuel; this fuel would come not only from the second generation of British nuclear power plants, the advanced gas-cooled reactors, but also from foreign light-water reactors. Contracts had already been signed with several foreign customers, in Japan, Spain and Sweden, for the reprocessing of light-water fuel; indeed their spent fuel was already accumulating in the ponds at Windscale after the failure of B204. But the new plan was of a different order entirely.

As details gradually emerged, the immediate proposal appeared to be to build a plant with a throughput of 1500 tonnes per year. It would be called THORP – for thermal oxide reprocessing plant. Fully half the capacity of this plant was to be dedicated to reprocessing spent fuel from Japan; accordingly, the nine Japanese electricity suppliers were to put up half the capital cost of the plant. Since the advanced gas-cooled reactors were still deep in the doldrums – none started up until 1976 – British Nuclear Fuels also proposed to offer reprocessing services to as many other foreign customers as it could find.

At first the British government viewed this plan with benign neglect, giving it a blessing but not much thought. There were, however, a few sceptics on the fringes. In October 1975 the *Daily Mirror* ran a lurid and inaccurate front-page story, whose black headline screamed 'PLAN TO MAKE BRI-

TAIN WORLD'S NUCLEAR DUSTBIN'. The resulting furore put the name of Windscale indelibly on the map – so much so that six years later British Nuclear Fuels changed the name of the site, presumably in an attempt to exorcize its unfortunate popular image.

Although in March 1976 the government duly gave British Nuclear Fuels the required investment approval for THORP, the controversy did not die down. Instead it escalated, because of the activities of the British wing of the environmental organization Friends of the Earth, and a steadily growing band of other unbelievers. Although all the other objectors were concerned primarily with the hazards of radioactive pollution, Friends of the Earth focused on what it saw to be the most serious problem – the separation of plutonium for commercial use, especially for foreign customers. What would become of the plutonium? Would it be returned to the foreign customers?

Britain already had a dubious track record in this area; despite being one of the three depositary countries of the Non-Proliferation Treaty, Britain had already returned separated plutonium to Italy and Japan, when neither was a party to the Treaty. Other questions also arose. If separated plutonium were to be returned to foreign customers, in what form would it be returned? Under what conditions? Would the form and conditions be proof against diversion of the plutonium to weapons use, either en route or in the hands of the customer? Neither British Nuclear Fuels nor the British government deigned to answer these questions.

In September 1976 the questions took on a new authority. The Royal Commission on Environmental Pollution was an official body chaired at the time by Sir Brian (later Lord) Flowers, a distinguished nuclear physicist and part-time board member of the Atomic Energy Authority. The Commission had been gathering evidence for more than two years, carrying out an independent study; the results of the study appeared as the Commission's sixth report, entitled *Nuclear Power and the Environment*. The Commission had construed its brief very widely, taking the environment to be human society in all its aspects. Many of its conclusions were in line with the official views of the nuclear establishment, albeit here and there with qualifications. What caught the eye, and media attention, however, was its stringent criticism of plutonium and the plans for its commercial use.

The Commission did not mince words:

> The dangers of the creation of plutonium in large quantities in conditions of increasing world unrest are genuine and serious. We should not rely for energy supply on a process that produces such a hazardous subject as plutonium unless there is no reasonable alternative. The abandonment of fission power would, however, be neither wise nor justified; but a major commitment to fission power and a plutonium economy should be postponed as long as possible. (Paragraph 535)

The Commission elaborated on the reasons with care and thoroughness, drawing particular attention to the unanswered questions about security and safeguards. The impact of the report shook the British nuclear community to its complacent foundations. Earlier in 1976 it had been widely anticipated that before the end of the year the government would give the go-ahead for construction of a full-scale 'Commercial Fast Reactor', for which the Atomic Energy Authority had been pleading since 1971. After the Flowers report nothing more was heard about this proposal for many months.

In the aftermath of the report the Windscale THORP controversy gathered fresh momentum. As noted earlier, the Secretary of State for Energy, Tony Benn, had granted investment approval for THORP in March 1976. In December 1976 he was outraged to learn that a leak of radioactivity had been discovered underneath a waste storage bunker at Windscale – the previous October. No one knew how to stop the leak of radioactivity; but the leak of information about it was effectively blocked for at least six weeks. When news of the leak and its subsequent cover-up at last reached Benn he was incensed, and made his feelings known in Cabinet. Moreover, the public outcry was by this time relentless. On 22 December 1976 Benn's colleague, Secretary of State for Environment Peter Shore, announced that there would after all be a public inquiry into the THORP plan.

The stubborn, inaccessible leak under building B38 was not the only technical problem at Windscale. The B205 chemical separation plant had been operating since 1964, reprocessing metal Magnox fuel. However, an unexpected chain of events had caught British Nuclear Fuels short of storage tanks for high-level liquid waste. The problem had been caused, ironically, by achieving higher burnup of Magnox fuel; when reprocessed this fuel produced more liquid waste than expected. From September 1973 until summer 1974 B205 had to be shut down, during which time a backlog of spent Magnox fuel elements accumulated in ponds at Windscale and at all the Magnox power plants. Stored underwater, the cladding on this type of fuel rapidly deteriorated, making it much more difficult to reprocess, and releasing a significant quantity of fission products into the pond water.

In January 1975, with too much corroding Magnox fuel already requiring urgent attention, the first Calder Hall reactor had to be shut down. Its spent fuel elements were left inside the core, with the carbon dioxide coolant still pressurized and circulating – de facto dry storage of the elements. They were to stay there for more than five years. British Nuclear Fuels refused to reveal the reason for the shutdown; it was to emerge only after painstaking cross-examination at the Windscale inquiry in 1977. In 1976, while proceeding with plans for a new oxide fuel reprocessing plant at Windscale, British Nuclear Fuels also applied to the government for investment approval for what it called 'refurbishment' of the Magnox reprocessing plant at the same site. The approval, and government support for the necessary finance – then estimated at £245 million – was granted without a flicker of critical attention by Parliament or the public. Only after the Windscale inquiry a year later did it emerge that the refurbishment amounted to the construction of a complete new Magnox plant on a different part of the Windscale site.

When plutonium people in the United States pointed across the Atlantic, they tended to skirt around the controversial aspects of the British reprocessing programme, feeling it sufficient to stress that Britain officially intended to press ahead. The same was held to be true for the fast breeder. American fast breeder proponents pointed to the British programme as proof that outside the United States the fast breeder was still the centrepiece of nuclear policy. They could offer in evidence a report by the British official Advisory Committee on Research and Development for Fuel and Power, chaired by Walter Marshall. Marshall was at the time both Deputy Chairman of the Atomic Energy Authority and Chief Scientist at the Department of Energy, a dual role which demonstrated the powerful influence of the nuclear establishment on official energy policy. The report, published in 1976, ranked the fast breeder and its support facilities as a five-star feature of British government energy research and development. Although the Authority's plans for a Commercial Fast Reactor continued to mark time, the British fast breeder programme continued to be much the largest single absorber of government energy research funds; expenditure was running at close to £100 million a year.

The prominence assigned to the fast breeder appeared to be in spite of rather than because of the results of work on the Prototype Fast Reactor at Dounreay. Several years late even in starting up, the plant thereafter accumulated a track record that, in any industry not so obsessively coddled, would have made it a national laughing-stock. In October 1974, for instance, a planeload of journalists had been flown to the remote Dounreay site. Contrary to their expectation, however, nothing of any particular moment happened while they were there. Only later did it emerge that the intention had been to switch power from the Prototype Fast Reactor to the grid during the visit. A fierce North Atlantic storm had torn loose vast quantities of seaweed along the north Scottish coast; hundreds of tonnes of it had blocked the plant's cooling water intakes, thwarting the planned switch-on. Needless to say the Atomic Energy Authority did not so inform the assembled journalists, who enjoyed the visit but left the site wondering why the Authority had chosen that particular occasion to fly them thither.

The reactor itself, by the Authority's account, was performing well. However, the turbo-alternator was a perpetual headache, and the steam generators were so prone to leaks that the Authority eventually got government backing to replace two-thirds of their internal plumbing with completely new hardware, while carrying out drastic repairs, tube by tube, on the remainder. As an example of the foreign threat to

100

American fast breeder leadership the Prototype Fast Reactor was scarcely ideal.

France: UP–2 and the Phénixes

Across the Channel the French, too, were pressing on with their plutonium plans. The UP–2 plant at Cap la Hague was one of the facilities which had come under the aegis of the new national fuel cycle organization, Compagnie Générale des Matières Nucléaires or Cogema, hived off from the Commissariat à l'Energie Atomique on 1 January 1976, as British Nuclear Fuels had been hived off from the Atomic Energy Authority in 1971. Cogema, nominally a private company, was in fact wholly owned by the Commissariat, in the same way that British Nuclear Fuels was wholly owned by the Authority. Cogema's interests and responsibilities were likewise essentially parallel to those of its British counterpart, although they were more extensive, encompassing uranium mining and milling, enrichment, fuel fabrication, and reprocessing.

Of all these sectors, reprocessing was proving the most troublesome. Even before the start-up of the oxide head end, UP–2 had come under attack from the Confédération Française du Travail, the main trade union on the site and the second largest in France. In July 1976 the union published a hard-hitting report on UP–2, alleging that there had been many dangerous events at Cap la Hague in recent years. The reasons cited included:

> deteriorating equipment, hastily repaired and strongly contaminated; additions poorly engineered and badly designed; an increasing drive for profitability and technical performance at the expense of safety; and a dramatic shortage of qualified personnel, to the point where newly engaged staff were set to work without training.

The oxide head end had been due to start up in 1975; but even as the first consignments of spent fuel, mostly from foreign customers, began arriving in the storage ponds, Cogema staff were busy with what the union called 'frantic', 'disorganized' attempts at rapid modifications. The unit eventually accepted its first spent fuel in May 1976. However, in September 1976, after only 17 tonnes had been reprocessed, handling of such oxide fuel – of much higher burnup and much more radioactive than the metal fuel otherwise reprocessed in UP–2 – under the conditions prevailing at Cap la Hague provoked the union to strike. To support its criticism the union even made a film about the working conditions at la Hague. It was entitled *Condamné à Réussir* – 'Condemned to Succeed', a nicely ironic comment that was totally lost on the translator who for the English version rendered the title as 'Sentenced to Success'. The management tried to start the plant up again unaided, but in vain. Even after the strike ended, relations between labour and management remained tense.

In 1976, therefore, even France, the only country with a plant that could handle commercial oxide fuel, was struggling to make it work at all. This did not prevent Barnwell boosters from warning that the French were forging ahead, and leaving the United States in the lurch. In truth, however, the French reprocessors were at best lurching ahead. Nevertheless, Cogema was pressing on with plans not only to double the capacity of the oxide head end to 800 tonnes per year, but also to construct a complete new reprocessing plant at la Hague. In due course it was intended to include two parallel process lines each with a capacity of 800 tonnes per year. This would raise the total reprocessing capacity at la Hague to 2400 tonnes per year by 1987.

It was estimated that the French nuclear programme would give rise to no more than 1000 tonnes of spent fuel per year by the mid-1980s. Accordingly, to fill all this capacity, the French reprocessors were soliciting business all over the world. When British plans for a new oxide-fuel reprocessing plant at Windscale ran into heavy weather, Cogema – partner of British Nuclear Fuels in United Reprocessors – intervened and came away with half the original order from the Japanese: up to 3000 tonnes, to be delivered to Cap la Hague over a period of ten years. The British reprocessors raised a dolorous public lament about the loss of this tonnage, claiming that the British government's delay in giving the go-ahead for the new Windscale plant was to blame. It was never made clear just how the two 'partners' in United Reprocessors were expected to behave toward each other when competing for business. In any event United Reprocessors gave an impression of only fragile unity from that time on.

Cogema continued to gather other contracts, with Sweden, Federal Germany and other foreign customers, in a bid to corner the world market for reprocessing of oxide fuel. The provisions of these contracts, especially the fate of the separated plutonium, were secret; even the reasons for this secrecy were secret. In due course some of the contract provisions were to leak out; they set few minds at rest.

The French were also, more or less by default, taking the lead in the fast breeder stakes. With the possible exception of the Soviets, fast breeder people elsewhere in the world were looking longingly toward France and Phénix. Phénix did, it is true, suffer a share of the technical troubles plaguing the short roster of fast breeder prototypes. From September 1976 until summer 1977 it was shut down to replace its intermediate heat exchangers, which had proved to be annoyingly leaky. But this hiccup did not interfere with progress on its much larger successor.

The Super-Phénix was to be a 1200-megawatt fast breeder power plant, at a site called Creys-Malville, about 40 km east of Lyons in southern France. It was owned by a consortium of electricity suppliers called Nersa, of which in turn Electricité de France owned 51 per cent, Enel of Italy 33 per cent, and the suppliers' group SBK – including suppliers from Federal Germany, Belgium, the Netherlands and Britain – the remaining 16 per cent. It was to be built by a French-Italian consortium called Novatome-Nira, whose leading shareholder was Framatome of France. The elaborate international network was set up to carry out plans that foresaw the construction of six further plants, replicas of Super-Phénix, to be ordered in France more or less forthwith, and a seventh, to be known as SNR–2, to be ordered in Federal Germany following the Kalkar prototype.

Work got underway on the Super-Phénix in 1975. However, the plant was attracting fierce opposition, both local and international, because of concern about its safety and radioactive releases; there was, however, little explicit concern about the implications of its use of plutonium fuel. In July

103

1976 the Creys-Malville site was the focus of a mass demonstration numbering tens of thousands of protestors. The official response was to send in a battalion of riot troops, waving batons and firing tear gas. A year of bitter local and national opposition was to ensue, culminating in an even bigger demonstration at the site, greeted by a yet more violent official response. In the frenzied battle that broke out one demonstrator was killed and many injured. Thereafter, protest swiftly subsided. The Super-Phénix rose in its place, taking shape as the flagship of the international fast breeder community. However, the blunt suppression of public protest in France did not mean that all would thenceforth be plain sailing.

12 Enter Carter

Outside the United States, as the mid-1970s came and went, the technical status and track record of reprocessing and the fast breeder were not all they might have been; but official enthusiasm for them continued unabated. Within the United States, however, 1976 was turning out to be a bad year for plutonium. The letter to the White House from Robert Seamans of the Energy Research and Development Administration, requesting a review of nuclear policy and plans, at first drew only a dismissive response. Secretary of State Henry Kissinger insisted that nuclear matters were all well in hand and required no extra attention. Many others, however, took a contrary view: as did an erstwhile peanut farmer from Georgia, Jimmy Carter. To the surprise and occasional disbelief of the political old guard, Carter had come out of nowhere to win a fervent following in the run-up to the Democratic National Convention. Carter had trained as a nuclear engineer in Admiral Hyman Rickover's nuclear navy; but Carter's speeches and pronouncements betrayed a notable lack of fervour for civil nuclear technology – especially that involving plutonium.

On 13 May 1976 Carter delivered a major address at the United Nations. In it he called for a reassessment of US domestic civil nuclear policy; until such reassessment, 'US dependence on nuclear power should be kept to the minimum necessary to meet our needs'. He noted the 'fearsome prospect' that civil nuclear power would lead to the spread of nuclear weapons, primarily because plutonium might be used for commercial power plant fuel. There should be collective international action to limit reliance on nuclear power, while supplying the energy needs of all countries; existing nuclear power plants and international arrangements for the transfer of nuclear technology and materials should be modified 'to make the spread of peaceful nuclear power less dangerous'. Above all, the sale of enrichment and reprocessing plants must be halted, by a 'voluntary moratorium' – one that should also cover the deals involving Brazil and Pakistan.

Carter's United Nations address attracted worldwide coverage, and forced the hand of the Ford White House. Ford appointed Robert Fri, deputy administrator of the Energy Research and Development Administration, to chair a committee drawn from all the branches of the federal government with nuclear axes to grind – the Energy Administration, the Nuclear Regulatory Commission, several subsections of the State Department, the Office of Management and Budget, and the Defense Department. The Fri committee was to review American nuclear policy, domestic and foreign, and to make recommendations for its clarification and improvement.

Two issues above all dominated the agenda: reprocessing, wherever and whoever; and nuclear export regulations. These issues were linked in a way which few at first were willing to acknowledge. The State Department wanted to restore American credibility as a reliable nuclear supplier internationally, and in so doing re-establish some leverage over nuclear affairs in other countries. It was apparent, however, that any American strictures on reprocessing in foreign countries would come up against the United States's own plans for commercial reprocessing, as symbolized by the Barnwell plant. The time was long past when the United States could adopt a 'nanny knows best' attitude, and claim that reprocessing might be acceptable in the United States but not elsewhere: that separated plutonium was safe in American hands but not in those of butter-fingered foreigners.

Although the Energy Administration had originally suggested the review, partly in the hope of bailing out Barnwell, the old guard there did not like the feel of this at all. However, within the Administration there was also a growing band of sceptics, whose faith in the traditional values espoused by the plutonium people had been steadily eroded, not least by the evident weapons implications. Similar divisions of opinion were also growing within some of the other bodies represented on the Fri committee.

In other circumstances the outcome of a study involving such a conflict of opinions would have been a fudged compromise, a document long on rhetoric and short on substance, worded to blur the outlines of controversy and perpetuate the status quo. The Fri review did not, however, go that way. In September 1976 its 150–page report was duly delivered to the White House. It laid out the position in thorough detail, identifying both the key issues facing the President and the policy options available, with their advantages and disadvantages. It began with the premise that American nuclear policy should be coherent, 'viewed within a broader framework of foreign and domestic policy', not least the desire to prevent the spread of nuclear weapons. It then considered how the United States could tighten international controls on sensitive nuclear material, and improve safeguards against diversion of the sensitive material and security against theft. It weighed the possibility of constraining nuclear exports, and indicated the need to have a response ready if an international agreement were broken. It asked whether existing agreements should be tightened, and if so how, noting the diplomatic difficulties which might ensue. Most specific of all, it suggested that the United States might offer alternatives to the currently accepted intention to reprocess commercial fuel in national facilities in the United States and elsewhere.

The report was careful not to define a specific policy. The outstanding issues, especially concerning plutonium, were incapable of resolution within the Fri forum. Furthermore, the final decision on policy would have to come from the President, who would have to put the decision forward and defend it. The necessity to do so was becoming clear. Carter, now running as the Democratic nominee for President against the incumbent Ford, was making visible capital out of non-proliferation. In a speech in September 1976, Carter even went on record that he would 'seek to withhold authority for domestic reprocessing until the need for, the economics, and the safety of this technology are clearly demonstrated'.

After more weeks of stubborn infighting at the White House, a sub-group of the Fri committee at last produced a draft presidential statement. On 28 October 1976, just before

107

the election, Ford issued a statement that made headlines all over the world. For the first time an American President declared that the separation and use of plutonium as fuel for power plants – hitherto the cornerstone of long-term civil nuclear policy almost everywhere – posed dangers so grave as to require equally grave countermeasures. The Ford statement called for an urgent international effort to devise such countermeasures. To emphasize still more the gravity of the situation, Ford announced that henceforth the United States 'would no longer regard reprocessing of used nuclear fuel as a necessary and inevitable step in the nuclear fuel cycle'. For the plutonium people this was tantamount to heresy – from the highest office in the land.

13 Carter speaks out – and back

A week later the highest office in the land was under new management. The change of administration did not excite any sense of relief in the hearts of the plutonium people: on the contrary. Carter's pre-election pronouncements had been no mere electioneering ploy. His concern about weapons proliferation appeared to be deep and genuine; and he was determined to do something about it. So were several of his closest and most influential advisors, among them Abraham Chayes of Harvard Law School and Joseph Nye, professor of government at Harvard.

Both Chayes and Nye were members of the Nuclear Energy Policy Study Group, convened earlier in 1976 under the auspices of the Ford Foundation. In the light of the growing public controversy about nuclear issues, the Foundation had brought together a panel of some two dozen high-powered academics, none of them known to have a strong prior position on such issues, to carry out an independent analysis of nuclear power policy. It was chaired by Spurgeon Keeny of the MITRE Corporation, a think tank in northern Virginia that administered the project. The report of the study group, entitled *Nuclear Power: Issues and Choices*, was delivered in January 1977, shortly before Carter's inauguration. It was to become the bible of the nuclear policy activists in the Carter administration – although, like the King James version, the Ford-MITRE report made it possible to quote nuclear scripture to back widely contrasting opinions.

The first three sections of the report discussed energy economics and supply, health, environment and safety, and nuclear proliferation and terrorism. The fourth identified and analyzed 'issues for decision'. In the words of the overview:

The United States faces a number of early decisions having an important bearing on the future of nuclear power and on the worldwide risks in the nuclear fuel cycle. These decisions, which are closely interrelated, must be considered in the context of the economic, energy supply, social costs, and international security issues. . . . The significant common thread in these decisions is the question of whether plutonium should be introduced into the nuclear fuel cycle. We have concluded that there is no compelling reason at this time to introduce plutonium or to anticipate its introduction in this century. Plutonium could do little to improve nuclear fuel economics or assurance here or abroad. This conclusion rests on our analysis of uranium supply, the economics of plutonium recycle in current reactors, and the prospects of breeder reactors. In the longer term, beginning in the next century, there is at least a possibility that the world can bypass substantial reliance on plutonium. If this is not the case, the time bought by delay may permit political and technical developments that will reduce the nuclear proliferation risks involved in the introduction of plutonium.

The policy implications of these findings were immediate, but fiercely controversial. The Ford-MITRE report and its findings were seized upon by nuclear commentators and critics both inside and outside the United States, and used both to support existing nuclear power policy and to attack policies directed towards the use of plutonium as civil fuel. In Washington, the advent of the Carter administration merely reinforced the intensity of the nuclear policy debate already hotly joined under Carter's Republican precursor. Behind the bureaucratic scenes the same combatants continued their bitter struggle over the same issues, especially American nuclear export regulations, the Clinch River breeder and the future of commercial reprocessing in the United States. Even among Carter's immediate entourage there were stubborn and deep-seated differences. One of the most intractable was the argument about how to deal with overseas clients, among whom were numbered some of the most important and valuable political allies of the United States, including of course Britain, France, Federal Germany and Japan.

The official nuclear policy in these countries was sharply at variance with that emerging in the United States, particularly with regard to the role of plutonium as a commercial power plant fuel. All those four countries, and several other American customers overseas, had gone on record repeatedly, emphatically and recently, to confirm their continuing commitment to reprocessing and the fast breeder reactor. Some – notably Federal Germany – also insisted that it was necessary and desirable to commence the use of mixed-oxide fuel in light-water reactors.

All these attitudes had been initiated by the American nuclear establishment, especially the Atomic Energy Commission, many years earlier. By the mid-1970s they had taken deep and tangled root. That they had become embedded virtually as articles of faith in the subconscious of nuclear planners all over the world was due in no small measure to the American nuclear missionary work of the 1950s and the 1960s, the Atoms for Peace programme, the Geneva conferences and the overseas licensing of American nuclear technology. If the United States was now to become not only an apostate but a proselytizing apostate, how should it present its lapse from virtue to its erstwhile converts? How would they react?

There was little prospect that the plutonium proponents outside the United States would as cheerfully shed their beliefs as they had once embraced them. Given that simple missionary work was this time unlikely to be either effective or swift enough to head off the mounting immediate threat, posed by contracts already signed and projects already under way, what could the new Carter administration do? One faction wanted Carter to invoke the legal powers written into existing contracts with countries such as Japan, and withhold permission to reprocess spent fuel enriched in the United States – essentially all of it. Others insisted that Carter could not twist foreign arms without arousing bitter resentment and antagonism; and that in any case it was more important to persuade foreign governments of the force of the rational arguments, especially about the urgent need to head off weapons proliferation. Australia, Canada, and the Soviet Union appeared likely to require little convincing on this point, and might be valuable allies in the endeavour to change the direction of civil nuclear policy worldwide.

The internal disagreement came to a public head on 7 April 1977. President Carter called a press conference to deliver a brief and succinct statement on his decisions following the review of nuclear power policy (see Appendix IV for the complete text). In it Carter said:

The benefits of nuclear power, particularly to some foreign countries that don't have oil and coal of their own, are very practical and critical. But a serious risk is involved in the handling of nuclear fuels – the risk that component parts of this power process will be turned to providing explosives or atomic weapons. . . . The United States is deeply concerned about the consequences of the uncontrolled spread of this nuclear weapon capability. We can't arrest it immediately and unilaterally. We have no authority over other countries. But we believe that these risks would be vastly increased by the further spread of reprocessing capabilities of the spent nuclear fuel from which explosives can be derived. . . . Therefore, we will make a major change in the United States domestic nuclear energy policies and programs which I am announcing today. We will make a concerted effort among all other countries to find better answers to the problems and risks of nuclear proliferation. And I would like to outline a few things now that we will do specifically.

First of all, we will defer indefinitely the commercial reprocessing and recycling of the plutonium produced in US nuclear power programs. From my own experience, we have concluded that a viable and adequate economic nuclear program can be maintained without such reprocessing and recycling of plutonium. The plant at Barnwell, South Carolina, for instance, will receive neither Federal encouragement nor funding from us for its completion as a reprocessing facility.

Second, we will restructure our own US breeder program to give greater priority to alternative designs of the breeder other than plutonium, and to defer the date when breeder reactors would be put to commercial use. We will continue research and development, try to shift away from plutonium, defer dependence on the breeder reactor for commercial use.

Third, we will direct funding of US nuclear research and development programs to accelerate our research into alternative nuclear fuel cycles which do not involve direct access to materials that can be used for nuclear weapons.

Fourth, we will increase the US capacity to produce nuclear fuels, enriched uranium in particular, to provide adequate and timely supplies of nuclear fuels to countries that need them so that they will not be required or encouraged to reprocess their own materials.

Fifth, we will propose to the Congress the necessary legislative steps to permit us to sign these supply contracts and remove the pressure for the reprocessing of nuclear fuels by other countries that do not now have this capability.

Sixth, we will continue to embargo the export of either equipment or technology that could permit uranium enrichment and chemical reprocessing.

And seventh, we will continue discussions with supplying countries and recipient countries, as well, of a wide range of international approaches and frameworks that will permit all countries to achieve their own energy needs while at the same time reducing the spread of the capability for nuclear explosive development . . .

It was a powerful and concise statement of policy, unambiguous in both content and intent. Unfortunately, however, Carter had not confined himself to the text as drafted. Instead, both in delivering the statement itself and in answering questions from the press afterwards, Carter interpolated comments which gave a significantly different feel to the administration's apparent attitude – sufficiently different that on this acutely sensitive issue Carter muddied the waters. They were to remain turbid virtually throughout his presidency.

A key departure from the written text was Carter's comment that 'We are not trying to impose our will on those nations like Japan and France and Britain and Germany, which already have reprocessing plants in operation. They have a special need that we don't have, in that their (there?) supplies of petroleum products are not available.' In answer to the first press question, Carter observed, 'I think that we would very likely see a continuation of reprocessing capability in those nations that I have named, and perhaps in others.' Later in the press conference he expanded this theme:

The one difference that has been very sensitive, as it relates to, say, Germany, Japan and others, is that they fear that our unilateral action in renouncing the reprocessing of spent fuels to produce plutonium might imply that we prohibit them or criticize them severely because of their own need for reprocessing. This is not the case. They have a perfect right to go ahead and continue with their own reprocessing efforts. But we hope they'll join with us in eliminating in the future other countries that might have had this capability evolve.

With these impromptu glosses on the original statement Carter vitiated drastically the impact the statement had been designed to produce on just those countries mentioned. He

113

made American renunciation of any commitment to the use of plutonium appear to be a purely domestic affair, instead of the dramatic international signal that had been intended. It was to say the least an unpropitious launch for a radically new policy on an issue of extreme delicacy – clumsy, confused, and open to wilful reinterpretation by those foreign governments that found its obvious import uncongenial. Britain, France, Federal Germany and Japan were to lose no time in seizing the policy initiative thus conceded to them.

Nevertheless, Carter's statement heralded a dramatically different approach to the issue of civil nuclear power and weapons proliferation. Moreover, it was being put forward by the country which, a quarter of a century earlier, had staked out the traditional approach subsequently endorsed and pursued by most other countries. However ineptly it had been unveiled, this new approach nevertheless addressed directly, for the first time, key questions which had long been fudged by nuclear policymakers:

– What really was the appropriate role for nuclear electricity?

– Would the growth of electricity use really require vast serried ranks of nuclear plants?

– Was uranium still a scarce strategic material? Would it ever be again?

– Were the original airy assurances about security and safeguards for civil technology valid? Could they be applied to separated plutonium? Or did reprocessing, separated plutonium and plutonium-fuelled reactors represent a proliferation threat beyond any control?

Although the Carter administration was not at one on these crucial questions, the balance of opinion in and around the White House was clearly different from that of five years earlier. The United States had abruptly parted company with almost every other government that had a significant nuclear power programme. The scene was set for international fireworks.

114

14   International fission

Within four months of his inauguration, President Carter found himself confronting not only traditional adversaries like the Soviet Union but also some of America's closest and most trusted allies. An additional irony was that on this issue of proliferation control Carter found more common ground with the Soviets than with Western friends. The confrontation had been a long time in building; allies of the United States could not in honesty pretend to be taken unawares. Carter, however, was the first political leader to meet the issue head on in public, with no prodding from political opponents.

True, the Ford administration had made known through diplomatic channels its acute displeasure over the German-Brazilian contract, and the French contracts to supply repro-cessing plants to South Korea and Pakistan. The South Korean deal had been cancelled only after strenuous pressure from the United States on both parties. Remonstrations from the Ford administration had also had a good deal to do with French foot-dragging over the supply of essential components for Pakistan's Chashma reprocessing plant, which slowed down its completion and left it on the international agenda.

This behind-the-scenes pressure from the United States had not, however, led to an open breach with either the West Germans or the French. On the contrary, both European allies had accepted the force of the American non-proliferation argument. Both had agreed to the June 1976 bulletin of the London Suppliers' Group; and both had declared in late 1976 that they would export no further reprocessing or enrichment plants beyond those in existing contracts. They would, however, honour the existing contracts, American displeasure notwithstanding; and they had braced themselves for the change of administration in Washington.

The possibility of an overt challenge from the incoming Carter administration triggered a European reaction even before the statement of 7 April 1977. Diplomatic meetings about plutonium policy were held with Federal Germany and Brazil in the early weeks of the Carter administration. The meetings were chilly to the point of hostility – albeit apparently more as a result of personality clashes than because of any American policy at the time. The ambiguities of the 7 April statement provided precisely the opportunity for which plutonium people in the United States and elsewhere had been waiting. They at once insisted that the Carter administration did not know what it was doing, and that its strictures against commercial use of plutonium were merely another instance of misguided ineptitude.

A conference in Persepolis, Iran, in April 1977, gave the plutonium people an excellent forum in which to stress this point. The conference had been planned many months earlier, but its theme was peculiarly timely: the transfer of nuclear technology, especially to developing countries. The Shah had committed Iran to an impressive programme of nuclear power. Many delegations at the conference came from countries with similar aspirations. The conference produced a nine-point discussion document which deplored any attempt to restrict access to peaceful nuclear technology. It underlined the requirement of the Non-Proliferation Treaty that nuclear industrial countries render every assistance to other countries pursuing nuclear programmes. According to the document,

1 The essential point is that most countries look upon nuclear power as the only route to energy independence. For those countries which do not have large resources of uranium this independence will come only with the breeder reactor. The reprocessing of fuel and recycling of fissile isotopes are essential to the operation of any breeder, no matter what the type. Hence any suggestion that reprocessing and recycling are unacceptable strikes at the very root of this motivation for adopting nuclear power, and naturally is viewed with alarm.
2 Although President Carter has concluded that the US can afford to defer the breeder, many other countries cannot afford such a course. They view the breeder as an imminent reality, and this view is supported by the rapid progress in LMFBR develop-

ment in Europe. They want to make firm plans for a nuclear
future now . . .

The conference document was widely reported internationally, not least in the United States, where proponents
brandished it as an indication that under Carter the country
was trying to break step with the rest of the world, and
breaking its treaty undertakings at the same time. Only later,
in the summer of 1977, did it emerge that this 'global
condemnation' of Carter's plutonium policy had been drafted
by delegates from the American nuclear industry.

From 2–13 May 1977, many of the same delegates joined
with hundreds more in Salzburg, Austria, for a conference
entitled 'Nuclear Power and its Fuel Cycle', organized by the
International Atomic Energy Agency. In all but title this
gathering was the direct lineal successor to the United
Nations conferences on peaceful uses of atomic energy. The
last had taken place in Geneva in 1971, while international
nuclear euphoria was still on the increase, and the hard
questions had still to attract top-level attention. By May 1977
the world nuclear community was on the defensive. Nuclear
opposition was rife virtually throughout western industrial
society; technical and economic troubles were mounting. The
last thing the nuclear community wanted was dissent within
its own ranks.

American government officials had had to submit their
papers to the conference months earlier. With the advent of
Carter they found themselves at Salzburg delivering texts
hastily revised to comply with the new stance adopted in the
White House. American delegates were backed up against
many a Salzburg wall by irate foreign colleagues, who demanded that nuclear believers in the United States disown
the Georgian upstart and his antinuclear foolishness. But the
conference was intergovernmental, and the delegates government delegates. Even those American participants who might
have heartily concurred with their overseas colleagues could
not do so openly.

The collision at Salzburg between the United States and
the rest was, as might have been expected, most acute over
reprocessing and plutonium fuel. Joseph Nye, US deputy

under secretary of state for security assistance, science and technology, had come with a brief from Carter to explain the new American policy: to attempt to mollify foreign allies and convince them that Carter's concern was valid, especially about plutonium. Nye made a courageous foray into the alien ranks. But he soon found himself catching the brunt of the flak thrown up by the plutonium people, in particular the Europeans and Japanese, and did as much listening as talking.

One of the talking points was nevertheless thoroughly unexpected. Nuclear opponents had arranged a 'Conference for a Non-Nuclear Future', coinciding with the official conference and just down the street. At the 'Non-Nuclear' conference a former United States Senate aide revealed a secret hitherto closely guarded by the international nuclear community. Nine years earlier, in 1968, a shipment of 200 tonnes of uranium yellowcake, supposed to be headed for Italy, had disappeared somewhere in the Mediterranean. It was widely believed to have ended up in Israel. Euratom, which is notified of any uranium leaving the European Community, had become aware of the disappearance several months later – but had said nothing about it in public, after the Council of Ministers secretly directed the Inspector General of Euratom not to pursue the matter further. The incident was hushed up for a decade. Its revelation at Salzburg, amid the fraught debate over safeguards and proliferation, raised the tension a further notch.

The formal proceedings at Salzburg had been organized to emphasize technical presentations almost to the exclusion of policy issues. The only nuclear critic on the programme was the Nobel Laureate Hannes Alfven, in a showpiece debate with Hans Bethe. But the lack of formal opportunity to debate policy did not seriously impede the discussions which took place in corridors and bars. The American delegation return-ed home without any doubt that plutonium had become a first-magnitude diplomatic problem.

Even before the conference was over, the issue was being addressed at the highest diplomatic levels. On 7–8 May 1977 President Carter and the leaders of the six other richest Western countries met in London at what quickly became known as the Downing Street Summit. Carter's statements of the previous month ensured that plutonium figured prominently on the summit agenda. At the Downing Street deliberations the world leaders adopted Carter's proposal to set up an International Nuclear Fuel Cycle Evaluation. Its avowed purpose was to carry out a technical assessment of various nuclear fuel cycles, to determine if there was one which posed less risk of spreading nuclear weapons.

In due course, some sixty countries and five international organizations were to participate in the Fuel Cycle Evaluation. An inaugural conference in October 1977 set up a Technical Coordinating Committee and eight Working Groups. But anyone assuming that the focal point of the Evaluation was to be the material that had caused the original international friction – plutonium – would have been hard put even to locate it on the agenda. In fact the countries participating in the Evaluation, except for the United States, had a rather different purpose in mind, as was soon to become apparent.

Back in the United States, the battle continued unabated. The Carter administration set up its own mini-Evaluation, called the National Assessment Study of Anti-Proliferation Alternatives. Congress was also moving on the issue, albeit with glacial slowness. The proposed Export Reorganization Act of 1976 was still grinding its way laboriously through the back rooms. Under pressure from the plutonium people on one side and the anti-proliferation activists on the other – both those within the Carter administration and those from public interest groups – it was undergoing a continual metamorphosis.

By mid-1977 the measure had been renamed the Anti-Proliferation Act. Its intentions were now both explicit and – to plutonium proponents – alarming. Its promoters, who had been watching the Carter administration fumble its way through one international confrontation after another, had drawn their own conclusions and embodied them in the Act. If the President and his advisors could not be relied upon to execute their non-proliferation function effectively, perhaps the only way to slow down the relentless spread of nuclear weapons capability was to lay down clearcut strictures with the force of law.

A year later, again renamed, the Nuclear Non-Proliferation Act became law. Among its requirements was the stipulation that any foreign country except a weapons state must accept full-scope safeguards on all its nuclear activities as a condition for receiving American exports of nuclear hardware or materials. The Act also imposed stringent constraints on the reprocessing of spent fuel that had originated in the United States. It committed the American government to renegotiate existing agreements for nuclear co-operation with other countries, in order to tighten American control over plutonium. Before long the Act had the Carter administration turning nuclear somersaults.

15   Plutonium and the public

Perhaps the biggest single factor in the falling-out between the American government and its allies and customers over the plutonium issue was the contrast in the nature of the policy advice being given to governments behind the scenes. In the United States those close to the President and the levers of government included senior advisors with impeccable credentials, academic and otherwise, but with no history of active involvement in the nuclear establishment. They had no long-standing association with traditional nuclear policy, nor with the presumption that plutonium fuel would have a crucial commercial role. Elsewhere in the key nuclear industrial countries this was not the case.

Throughout most of the Carter years, his non-proliferation team of well-meaning but inexperienced academics was no match for the seasoned, hard-nosed European and Japanese plutonium proponents. In Britain, France, Federal Germany and Japan, government nuclear policy was shaped almost completely by bureaucracies permeated to the highest level with nuclear alumni. In Britain, for example, as noted earlier, the Chief Scientist at the Department of Energy in the mid–1970s was Dr Walter Marshall, also deputy chairman of the Atomic Energy Authority. The corridors of Whitehall were heavily populated with ex-Authority staff, who formulated almost all the nuclear policy advice given to successive governments. The views of these advisors hewed faithfully to the attitudes they had held since the 1950s, if not the 1940s, in which plutonium fuel held pride of place.

A similar situation prevailed in France. The Commissariat à l'Energie Atomique was the cradle of influence, long personified by its chairman Bertrand Goldschmidt. Indeed, in 1978 President Giscard d'Estaing moved André Giraud from the chairmanship of the Commissariat to become Minister for Industry. Even in Federal Germany, although its nuclear industry was dominated by private companies like Kraftwerk Union and the electricity suppliers, official nuclear policy originated within the Federal Ministry for Research and Technology, particularly within the Ministry's nuclear laboratories at Juelich and Karlsruhe – always in close consultation with the private sector. Much the same state of affairs prevailed also in Japan.

These four countries – Britain, France, Federal Germany and Japan – took the lead in confronting and defying the Carter administration. They had good reason to: not only because of the long-standing mind-set of their policy advisors, but also because they were all involved, individually and collectively, in immediate plans which ran directly counter to the Carter initiative on plutonium. However, while the nuclear insiders dictated official policy in these countries, they were facing a challenge from outside their secretive precincts, not only from the American government but also from the general public in their own countries.

THORP and the Windscale Inquiry

The Windscale Inquiry opened on 14 June 1977. No nuclear issue in Britain had ever been subject to such a searching public examination. Indeed, there was no administrative precedent; the inquiry had to be held under an act governing a 'public local inquiry', more commonly applied to issues like whether or not a local citizen could build a shed in his garden. The inquiry was led by an 'Inspector', a High Court Judge named Roger Parker, assisted by eminent 'technical assessors' to amplify matters concerning radiology and engineering.

The inquiry ranged the supporters of the proposed Thermal Oxide Reprocessing Plant (THORP) – including British Nuclear Fuels, the Central Electricity Generating Board, the Department of Energy and the National Nuclear Inspectorate – against an array of objectors including Friends of the Earth, the Town and Country Planning Association, the British section of the International Commission of Jurists and many others.

The inquiry sat for exactly 100 days. British Nuclear Fuels, backed by the other official bodies, opened its case by arguing that the reprocessing of oxide fuel recovered valuable uranium and plutonium for re-use; that it was in any case essential for the management of radioactive waste; that the cause of non-proliferation would be advanced by having foreign fuel reprocessed at Windscale rather than in reprocessing plants in other countries; that THORP was necessary in any case to deal with the oxide fuel from Britain's own nuclear programme; and that contracts to reprocess foreign fuel would reduce the cost of reprocessing for British electricity suppliers and benefit the British balance of payments.

Be that as it might, the involvement of the Central Electricity Board in the inquiry was both belated and breathless. It appeared to consist, in toto, of a letter less than three lines long, dated 6 May 1977 – only five weeks before the opening of the inquiry, stating baldly that the Board wished to reserve half the proposed capacity of THORP. Objectors, reading this perfunctory epistle, drew their own conclusion: the fuel company had realized at the last minute that to present THORP purely as a facility to serve foreign customers would leave it acutely vulnerable politically. Some of the most intemperate criticism had had nothing to do with nuclear issues at all but had had an ugly undertone directed at the Japanese. Objectors decided that the fuel company must have asked the Electricity Board to go on record with some preliminary indication of interest in THORP for reprocessing of British spent fuel. As it turned out, the Board's commitment to THORP was to prove even more tenuous than the three-line letter suggested.

Objectors met the fuel company's case head-on. They pointed out that despite the company's breezy assurances no one, anywhere, had been able to demonstrate even the technical feasibility of reprocessing high-burnup oxide fuel on a commercial basis. Those who had tried – Nuclear Fuel Services at West Valley, General Electric at Morris, Eurochemic at Mol, and British Nuclear Fuels themselves with their own Head End Plant at Windscale – had met with expensive and messy failure. Even the French head end unit at Cap la Hague was operating far below design specifica-

123

tions, and its true commercial status was a mystery. The Barnwell plant, the only other plant comparable in scale to THORP, was already astronomically far over budget, and still in need of further vast investment. Objectors asked how British Nuclear Fuels could be so confident of technical feasibility when key design parameters for THORP, in areas which had been responsible for previous plant failures, like the removal of fission-product granules, were still uncertain.

In evidence and cross-examination objectors established that the value of the uranium recovered from THORP would be substantially less than the cost of its recovery, and that only a dramatic rise in the price of uranium would make this recovered uranium even marginally competitive with existing power plant fuel. The 'value' imputed to the plutonium was hypothetical until there were fast breeders in which to burn it. THORP would be producing plutonium far sooner than any plausible fast breeder programme could require. Furthermore, the higher-quality plutonium recovered from Magnox fuel would be ample for the largest fast breeder programme that could be foreseen even decades hence. According to the fuel company's own evidence the plutonium separated in THORP would remain unused, and its putative resource value unrealized, until well into the twenty-first century.

Objectors also challenged the company's assertion that reprocessing was a necessary stage in waste management. On the contrary, they insisted: reprocessing complicated waste management. It took an intact spent fuel element of high structural integrity, and chopped it up and dissolved it, creating a smörgasbord of radioactive wastes. Some of these wastes were released directly into the environment through stacks and outfall pipelines. Others were much more difficult to store with safety than the original fuel elements would have been. The high-level liquid waste thus produced had then to be turned back into a solid by vitrification – yet another technical process whose feasibility was far from fully established.

Surely, said the objectors, so long as no one knew for certain what arrangements would eventually be made for final disposal, it made more sense to keep the spent fuel intact, do nothing irreversible like chopping it up, and reserve all the

124

options. In any case storage of spent fuel must surely be technically less demanding than reprocessing and all its consequences. In response to this argument, the company went to remarkable lengths to asseverate that although reprocessing and its consequences were all technically straightforward, the storage of intact spent fuel posed all manner of difficulty. It was an extraordinary performance.

Many objectors laid great stress on the hazards of low-level radioactivity released from THORP. But Friends of the Earth focused its concern on a quite different issue. If Britain, with its North Sea oil and gas, its coal and indeed its thermal nuclear plants, were to insist that it must use plutonium fuel, so could every other country – including some like Pakistan, Argentina and several others, whose desire for separated plutonium might be dismayingly ambiguous. Friends of the Earth pointed out that the fuel company refused to explain clearly how it would manage plutonium separated on behalf of its foreign clients – that is, at least half the expected output from THORP. Would the plutonium be returned to overseas customers? If so, when? On what basis, and in what form? The company declared that these were matters for the government, and would be decided when the time came. The company was confident that all the necessary safeguards would be imposed, and that it could be easy in its corporate mind about its role as plutonium supplier to the world.

At the end of the 100 days of sittings, the Inspector withdrew into purdah to write his report. When on 6 March 1978 the Parker report was finally published, it dropped into the comparatively placid waters of the British nuclear scene like a depth charge. It accepted virtually without question all the arguments originally advanced by the company, and dismissed those of objectors out of hand. It polarized the nuclear controversy in Britain as never before, and drastically undermined the whole role of the 'public inquiry' in dealing with major policy issues.

The report drew furious rebuttals from objectors – particularly its commentary on the proliferation issue. Parker discounted the Friends of the Earth view that Britain should not set a dangerous international example by separating plutonium. On the contrary, he declared that Article IV of the

Non-Proliferation Treaty obliged Britain to offer reprocessing services to any foreign customer: 'All the Parties to the Treaty undertake to facilitate, and have the right to participate in, the fullest possible exchange of equipment, materials and scientific and technological information for the peaceful uses of nuclear energy.'

Parker's interpretation of this clause was at once contradicted by leading international lawyers, among them James Fawcett, Professor in international law at King's College, London, and president of the European Commission on Human Rights. He pointed out that Article 4 could only be read in conjunction with Article 1, according to which parties to the Treaty undertook 'not in any way to assist ... any non-nuclear weapon State to manufacture or otherwise acquire nuclear weapons ...'. If Parker's chapter on the proliferation issue was, as it appeared to be, a faithful reflection of official British thinking on the relationship between 'peaceful' plutonium and weapons proliferation, it was a worrying augury for the future.

Since the existing legal framework could not cope with the issue, the Secretary of State for the Environment, as the minister responsible for planning, had to resort to an absurdly convoluted procedure. According to the law under which the inquiry had been held, the Secretary of State had simply to announce his decision, with no reference to Parliament. This would have been politically unacceptable. Therefore, to allow a House of Commons debate on Parker's report, the Secretary of State first refused planning permission, artificially terminating the matter under the relevant law. Then, after one debate on 22 March 1978, he laid a 'Special Development Order' authorizing THORP after all.

This in turn was debated on 15 May, and gained a majority of 224 votes to 80. Nevertheless, the 80 'Nays' were by far the most ever recorded against any civil nuclear proposal in Britain, and represented the entire range of Members of Parliament, across the whole political spectrum regardless of party. High on their list of concerns was the proliferation impact of the decision. Anti-proliferation activists in Britain had thus acquired for the first time a visible and vigorous constituency in Parliament, akin to that already well-established in the United States Congress. Members who disagreed completely as to whether Britain itself should possess nuclear weapons nevertheless agreed wholeheartedly that it would be preferable if as few other countries as possible had them. They further agreed that Britain ought not to be providing other countries with an excellent cover story for weapons acquisition.

Federal Germany: Gorleben

Across the Channel, the German would-be reprocessors were likewise finding that their proposed activities entailed not only technical but also political complications. When, as mentioned earlier, the consortium of four German chemical companies pulled out of the reprocessing business in 1974, the twelve electricity suppliers reluctantly recognized that they themselves had to deal with their own spent fuel. To do so, they set up a company which eventually acquired a name about a sentence long: die Deutsche Gesellschaft für Wiederaufarbeitung von Kernbrennstoffen. Fortunately, its German acronym was much more euphonious – DWK, pronounced 'dayvaykah'. The Bonn government, however, was still very much in on the act. The Ministry for Research and Technology continued to press for adoption of its Entsorgungszentrum concept. In November 1975 the federal government asked the Premier of the state of Lower Saxony to choose from a short list of possible salt-dome sites a preferred location for the Zentrum.

The State Premier, Ernst Albrecht, a leading member of the Christian Democrats, was far from eager to take political heat on behalf of a nuclear policy promoted by the Social Democrats in Bonn. Albrecht instead suggested a site near the village of Gorleben, in a remote corner of the state, only about five kilometres from the East German border – and for that reason a location that failed signally to meet the criteria for acceptability that the Ministry itself had laid down when drawing up the short list. The federal government nevertheless – probably to Albrecht's surprise – at once accepted Gorleben.

The people of Gorleben and vicinity did not, however, accept the federal government's decision or its Zentrum. A

127

deputation called on Albrecht to ask him to commission an independent review of the federal plan. Albrecht, facing a state election, agreed. Having won the election he was as good as his word. At his behest some twenty nuclear specialists and experts from Britain, France, Norway, Sweden and the United States took part in a Gorleben International Review. During a week of hearings in the spring of 1979 in Hanover, in the presence of Albrecht, many other state politicians, nuclear industry representatives, and press, radio and television reporters and commentators, the Review panel raised many queries.

Only a handful of people from the Gorleben area were admitted; and at the last minute DWK, which had proposed the project, declined to take part. The hearings, however, opened at almost the precise instant – 9.00 A.M. European time, Wednesday, 28 March 1979, corresponding to 4.00 A.M. Eastern Standard Time – that the feedwater pumps failed at Three Mile Island. The week of hearings therefore took place in the shadow of the industry's worst accident, while no one was sure what might happen. The drama was heightened by a trek of protestors from Gorleben that arrived in Hanover on the Saturday to take part in a mass demonstration. Some estimated the crowd at 140 000 – much the largest anti-nuclear manifestation in Federal Germany to that time.

One key issue addressed by the Review panel was the 3000-page Safety Report prepared by DWK. On the basis of this report the Reactor Safety Commission and the Radiation Protection Commission had declared the facility adequately safe. After a heated bureaucratic struggle the director of the International Review at last obtained a copy of the report. It proved to consist of page after page of floor plans of buildings, with virtually no hardware mentioned.

On one particular point the German authorities were even less forthcoming than their British counterparts had been at the Windscale hearings. Despite repeated queries from the International Review panel neither DWK nor the Bonn government would answer key questions, questions closely akin to those about THORP that had likewise gone unanswered. The Gorleben reprocessing plant was intended to have a design capacity substantially larger than would be

128

required to handle all the spent fuel from even the most rapid feasible expansion of the German civil nuclear programme. Was this extra capacity to be taken up by foreign customers? If so, which? and what would become of the plutonium separated for foreign customers?

The German authorities would not even address the question of possible foreign customers at Gorleben. On the other hand, it was clear what would become of the domestic plutonium separated at Gorleben: it would be used for mixed-oxide fuel for domestic nuclear power plants, thermal plants as well as breeders, more or less immediately. Some German nuclear plants had already loaded experimental mixed-oxide fuel elements; and German fuel manufacturers were eager to move into the plutonium fuel business as soon as possible. Whether the private German electricity suppliers were prepared to pay the true commercial price for plutonium fuel was quite another matter, given the state of the world uranium and enrichment markets, where suppliers were begging for business and prices dropping steadily. None of these matters was ventilated during the Gorleben hearings, whose primary concern was plant safety, narrowly if obscurely defined. Whether the plant made any industrial sense at all was not on the agenda.

At the end of the hearings the leader of the opposition Social Democrats in Lower Saxony declared that, after what he had heard, he and his colleagues could no longer maintain their previous bipartisan support for the Gorleben proposal. Albrecht, however, reserved his decision for six weeks. Then, on 16 May 1979, in a half-hour live broadcast on national German television, he declared himself convinced that the proposed reprocessing plant would be safe. Nevertheless, the project was not politically acceptable; and he was accordingly refusing permission even to begin the licensing procedure for a reprocessing plant at Gorleben.

What he meant by 'not politically acceptable' was open to debate; but one aspect was amply clear. A go-ahead for the plant would have caused a furious public outcry; and Albrecht, a Christian Democrat, was not going to carry the can for the policy of the Federal Social Democrats if he was to find himself simultaneously under attack from the state Social

Democrats in Lower Saxony. Until the Federal Social Democrat Chancellor Schmidt in Bonn could get his state Social Democrat colleagues in Hanover back into line, Albrecht was not going to play.

Albrecht's rejection of the Gorleben reprocessing plant flabbergasted even the members of the International Review panel which had so recommended. Its impact on the West German nuclear establishment can only be imagined. Reprocessing was for them not only an article of faith, but – by their own insistence – a legal requirement for the further operation even of existing West German nuclear plants. The consequent confusion was for many months virtually absolute.

16 I reprocess, you reprocess, he reprocesses . . .

In the nuclear circumstances of the late 1970s it would have been understandable had the world nuclear community collectively shrugged its shoulders, muttered 'Oh, the hell with it' and shelved the whole idea of reprocessing until a more propitious time. More and more factors were entering the reckoning, all of them unfavourable to reprocessing. The technology itself was still throwing up one unpleasant surprise after another: leaks, breakdowns, design flaws, materials problems, maintenance headaches. The resource-recovery role of reprocessing was becoming steadily more difficult to defend. Fresh high-quality uranium was pouring on to the market. New mines in Australia, Canada and many other places were competing frantically for sales to a world nuclear market whose expansion had abruptly slowed to near-standstill. The competition brought the world price of uranium tumbling, from a high of over $40 per pound to less than $20. The uranium recovered from spent fuel was poorer in isotopic quality, and harder to use in new fuel than fresh uranium; even without taking into account the cost of its recovery it was less and less interesting as a fuel resource.

Moreover, in the aftermath of the United States enrichment-policy confusion of the early 1970s, and the fall-off in orders for new nuclear plants, there was also a buyers' market for enrichment services. With low-cost enrichment available, electricity suppliers were unlikely to bother 'recycling' plutonium in thermal reactors, given the additional complications and expense that this would entail. Plans for the long-awaited second generation of fully-fledged fast breeder power stations were bogging down everywhere but in France. Arrangements for final disposal of high-level waste were falling apart, beset with uncertainties. Potential reprocessors were asking for the moon, with no money-back guarantee. Details of the THORP contract with the Japanese, for instance, had been revealed under protest to objectors at the Windscale inquiry. According to the contractor the Japanese had to pay in advance for the services of THORP, even before it was built. British Nuclear Fuels, however, was under no obligation even to reprocess Japanese fuel, and could simply return it to Japan in the 1990s – while keeping every yen.

Electricity suppliers, alarmed by the build-up of spent fuel in power-plant ponds, and alarmed likewise by the demands of the reprocessors, were beginning to look for other ways to empty the ponds. They had realized, belatedly, that all they really needed was to be rid of their spent fuel. It mattered not a whit to them whether the fuel was reprocessed or simply stored out of their way. Nevertheless, despite all these setbacks, reprocessing was gaining, not losing, enthusiasts, particularly in the national nuclear organizations of Japan, India, Pakistan, and a roster of other countries. Their enthusiasm gave rise to increasing unease.

Japan

Japan's first power reactor was a small Magnox reactor at Tokai Mura, imported from Britain in the late 1950s. The contract for the Tokai Mura station stipulated that its spent fuel would be returned to Britain for reprocessing at Windscale, and – so far as can be ascertained – that the recovered plutonium would be returned to Japan. True to British official practice contract details remain secret; but Britain apparently did not even attempt to include any contract provisions akin to those in American export agreements, giving the exporter rights over the plutonium in clients' spent fuel. By 1975 the Atomic Energy Authority, and later British Nuclear Fuels, had delivered more than 250 kilograms of separated plutonium to Japan. During this time Japan was not a party to the Non-Proliferation Treaty, because a stubborn faction in the Japanese Diet was determined to reserve the option of acquiring Japanese nuclear weapons.

The plutonium thus returned was used, at least in part, to fabricate the first core for the Joyo experimental fast breeder, which started up in 1977. This early experience, with metal

Magnox fuel like that used both in the British weapons-plutonium reactors and in the first British nuclear power programme, undoubtedly helped to establish in Japanese nuclear minds as it had in British the conviction that spent fuel had to be reprocessed. Although every subsequent Japanese reactor used not metal but oxide fuel, the nine Japanese electricity suppliers set about arranging for the reprocessing of the spent oxide fuel from their lengthening catalogue of light-water plants.

At the beginning of the 1970s the only reprocessors that had been tendering for business were the British and the French. Accordingly, the Japanese suppliers had contracted to deliver spent fuel to Windscale and Cap la Hague. However, the Japanese nuclear programme expanded rapidly, albeit not as rapidly as the planners expected, requiring more comprehensive measures, indeed a double-tracked approach. On the one hand the nine suppliers, through their umbrella company, Enrichment and Reprocessing Group, planned to participate with British Nuclear Fuels in the THORP project in Britain, and in due course with Cogema in the add-on units at Cap la Hague. At the same time the Japanese suppliers supported, at least verbally, plans to construct a pilot reprocessing plant at Tokai Mura, adjoining the old Magnox station. The Tokai Mura reprocessing plant was built by the French firm of St Gobain Techniques Nouvelles, and financed by the Japanese government Power Reactor and Nuclear Fuel Development Corporation. It was to have a design capacity of 210 tonnes of spent fuel per year, and use more or less straightforward Purex technology.

However, both of the double tracks – the foreign contracts and the domestic reprocessing programme – quickly ran into trouble. All the fuel used in the Japanese light-water power plants had been enriched in the United States, and was subject to an agreement that allowed reprocessing only with prior permission from the American government. Such permission had always been treated as a formality; but the rise of the antiproliferation activists in the United States put the requirement in a new and – to the Japanese – irritating light. During 1976 the paperwork had begun to take longer to emerge from Washington; after Carter's statement of 7 April

1977 each request, considered 'case by case', took longer still.

By this time, American and Japanese officials were holding high-level diplomatic discussions, not only about Japan's reprocessing contracts with the British and French, but also about the Tokai Mura pilot plant. The American government also approached the British government about THORP, suggesting that while the international proliferation-controllers were trying to get a grip on the problems of separated plutonium it might be better if THORP were at least delayed. The British government responded with an unceremonious rebuff; they did not even want to discuss the matter, which was in any case no business of the United States. This official British attitude angered American antiproliferation activists, among them the Natural Resources Defense Council, which had been working with British objectors to the THORP plan. The American activists pressed their government even harder to exercise its legal right to refuse Japan permission to ship fuel to THORP.

At the same time the United States was leaning on Japan about the Tokai Mura plant. The American proposals were all unpopular with the Japanese, none more so than the basic proposal that Tokai Mura should not start up at all. Failing Japanese acceptance of this proposal – which indeed they stoutly refused – the Americans invited the Japanese to modify the plant: to change its technology from the traditional Purex layout to one which did not separate the uranium from the plutonium, but produced instead a mixture of the oxides, suitable for fuel fabrication if desired. This technology was called 'coprocessing'. It had been around for many years, but the dominant role of Purex technology, and the assumed need to recover uranium, had kept coprocessing on the shelf. The Japanese wanted to leave it there; but the United States at last applied so much pressure, with reference to its legal rights, that the Japanese reluctantly agreed to study coprocessing, and in the meantime to operate the Tokai Mura plant under an experimental régime limited to two years, and to 99 tonnes of spent fuel. In due course the Tokai Mura plant did start up. Its performance was to prove anything but reassuring.

India

Reprocessing also figured centrally in India's plans. The 50-tonne-per-year reprocessing plant in Trombay, in operation since 1965, was essentially experimental. But it had produced the plutonium for the Indian explosion in 1974; and the Indians were pressing ahead with more plans for reprocessing. Their power plant programme was based on heavy-water reactors of the Candu design, which used natural uranium fuel, requiring no enrichment and therefore no plutonium. However, the longer-term Indian nuclear programme still anticipated introducing fast breeders in quantity, fuelled with plutonium as well as India's abundant thorium. Reprocessing was an essential part of this package.

The one Indian plant that did require enriched fuel was the Tarapur plant, which had two small General Electric boiling-water reactors. According to the Tarapur agreement between the United States and India, signed in 1963, the United States would supply reload fuel until 1993. By 1976, however, it had been acknowledged in Washington, after investigation and pointed inquiries from Capitol Hill, that the original heavy-water inventory of the CIRUS reactor had come from the United States. The Indians had thus used American nuclear assistance to produce their explosive.

At this point some Americans began to have second thoughts about supplying more fuel to Tarapur. Antiproliferation activists in Washington, including the Natural Resources Defense Council, Friends of the Earth, and a number of Senators and Representatives, believed that India had contravened the 'peaceful use' provisions in the nuclear agreement with the United States covering operation of the CIRUS reactor. They declared that the United States should react as Canada had done, and cut off further nuclear cooperation with India – which would mean refusing to supply any more reload fuel for Tarapur.

The Indians responded to this suggestion with righteous indignation. If the United States unilaterally abrogated its agreement with India, India would no longer be bound by it either. In particular, India would then be free to reprocess spent fuel from Tarapur, without prior consent by the United States; nor would the fuel any longer be subject to IAEA safeguards. Furthermore, India could then take its nuclear business elsewhere – for instance to the Soviet Union. And indeed, despite its strong advocacy of control of proliferation, the Soviet Union could not refrain from taking advantage of American discomfiture, by insinuating itself into the controversy on the side of India. The Soviets let it be known that they would discuss with the Indians the supply of essential nuclear material, especially heavy water. India did, to be sure, have its own heavy water plants, but they were operating sporadically at best.

Behind the scenes, the American government, remarkably, helped to arrange that the Soviets take over as suppliers of heavy water to India. Nevertheless, the prospect of losing what little American influence still remained over Indian nuclear activity – and losing it, what was more, to the Soviet Union – left the American administration in a quandary. Should it allow the shipment of fuel for Tarapur, and in so doing concede that the Indian nuclear explosion was within the bounds of diplomatic acceptability? Or should it ban the shipment, and in so doing surrender any further control over Indian nuclear policy – leaving the way clear for the Indians to separate the plutonium already accumulated at Tarapur, and driving India into the Soviet camp? Opinion in Washington was deeply and bitterly divided.

The passage of the Nuclear Non-Proliferation Act by Congress in 1978 complicated matters yet further. Under its provisions, the Nuclear Regulatory Commission was empowered to determine whether a nuclear export should be licensed; but the President could override the Commission, and Congress in turn could override the President. In the case of Tarapur, the Commission had to determine whether the safeguards provisions permitted licensing the shipment of reload fuel. The Indians refused to provide assurances that safeguards would be applied in perpetuity – that is, beyond the expiration of the bilateral agreement, either in 1993 or earlier in the event that the United States discontinued fuel shipments because of future disagreements. In April 1978 the Commission split 2–2 on whether to license the Tarapur shipment, thereby holding up the licence. Carter then overruled the Commission and authorized the shipment; he justified his action by claiming that to ban the shipment would frustrate American attempts to persuade India to accept full-scope safeguards by March 1980, the deadline imposed by the Non-Proliferation Act. At this stage Congress did not intervene.

However, the American administration found itself in a further bind. India was not the only Asian nation with ambiguous nuclear plans. There was also Pakistan, another client of the United States. Since even before the Indian explosion, successive Pakistan governments and political leaders had left no doubt that they intended to match India bomb for bomb. Pakistan's reprocessing plant at Chashma could not by any plausible argument be justified as a civil facility. Even the French had at length come round to this view; at the last minute, in 1978, they withheld delivery of crucial components, including the 'shear pack' for chopping up fuel elements.

Pakistan's indignant outrage at this French affront was subsequently muted when, in early 1979, it was revealed that Pakistan was also constructing, under conditions of fierce secrecy, a uranium enrichment plant. A Pakistani scientist working at the Urenco facility at Almelo in the Netherlands had stolen key technical information on gas centrifuges, while an aggregation of dummy 'front' companies in western Europe had bought much of the necessary hardware, under the cover of specifications purporting to relate, for instance, to textile mills. Diplomats and a journalist who tried to learn more about the mysterious plant at Kahuta were viciously beaten up by thugs apparently on the government payroll. Pakistan ignored requests to open the enrichment plant to international safeguards. The American government, in compliance with the Symington amendment, forthwith suspended all nuclear aid to Pakistan: whereupon the Soviet Union invaded Afghanistan. The United States found itself regarding Pakistan as an essential ally, despite the alarming nuclear goings-on at Kahuta and Chashma.

As for India and Tarapur, the wrangles dragged on. In May 1980, the Nuclear Regulatory Commission voted again, and this time decided unanimously against licensing further fuel shipments, since India still refused to accept full-scope safeguards on its nuclear activities. In June 1980 President Carter, floundering in the ruins of his foreign policy while American hostages languished in Iran, again ordered that the Tarapur shipment go ahead. But in September 1980 the House of Representatives, past placation by Carter, voted by an overwhelming majority to overturn his order and ban the shipment under the Non-Proliferation Act. In the dying weeks of his administration, Carter launched a last-ditch campaign to win the Senate vote. It succeeded – barely. By 48 votes to 46, the Senate agreed to permit the shipment.

It was not to be the last of the Tarapur problem; but it was certainly an inglorious finale to Carter's campaign against the plutonium people. The civil nuclear programmes in both India and Pakistan were by this time – through no fault of the United States – virtually at a standstill, with existing power plants shut down and those under construction far behind schedule. But both countries pressed on with their plans to separate and use plutonium. What they might decide to use it for was a question uncomfortably easy to answer.

Next?

The situation in Argentina prompted the same question – and the same answer. Like India and Pakistan, Argentina was building heavy-water reactors – albeit not many. The Argentines, too, had no plausible reason – no civil reason, at any rate – to want separated plutonium. They were nevertheless proposing to produce it, in a new reprocessing plant at Ezeiza, within easy reach of Buenos Aires airport. The Ezeiza plant was to use technology originally supplied by Federal Germany, for a small experimental reprocessing plant which had been operated by Argentina from 1969 to 1972. Despite this foreign assistance, in design and possibly even in supply of components, the new Ezeiza reprocessing plant would not be subject to IAEA safeguards, since the Argentines considered it fully indigenous technology, with no foreign content; and their claim could not be challenged. Nor did they show any inclination to accept safeguards on the plant, even when they came back into the international nuclear marketplace to order both a third nuclear power

138

plant and a heavy water plant. The deal they struck did nothing to reassure those looking askance at Ezeiza.

Elsewhere around the world more new reprocessors were edging on to the scene. South Korea was thwarted by American intervention in its plan to acquire a reprocessing plant from France. Taiwan had completed a 'hot cell' – a laboratory-scale reprocessing facility – in 1975; but the facility was shut down in 1977, in response to American pressure. Nevertheless both countries continued to suggest that their growing nuclear programmes would sooner or later necessitate reprocessing.

Italy's nuclear programme seemed to be, if anything, contracting; but it too continued to operate a small reprocessing facility at Saluggia, keeping its options open. Italy's own nuclear aspirations might have been above reproach; but in 1979 Italy also agreed to supply a similar unit to Iraq – a country with no power reactors at all, but only two research reactors, and no plans for any more. Brazil's nuclear programme was in disarray, with the Angra 2 plant far behind schedule, Angra 3 even more so, and later stations fading from the drawing boards. Yet Brazil was pressing ahead with work on the reprocessing plant being supplied under the contract with Federal Germany.

In those countries some information was at least available. In Israel and South Africa no one outside tight official circles knew for certain what was going on beyond the fences and the guards. The stubborn rumour was that South Africa, with only one nuclear power plant not yet completed, and Israel, with none at all, were working together on covert nuclear activities; and that Israel had a top-secret reprocessing plant. In September 1979 an American Vela surveillance satellite designed to monitor atmospheric nuclear explosions detected a flash over the south Atlantic, near South Africa. Many observers concluded that it had been a secret nuclear test, possibly conducted jointly by South Africa and Israel; but the American government at length concluded otherwise.

Most of the new generation of reprocessors emerging at the end of the 1970s appeared to share one distinguishing characteristic. With the possible exceptions of Italy, Japan, South Korea and Taiwan, none of the new reprocessors had a civil power programme which could possibly justify separating plutonium. To a dispassionate onlooker the conclusion was obvious. Reprocessing was coming full circle, a one-time military technology re-emerging as a military technology. In precisely those countries where it could not by the remotest stretch of credibility be labelled 'civil', reprocessing was alive and advancing.

Civex

To be sure, most of the world nuclear community, especially those in the national nuclear organizations, did not see the situation in that light. One curious notion epitomized their world view. It was conceived by two of the nuclear élite: Walter Marshall of the United Kingdom Atomic Energy Authority and Chauncey Starr of the Electric Power Research Institute in the United States. At the International Atomic Energy Agency conference in Salzburg in May 1977 Marshall had been heard to worry about the stocks of spent fuel accumulating in power plant cooling ponds around the world. In his view these stocks constituted 'plutonium mines': as the radioactivity gradually decayed, the plutonium in the spent fuel would become progressively easier to extract, and more susceptible to misuse. Reflecting on this problem, Marshall and Starr came up with a concept they called Civex, which they revealed to the world in February 1978.

Civex, for 'civil extraction', was a reprocessing technology, a form of coprocessing. What made it novel was the way its originators envisaged its application. Certain countries would have Civex plants – by implication, those countries which either already had nuclear weapons or could be trusted not to acquire them. These countries would also have fast breeder power plants. The rest of the world would have conventional nuclear plants. The spent fuel from the world's conventional nuclear plants would be delivered to the Civex plants, which would produce a mixture of uranium and plutonium in the form of fast breeder fuel. This fuel would be burned in the power plants of the Civex countries. The non-Civex, non-fast-breeder countries would receive, in exchange for their spent fuel, fresh low-enriched uranium fuel of fissile content equivalent to the plutonium in their spent fuel. In this way, said Marshall, reprocessing and fast breeders would burn up the stocks of plutonium, instead of letting them accumulate.

This proposal received wide publicity internationally, presumably because of the eminence of its progenitors. Indeed, Marshall and Starr evidently regarded the proposal as a genuine attempt to get to grips with the plutonium problem. No one, apparently, asked Marshall and Starr how they proposed to organize the entire world to comply with their scheme, on a time-scale of decades; nor who would put up the astronomical sum of capital required just to build the staggering array of special plants involved; nor what security could cope with the thousands of tonnes of separated plutonium that would be in circulation in the Civex countries themselves. As an example of nuclear megalomania of epic grandiloquence, the Civex concept would be hard to beat. As a serious attempt to come to terms with the plutonium problem, it served only to demonstrate how little realistic help would be forthcoming from the plutonium people themselves.

Evaluation, of a sort
Walter Marshall, as it happened, was chairman of Working Group 4 of the International Nuclear Fuel Cycle Evaluation, on reprocessing. As the months slipped by, and with them the original deadline for the Evaluation to report, leaks from within suggested that all was well; no johnny-come-lately from Georgia was going to upset the international plutonium cart. The issues, to be sure, had not been resolved. The difficulty of safeguarding reprocessing plants continued to arouse concern. Within and outside the Evaluation much discussion was devoted to the concept of international and regional reprocessing centres. Unfortunately, however, this concept suffered from much the same problem of actual implementation as did Civex, albeit admittedly on a more modest scale.

Furthermore, even if safeguards for reprocessing facilities were satisfactory, the crucial question of access to separated plutonium remained. What should be the criteria, and how administered? The possibility of international plutonium storage was also discussed; but again the root question remained. What would release the plutonium again? The obvious answer, repeated by rote whenever the question came up, was a 'demonstrable need' for it. In terms of demonstrable need for plutonium, nothing could touch the fast breeder. It would be the key to unlock the plutonium store.

At the end of February 1980 the report of the International Nuclear Fuel Cycle Evaluation at long last appeared. By that time it was, even in the eyes of the nuclear establishment, a non-event. For the international nuclear community the report was a non-event because the Carter administration had already conceded in the various Working Groups almost all the points of policy at issue. The separation and use of plutonium as civil power plant fuel, over which the international disagreement had first arisen, was accepted and endorsed, particularly for fast breeder reactors. Even the recycling of plutonium in thermal reactors was considered to be acceptable, if economically doubtful. For the rest of the world the Evaluation was a non-event partly because of its pretence of unconcern about policy issues, and partly because, when the public noticed it at all, it was seen as a nuclear establishment talk-in, with believers talking to believers and no genuine sceptics allowed.

The report bore out these early suspicions. It proved to consist of the lowest common denominator of the policy arguments in every category, minimizing any disagreement by conceding the admissibility of anything anyone wanted to do:

> The extent to which the possibilities of misuse vary as between fuel cycles is not easy to judge. Taking into account the qualitative nature of the evaluation, the different stages of development of the various fuel cycles, the extent to which complete fuel cycles are present within individual countries and the evolutionary nature of the technical safeguards and institutional improvements that may be implemented, no single judgement about the risk of diversion from the different fuel cycles can be made that is valid both now and for the future.

In other, and fewer, words, all nuclear technologies and fuel cycles were found to be more or less equally proliferative; therefore each country might as well go ahead and do what it had first thought of. The Summary volume put it like this:

... (A) decision by a government to construct nuclear weapons is obviously a political decision motivated by political considerations that are beyond the scope of this study.

The press summary prepared by the Technical Coordinating Committee summed up all the verbiage in just ten words:

Proliferation is primarily a political and not a technical matter.

The politicians, not the plutonium people, would have to deal with it.

The Evaluation report – all nine expensive volumes of it – ushered in the 1980s with a vision of the quintessential nuclear dream: energy use multiplying manyfold, electricity use likewise, and nuclear electricity leading the way. In this best of all possible nuclear worlds, every cloud had a plutonium lining.

PART THREE

Plutonium addiction: curable or terminal?

1980 and after

17 Reagan restores the faith

The 1970s thus ended with the ignominious collapse of the first real top-level government initiative aimed at reining in the runaway plutonium bandwagon. In short order the incoming Reagan administration served notice that its attitude to plutonium, like its attitude to nuclear technology in general, was going to be very different from that of President Carter. Under President Ronald Reagan the American government would look upon plutonium with the fervour of true believers.

Another factor, however, had come into the reckoning. The general public, in the United States, Britain and elsewhere, had begun to demand a voice in nuclear policy – much to the irritation of the international nuclear establishment. Throughout the 1970s, on one issue after another, the public had been making itself heard, almost always with difficulty, and almost invariably with views sharply diverging from those of the nuclear establishment. The issues which provoked public involvement included low-level radiation and its effects; the safety of nuclear power plants and other installations; the disposal of radioactive waste; and the true, as distinct from hypothetical, economic status of nuclear electricity. However, the link between the civil and military aspects of nuclear technology and policy only began to register on the public consciousness toward the end of the 1970s.

When it did, it virtually coincided with the sudden resurgence of public concern about nuclear weapons per se; and the plutonium people viewed this development with mounting unease. If civil nuclear opponents joined forces with those opposing nuclear weapons, an obvious target for their combined efforts would be plutonium and its alternative uses. This could make the lives of plutonium supporters distinctly more difficult. It was one thing to outflank a President; it was quite another to outflank an international mass movement, decentralized, diverse and impromptu. The public had already shown that it could exert impressive, unwelcome pressure on nuclear decision-making, by lawsuits, lobbying and media impact. As the plans to use a nuclear explosive as fuel emerged reluctantly into the public daylight, plutonium advocates realized that their activities might be more and more impeded.

Even so, the advent of the Reagan administration gave new life to the plutonium business in the United States, at least psychologically. Instead of having to weather steady flak from high promontories, advocates of reprocessing and the fast breeder were once again welcome in the White House, even though they tended to arrive with palm extended, a characteristic that the Reagan administration chose to ignore. Although the administration's rhetoric stressed the importance of non-proliferation, it saw no difficulty in reconciling this rhetoric with vigorous efforts to resuscitate the plutonium business in the United States, and indeed to promote it internationally.

With the delighted encouragement of its opposite numbers in Europe, Japan and elsewhere, the American government declared itself once again in favour of reprocessing, fast breeders and plutonium fuel for power plants. To restore American leadership in world nuclear policy, the United States would once again become a 'reliable supplier': no more unilateral interference with the legitimate nuclear activities of other countries. On 16 July 1981 President Reagan released a policy statement that redefined American non-proliferation policy in such terms:

> The United States will cooperate with other nations in the peaceful uses of nuclear energy, including civil nuclear programs to meet their energy security needs, under a regime of adequate safeguards and controls. . . . We must reestablish this nation as a predictable and reliable partner for a peaceful nuclear cooperation under adequate safeguards . . .

The United States would:

> . . . continue to inhibit the transfer of sensitive nuclear material, equipment and technology, particularly where the danger of

148

proliferation demands, and to seek agreement on requiring IAEA safeguards on all nuclear activities in a non-nuclear-weapon state as a condition for any significant new nuclear supply commitment.

However, the United States would not seek to:

inhibit or set back civil reprocessing or breeder development abroad in nations with advanced nuclear power programs where it does not constitute a proliferation risk.

In a major nuclear policy statement on 8 October 1981 Reagan called for a resumption of reprocessing in the United States. Specifically lifting the Carter ban, he declared that his administration would pursue consistent long-term policies designed to eliminate regulatory impediments to commercial participation. He further requested a feasibility study to see whether the Department of Energy might obtain plutonium supplies economically by competitive bidding:

By encouraging private firms to supply fuel for the breeder program at a cost that does not exceed that of government-produced plutonium we may be able to provide a stable market for private sector reprocessing and simultaneously reduce the funding needs of the US breeder demonstration program.

In June 1982, after the press got wind of a further shift in policy, the State Department confirmed that Japan and other nations presenting 'no risk of proliferation' that used fuel from the United States could henceforth negotiate for blanket permission to have it reprocessed as desired; Carter's 'case by case' approach would no longer apply.

Barnwell again

While cheering from the sidelines, the Reagan administration endeavoured to leave it to private industry to bring about the called-for renaissance of reprocessing in the United States. Private industry, alas, was not interested. At Barnwell, for instance, the chemical separation plant, spent fuel ponds and uranium finishing plant were all in place. However, before the facility could be licensed it would be necessary to build a plutonium finishing plant and a plant to turn the liquid high-level wastes into glass; these plants would entail further capital investment of $700 to $900 million.

Shell, Gulf and Allied Chemical, co-owners of the Barnwell plant, announced that they could see little future in their
South Carolina misadventure. They were tired of waiting for
officials to agree a policy and stick with it; nor did they fancy
investing the further major sums required just to reopen the
licensing process for Barnwell. Instead, they declared that
they would prefer to write the plant off against tax, cut their
losses and get out.

Although the partners in Allied General shied away from
the prospect of pouring more money into Barnwell, other
organizations spoke out in favour, notably Bechtel. However,
Bechtel was not offering to put up the capital itself. What it
had in mind was – surprise – turning Barnwell into a
demonstration plant, with most of the funds to come –
surprise again – from the government, through contracts to
purchase the plutonium. Bechtel also pointed out that the
German consortium of DWK had expressed a tentative
interest in a co-operative reprocessing venture with the
United States: surely Barnwell would fit ideally into such a
scheme. Alas, despite all the advantages everyone appeared so
ready to identify, no one actually came forward with cash in
hand. With Federal funds cut off by Congress, Barnwell
continued to languish, a nuclear pariah.

Clinch River again

Unlike Barnwell, the Clinch River fast breeder was not even
so much as a hole in the ground when the Reagan administration came to power. But its supporters, with their tenacious
rearguard action in Congress throughout the Carter years,
had kept it not only in the budget but also on the order books.
By 1981 several hundred million dollars' worth of hardware
had been manufactured and paid for. It might have been
expected that the new administration could simply have given
Clinch River the green light, stood back and watched it take
shape. However, although the government's attitude toward
fast breeders in general and Clinch River in particular had
shifted dramatically in their favour with the change of
presidents, other circumstances had also changed, in a much
less favourable direction.

For a start, the estimated cost of Clinch River had risen like an express elevator. By 1982 even its backers were admitting that it would probably cost $3500 million to complete; critics believed this figure to be unrealistically low. Clinch River supporters watched in dismay as an improbable coalition materialized. Those who had criticized the project in the 1970s had been moved by the argument that it was thoroughly dangerous to advocate the use of a nuclear explosive as fuel. These critics came in the main from the liberal range of the political spectrum. At the beginning of the 1980s, however, new voices joined the critical chorus: the political and fiscal conservatives, who considered it thoroughly dangerous to provide open-ended government funding for any research project, especially one whose costs were rising so rapidly into the stratosphere. Activists who would in almost every other respect have found themselves on opposite sides of a vast ideological chasm linked arms and advanced on Clinch River with murderous intent.

In response to this remarkable and ominous twin-pronged onslaught, supporters pointed to France and Super-Phénix. They not only pointed, they journeyed thither, returning from their pilgrimage fired with fervour. If France could build a full-scale fast breeder power plant, surely the United States must not be left behind. Not only nuclear industry people but also Senators, Representatives, and journalists from industry publications made their way to the shrine and came away with faith renewed.

Supporters of Clinch River were bolstered by a fortunate coincidence: Clinch River was in Tennessee, the home state of Senator Howard Baker, the Senate majority leader. In his eyes it was not only an essential element of American energy policy but also a prestige project on his own turf; and he defended it doggedly. The White House would need Baker's backing to get its legislative programme through Congress. Baker made it clear that in return he expected unstinting White House backing for Clinch River; and he got it. The powerful Office of Management and Budget reluctantly agreed to support the project, although Office head David Stockman had bitterly opposed it while a Congressman. Baker twisted Congressional arms relentlessly on its behalf; and in one crucial vote after another Clinch River survived, if narrowly.

Blurring the boundaries

In late 1981 the Reagan administration came up with two ideas which further fuelled the plutonium controversy. Across the nation the cooling ponds at nuclear power plants were relentlessly filling with spent fuel. Some power plants faced having to shut down because they had not enough room left in their ponds. At the same time the American military was tooling up to produce a new generation of nuclear weapons, a plan endorsed by Carter in the final year of his term and espoused enthusiastically by Reagan. The bomb-makers claimed, however, to be short of plutonium. The military plutonium production reactors at Hanford and Savannah River were out of service, most of them permanently; bringing even two or three back into service would take years.

Reagan officials suggested solving the two problems simultaneously: the Department of Energy should take the spent fuel from power plant ponds and reprocess it at Hanford and Savannah River, to recover the plutonium for use in weapons. The officials might have expected the electricity suppliers to welcome this tidy solution to their spent fuel problem; but the suppliers were aghast. For more than two decades they had been trying to convince the public that there was no relation between nuclear power plants and nuclear weapons. But here was the federal government itself underlining just such a relationship, in the most blatant way imaginable. Nuclear Regulatory Commissioner Peter Bradford summed up the reaction:

> The average nuclear utility realizes that it does not need the controversy and that most of its customers do not want the feeling that when they turn on their lights, they are also turning on the local atomic bomb factory.

Antiproliferation activists were likewise outraged. If the United States were to recover plutonium from civil spent fuel for use in weapons, it would be inviting every other country to do likewise – sounding the death-knell for 'safeguards', and possibly for the entire planet as well.

While the Reagan administration was thus getting its domestic nuclear affairs into a tangle, it was also upsetting some foreign friends. In its search for new sources of

152

plutonium the American government also looked across the Atlantic to Britain. In October 1981 the British media revealed that the United States had approached Britain with an offer to purchase some five tonnes of plutonium. When the offer came to public attention the response was wrathful, not only from nuclear opponents but also from senior staff of the Central Electricity Generating Board and eventually from the Electric Power Engineers' Association, the leading trade union proponent of civil nuclear power in Britain. The Association even declared that the sale of plutonium to the United States might cause the union to withdraw its support from the entire British civil nuclear programme.

Nuclear officials in both countries insisted that the plutonium involved would be exclusively for civil purposes, not weapons; but the critics were not appeased. They pointed out that provision of plutonium from Britain to fuel Clinch River – the declared destination of the material – would allow the United States to use its own ostensibly civil plutonium in its new warheads. While British plutonium might not actually wind up in American bombs, it would undeniably assist the United States to add to its stockpile of nuclear arms. After several months of wrangling on both sides of the Atlantic, the Reagan administration went out of its way to assert, both at home and abroad, that it had withdrawn its request to purchase plutonium from Britain, and that it had no intention of separating plutonium from American power plant fuel. But both episodes reinforced the feeling of many that the American government's attitude toward plutonium was entirely too casual.

Plutonium in trouble

By 1982 Clinch River was facing the most serious Congressional challenge yet. Antiproliferation activists and financial conservatives had come together under the banner of the National Taxpayers' Coalition Against Clinch River. Liberal Democrats and conservative Republicans shared the same platform to hammer home the message: Clinch River was a nonsensical way to spend taxpayers' money. It was a 'technological turkey', a plant whose design was already obsolete, and whose ostensible purpose was no longer relevant to national energy policy.

American fast breeder people found some respite from the onslaught in June 1982, by thronging to a major conference in France to discuss fast breeder safety. They came away proclaiming that the fast breeder was turning out to be the safest reactor of all. They also made the obligatory side-trip to Creys-Malville, to pay their respects to Super-Phénix. But they did so with mixed feelings. While they might be satisfied that the fast breeder was impressively safe, a prior problem was looming all too obtrusively. In the early summer of 1982 the Commissariat à l'Energie Atomique had conceded that electricity from Super-Phénix would cost about twice as much as that from conventional French nuclear plants.

The French plan had been to follow Super-Phénix with six more plants, replicas of the original. Yet another replica, designated SNR–2, had been planned to follow the SNR–300 at Kalkar in Federal Germany. However, Electricité de France was by its own admission facing its worst financial crisis in thirty years, the result of a fall-off in electricity demand, coupled with the high cost of foreign borrowing to finance its nuclear programme. The prospect of ordering a series of fast breeder power plants whose output would be not only surplus to requirements but also twice as expensive appealed to the company not at all. The French government let it be known that it proposed to wait until Super-Phénix had been in operation for a year or more before deciding on the next stage of the programme. By this time Super-Phénix was some two years behind schedule. Instead of proceeding with plans to replicate it, the Commissariat engineers embarked on fundamental redesign, aimed at producing not 1200 but 1500 megawatts from the same size of reactor core. The erstwhile flagship of the international fast breeder effort had begun to show signs of foundering.

In the autumn of 1982 the battle over funds for Clinch River was joined afresh. However, when American fast breeder people reiterated in autumn 1982 their favourite catch-phrases about 'losing the lead in fast breeders to the French', their ever more vociferous opponents pointed in rebuttal to the mounting confusion across the Atlantic. In vain

154

the proponents resurrected all the time-honoured chestnuts about the glittering promise of the fast breeder: the savings in costs of uranium, the guaranteed infinite supply of energy, the relief from the grip of grasping oil sheikhs, even the comparatively recent claims about using the fast breeder to burn up the dangerous accumulations of plutonium. Against a background of falling energy demand, a glut of oil, and even an incipient glut of uranium, the claims for the fast breeder had an ever more hollow ring.

Probably the most damning vote of no confidence came from those who had always been proclaimed the beneficiaries of the breeder boon: the electricity suppliers. The suppliers, in the United States, Belgium, Britain, Federal Germany, the Netherlands, Japan, and elsewhere, did not to be sure proclaim aloud their disillusion with the fast breeder and plutonium fuel. They simply sat back and watched the costs of fast breeder research continue to climb, while they kept their money in their pockets and let governments pay the bills. The bills – by now including over DM6 billion for the Kalkar plant, and upwards of $3.5 billion for Clinch River, in other words from $5000 to more than $10,000 per kilowatt – grew ever more impressive.

18　Piling up plutonium

The world plutonium industry is as yet embryonic. It has yet to become a true ecónomic activity commercially connected to others, producing goods and services and selling them in a genuine market. The plutonium business is still almost completely dependent on government support and finance everywhere. There is, nonetheless, a world plutonium establishment, with a vast budget and a long payroll of highly skilled staff. What is the current status of this plutonium establishment? How much plutonium is currently stockpiled? How might the stockpiles grow? What production facilities are currently in operation, and planned? What are the prospects for using plutonium as fuel – and for ensuring that it does not find a different and devastating use?

The plutonium inventory
Although plutonium is a manufactured material, no one – literally – knows how much plutonium there is in the world in 1984. Even within individual countries national inventories are known by at most a handful of individuals, because of the military importance both of the material and of information about it. Some governments and industries have published information about their existing and anticipated stocks of nominally 'civil' plutonium. A compilation and analysis of this information was published in mid-1983 by the Nuclear Control Institute, Washington, D.C., in *World Inventories of Civilian Plutonium and the Spread of Nuclear Weapons;* see Tables 3 and 4 for key findings. In the non-communist world the conventional nuclear plants now in operation are able to produce about 40 tonnes of plutonium a year – enough for at least 6000 bombs, if separated out of spent fuel in reprocessing plants. By the year 2000 the cumulative inventory of

156

non-communist commercial spent fuel will have included up to some 1700 tonnes of plutonium, produced in up to 31 countries; if all present plans proceed, some 600 tonnes will have been separated. Through 1982 the existing reprocessors had separated some 44 tonnes of 'commercial' plutonium, enough for some 6500 atom bombs.

There is moreover a problem with all such information. In

Table 3: Plutonium in All Commercial Spent Fuel
Cumulative Total (metric tons)

Country	Through 1982	Through 1990	Through 2000 (maximum estimate only)
Argentina	⅛.½	5.7	15
Australia	–	–	.9
Belgium	2.5	11	24
Brazil	–	2.1	18
Canada	19	60	140
Chile	–	–	.7
Denmark	–	–	.9
Egypt	–	–	2.4
Finland	1.2	5.5	13
France	15	106	307
Germany, West	12	41	117
Greece	–	–	1.7
India	1.9	6.4	18
Italy	3.0	6.3	21
Japan	17	63	200
Korea	.39	8.4	36
Mexico	–	1.4	7.8
Netherlands	1.1	2.2	4.6
Pakistan	.56	1.0	2.6
Philippines	–	.54	2.8
Portugal	–	–	1.3
Romania	–	.85	13
South Africa	–	2.7	9.6
Spain	1.4	11	42
Sweden	4.6	20	43
Switzerland	3.5	8.6	20
Taiwan	.86	8.5	24
Turkey	–	–	1.5
United Kingdom	15	43	88
USA	74	242	546
Yugoslavia	–	1.2	8.4
TOTALS	175	660	1700

Table 4: Amount of Commercial Plutonium Separated by Major Reprocessors Through 1982

Country	Facility	Fuel Type	Amount (kg)
Belgium	Eurochemic-Mol	metal & oxide	683
France	La Hague	oxide	4,100
		metal	8.700
		mixed oxide	600
	Marcoule	metal	2,700
		mixed oxide	900
		French Total:	17,000
Germany, West	WAK – Karlsruhe	oxide	540
India	Tarapur	oxide	–
Japan	Tokai Mura	oxide	690
USA	West Valley	oxide & metal	1,886
United Kingdom	Windscale	metal and .small amount of oxide	23,000
	Dounreay	mixed oxide	360
		Total:	44,000

NOTE: Reflects reprocessing through 1982 only.

Britain, for example, the government, in answer to questions in Parliament, declared that the stock of separated 'civil' plutonium in 1982 was 21 tonnes, with another 12 tonnes still in fuel elements. This does set a lower limit of sorts on the total stock; but there is no way to cross-check the figures independently. In 1982, independent analysts in Britain began trying to reconcile the declared stocks of civil plutonium with the known operating history of British civil reactors. They pointed out that the civil Magnox plants were refuelled continuously without shutting down. In the early years of operation they would therefore have discharged significant quantities of low-burnup plutonium of high purity – 'weapons-grade' material suitable for use in sophisticated nuclear weapons. But the government told Parliament that none of the plutonium in the civil stockpile was weapons-grade.

What had become of the low-burnup material? Had it been sent to the United States, under a military nuclear agreement signed in 1959? Government ministers stoutly and repeatedly denied that any plutonium from British civil reactors ever found its way into American nuclear weapons; but the figures and the documents could not support the official line. Whatever the truth, it serves to underline an insuperable difficulty when trying to take inventory of civil plutonium: the dividing line between 'civil' and 'military' depends more on semantics than on physics, a point to keep in mind about Table 4.

It should also be noted that calling some plutonium 'weapons-grade' does not mean that the rest cannot be used for bombs. Even plutonium from fuel that has been in a power reactor for several years can be used as a nuclear explosive. Its performance is not so precisely predictable, and it is somewhat riskier to handle. But it will nevertheless explode; indeed expert design will produce a bomb almost as powerful as one made from the highest-purity 'weapons-grade' material. Like calling plutonium 'civil' or 'military', calling it 'weapons-grade' or otherwise is a matter more of semantics than of substance.

Reprocessing plants

By 1984 there were military reprocessing plants in operation in the United States, the Soviet Union, France and presumably China. There were dual-purpose military-civil reprocessing plants in operation in Britain and France. There were civil – at least nominally civil – reprocessing plants in operation in Britain, France, Federal Germany, Japan and India. There were civil reprocessing plants out of or not yet in operation in the United States, Belgium, Argentina, Brazil, and Pakistan. (See Table 1.) Many commentators also assumed or suspected the existence of a secret military reprocessing plant in Israel. Every country engaged in civil reprocessing faced continuing controversy.

United States

In the United States, in 1984, Allied General Nuclear Services had begun to mothball the Barnwell reprocessing plant. It had been struggling to stay afloat with the support of federal funds for a 'safeguards demonstration' programme, designed to tackle the difficulty of safeguarding reprocessing plants. In March 1983, however, Congress refused to extend the programme or the funding. The company forthwith sued the federal government for $500 million; the company charged that the government had induced private industry to get into the reprocessing business, and then – under the Carter administration – reversed its policy, effectively taking private property without just compensation. Bechtel, the major multinational construction firm, continued to press the government to use money from the Waste Management Fund, set up under the new Waste Policy Act of 1983, to complete and commission Barnwell. But by autumn 1983 Allied General were laying off staff; by 1984 they had begun to sell off the plant's usable components.

Britain

In Britain, by 1984, ground had not yet been broken for the Thermal Oxide Reprocessing Plant (THORP) at the Windscale site of British Nuclear Fuels, although it had been given the go-ahead more than five years earlier. Despite its three-line letter of May 1977 asking to reserve half the capacity of THORP, by 1984 the Central Electricity Generating Board (with its smaller equivalent, the South of Scotland Electricity Board) still had not signed a contract for reprocessing the first 1850 tonnes of spent oxide fuel from the advanced gas-cooled reactors, and was letting it be known that it found the company's terms unacceptable.

At the Windscale inquiry in 1977 the cost of reprocessing in THORP had been given as £160,000 per tonne of uranium in the contract with the Japanese, and £230,000 per tonne of uranium in the proposed contracts with the British Electricity Boards, each figure embodying an unspecified profit to the company. The difference was explained as arising from the prepayment by the Japanese, excluding financing charges. In mid-1983, however, the fuel company's deputy chairman, giving evidence at the inquiry into plans for a new nuclear power station at Sizewell, Suffolk, said that the corresponding figure for reprocessing British oxide fuel in THORP was by that time £425,000 per tonne of uranium in March 1982 money values. This cost referred only to reprocessing itself, and excluded storage and dismantling of British spent fuel, waste conditioning including vitrification, and final disposal.

In its annual report, published in August 1983, the company announced that it had contracts to reprocess 1200 tonnes of spent fuel in THORP between 1990 and 2000. This had to be set against the original planned capacity of 6000 tonnes over the period. The annual report gave the latest estimated cost of THORP as £1.2 billion. In December 1983, however, the company revealed that in the light of further design work the capital and operating costs had risen considerably. The American industry newsletter *Nuclear Fuel* suggested that the operating costs had risen as much as 60 per cent, and that the company's customers were complaining. For its part the company announced that it had proposed to its customers price rises of 30 per cent or more. One customer who had signed a contract earlier in 1983 declared that it 'would not have done so had it been warned of the impending price increase'.

At the same time, British Nuclear Fuels was also endeavouring to renegotiate its existing contracts for reprocessing metal Magnox fuel from the British Boards. But the Central Electricity Generating Board was proving a distinctly obstreperous customer. Worse still for the company, the Board had completed its third dry-storage facility for spent fuel at its Wylfa Magnox plant, and was delighted with the performance of all three – one cooled by carbon dioxide and two by natural circulation of ordinary air. If Magnox fuel could thus be stored indefinitely, so could the more durable oxide fuel – making reprocessing even less important to the Board.

Its waning interest in reprocessing was underlined in February 1983. Giving evidence at the Sizewell inquiry, a senior Board witness revealed that the Board intended to seek approval to build a central facility for long-term storage of spent fuel, at an estimated cost of £100 million. The Board noted that British Nuclear Fuel's own design lifetime for THORP indicated that it would be in service only between 1990 and 2000. Allowing for the time needed to cool spent fuel after discharge, this meant that the existing advanced gas-cooled reactors and the proposed pressurized-water reactor at Sizewell would be in service long after THORP had expired. The fuel company had not, at least in public, addressed the question of reprocessing plants to follow THORP. The Board recalled its experience in the 1970s, when the company's Magnox reprocessing troubles led it to refuse to meet its contractual commitments, and decline to accept spent Magnox fuel from the Board's ponds. The Board was evidently not prepared to give any more hostages to the fortunes of the reprocessors.

Meanwhile, the first shipments of spent fuel from Japan and elsewhere, feedstock for THORP, had already begun to arrive for storage in the ponds at Windscale. There was, however, still no public word on what would become of the plutonium from it. As far as could be ascertained, plutonium separated from Spanish spent fuel in the Head End Plant before its demise ten years earlier was still stored at Windscale; the company's failure to return it to Spain was believed to be linked with Spain's continuing refusal to ratify the Non-Proliferation Treaty.

The site, as it happened, was no longer officially called Windscale. In May 1981 the company had changed its name to Sellafield. Many commentators assumed – despite the company's protestations to the contrary – that the name change was an attempt to exorcize the site's unfortunate public image. Since the reprocessing plant and its associated facilities were still on the part of the site called the Windscale Works, commentators tended to ignore the official name-change and stick with Windscale.

The Atomic Energy Authority, for its part, continued to operate its pilot reprocessing plant for spent fast breeder fuel at Dounreay. But any further development along that particular line seemed very far off indeed.

France

In France, in 1984, Cogema was continuing to operate the original oxide head end plant at Cap la Hague, albeit with difficulty. Its design had left a great deal to be desired. It required far too much maintenance, and the capacity of its components was poorly matched to the size of spent fuel elements. In consequence, the plant was operating with process vessels only partly filled, and thus well below maximum efficiency. Cogema massaged the figures with every variety of ambiguity, but the underlying implication remained clear. The true capacity of the first head end plant was nearer 250 tonnes per year than the 400 originally claimed. This in turn meant that the capital cost of the plant per unit of capacity was proportionally higher, casting further doubt on its economic status. Cogema officials, to be sure, denied vehemently all suggestions alleging technical difficulties at la Hague. They claimed that only a shortage of suitable feedstock caused the low throughput, and that all would be well once the spent fuel on hand was of the right size and kind.

Work continued meanwhile on the next two instalments of capacity at la Hague. Designated UP2–800 and UP3, each was to have a design throughput of 800 tonnes of spent fuel per year. The planning history of these further plants was convoluted even by comparison with reprocessing elsewhere. In 1977 Cogema was planning to enlarge UP–2 from a stated capacity of 400 tonnes per year to 800 tonnes per year by 1979. It was to be followed by UP–3A, a new 800-tonnes-per-year plant in operation by 1985, and UP–3B, another of the same capacity a year later. By the mid-1980s Cogema was thus expecting to be reprocessing 2400 tonnes of spent fuel annually. After 1977, however, the anticipated upsurge in reprocessing business failed to materialize. By 1984, UP–3A – now just called UP–3 – is not expected to come into service until 1987, UP–2/800 a year later. The two plants are not to reach their full design throughput of 1600 tonnes per year until 1992.

Both of these units were ordered on the basis not only of the spent fuel expected from French power plants, but also of commitments from foreign customers, including Federal Germany, Japan, and Sweden. Indeed, UP3 was to be financed entirely by advance payments from foreign customers. The contract terms were extraordinarily one-sided – like that between British Nuclear Fuels and the Japanese – as became clear when a contract with Sweden was leaked to the Swedish media. It was abundantly clear that the overriding concern of customers was to rid their ponds of the embarrassing accumulation of spent fuel. What later became of the fuel was of secondary importance to the customers. It is, however, still uncertain what will happen to plutonium separated at la Hague from foreign spent fuel. According to one interpretation of the leaked Swedish contract, all the high-level waste is to be returned to Sweden, but not necessarily all the separated plutonium.

In January 1983, an official report from a top-level French government committee cast the faintest of shadows over Cogema's rosy prognosis. The committee, called the Conseil Supérieur de la Sûreté Nucléaire, had been appointed in November 1981 by the Socialist government of President François Mitterrand. Some saw it as a way to take the heat out of the reprocessing issue, to appease voters waiting for Mitterrand to keep his campaign promise to slow down the headlong French nuclear programme, while not upsetting the powerful French nuclear lobby. The committee was chaired by Professor Raymond Castaing, a nuclear physicist at the University of Paris, and included both keen reprocessors and some more sceptical.

The Castaing report was delivered to the government at the beginning of January 1983 and published on 11 January. It proved to be broadly sympathetic to reprocessing, endorsing Cogema's activities at la Hague and its plans for expansion. But the report also called for advanced reprocessing, involving more thorough removal of long-lived radioactivity, to reduce the hazards associated with final disposal of long-lived wastes. Such technical innovations would significantly strengthen the case for reprocessing as a waste-management measure, as the Castaing committee stressed. Unfortunately, it would also undoubtedly increase the cost of reprocessing, at a time when electricity suppliers were already showing signs of rebellion against the Hobson's choice the reprocessors were offering.

For the reprocessors, the most ominous section of the Castaing report was that which advocated – for the first time in France from an official source – serious investigation of interim and long-term storage as an alternative to immediate reprocessing. The suggestion was put forward, to be sure, in the light of indications that capacity at la Hague might not be adequate to cope with the anticipated quantities of French spent fuel beyond the 1990s, to say nothing of commitments to foreign clients; and the report was careful to stress that reprocessing and long-term storage were not mutually exclusive. It was nevertheless a clear departure from previous French nuclear policy. It could also be construed as an oblique and intriguing comment on the changing nature of French plans for the fast breeder:

> Until very recently in the great majority of countries engaged in electronuclear programmes, it was considered that immediate reprocessing represented the best, if not the only available method to close the fuel cycle. . . . It has become ever clearer that reprocessing is a complex operation which is much more costly than it was thought at the beginning (the estimation of costs by the Commission on the Production of Nuclear Energy has been multiplied by 9 in constant francs between 1970 and 1982). For a long time, the capacities of reprocessing will probably remain greatly inferior to the tonnages discharged from reactors, even if for a while the plutonium extracted is in excess of the needs of fast breeders. It is expected that there will be a world stock of 20 000 tonnes of spent fuel in the year 2000+ (IAEA estimation); even in France . . . after 1990 there will be a permanent stock of 9000–12 000 tonnes of unreprocessed spent fuel, unless new reprocessing plants are commissioned.
> A growing number of countries have therefore begun to take measures to extend their long-term storage capacity, in particular in the USA and Canada, where large quantities are currently stored by the reactors. . . . In Europe, there are projects, and even sites for long-term storage (UK, W. Germany, Sweden).
> The option not to reprocess immediately is reversible. . . . The uncertainties relative to the safety of long-term storage in deep geological layers, be it of glasses subsequent to reprocessing or of spent fuel itself, should be answered before any decision to bury (spent fuel et cetera).
> On the other hand, not reprocessing immediately is in keeping with the hypothesis that commercialization of the fast breeder, for economic or political reasons, or for reasons of the safety of the reactor and its cycle, would not be considered desirable over the next few decades . . .

In France this was verging on nuclear heresy, with an official imprint. The Castaing committee seemed likely to give French plutonium people their first genuinely uneasy moments.

Federal Germany

In Federal Germany, in 1984, the reprocessing situation continued to mirror the confusion that had prevailed ever since Lower Saxony Premier Albrecht decided against the Gorleben project in May 1979. One clear casualty of the decision had been the concept of a single vast reprocessing plant to service the entire country. In the months that followed Albrecht's bombshell decision, DWK and the individual electricity suppliers came up with one potential site after another, scattered all over the Republic. In each case, the proposal was not for a sprawling 'Zentrum' on the original Gorleben model, but just for a reprocessing plant – one of comparatively modest size, usually of the order of 300 tonnes of spent fuel per year capacity.

Some state governments and premiers welcomed the preliminary proposals and encouraged site investigations. Others were less enthusiastic, their constituents still less so; opposition groups sprang up and spoke out wherever the reprocessors turned their gaze. For either political or geological reasons one site after another was eliminated. At the same time DWK and the suppliers also looked farther afield, signing contracts with Cogema to deliver more spent fuel to la Hague. DWK also made an approach to interested parties in the United States, with a view to turning Barnwell into a cooperative international facility; but nothing came of these discussions because no one was prepared to put up the necessary finance.

By late 1982 the hunt for a reprocessing site had apparently narrowed down to three locations, in the provinces of Hesse, Rhine-Palatinate, and Bavaria. Then, in November 1982, Albrecht proposed a site at Dragahn. The proposal dumbfounded many, because Dragahn was only some thirty kilometres from Gorleben, the site Albrecht had turned down in 1979. Local opponents, however, found the decision unsurprising. They pointed out that, although Albrecht had refused permission for a reprocessing plant, he had permitted continuing investigation of Gorleben as a possible site for final disposal of radioactive waste. Albrecht's original rejection of the proposed reprocessing plant had been because it was 'politically unacceptable'. By 1983, the Bonn government was

Christian Democrat, like Albrecht; and plans originating in Bonn were therefore suddenly more 'politically acceptable', even if they were virtually the same plans.

The Federal Ministry for Research and Technology was still pushing its long-standing concept for 'closing the fuel cycle' by recovering plutonium and using it as power plant fuel. From their viewpoint, it would still obviously be preferable to site any reprocessing plant as close as feasible to the final repository for radioactive waste. The local population of Gorleben and environs thus, albeit with a measure of hindsight, found Albrecht's proposal of Dragahn as a reprocessing site predictable. With the offer of Dragahn on the table DWK dropped the Hesse and Rhine-Palatinate sites, keeping the site in Bavaria for a second 350-tonne unit. But a long legal and political process lies ahead, before either site produces its first plutonium.

In the meantime the twelve suppliers which had banded together as DWK also pooled their efforts to press on with the manufacture and use of plutonium fuel. Using plutonium separated from German fuel at Cap la Hague, they contracted with the Alkem subsidiary of Kraftwerk Union for the manufacture of mixed-oxide plutonium fuel for their existing conventional nuclear power plants. The small plants at Obrigheim and Gundremmingen had used such fuel since the early 1970s, albeit only on an experimental basis. In 1984 the manufacture of fuel for the SNR–300 fast breeder at Kalkar was the top priority; but the suppliers were also planning for thermal recycle. Indeed, they appeared more willing to pay a premium for mixed-oxide fuel for conventional reactors than to increase their contribution to the cost of Kalkar.

Needless to say mixed-oxide plutonium fuel was substantially more expensive than conventional low-enriched uranium fuel. But no one was prepared to put a figure on the actual cost, because no one had either manufactured or burned mixed-oxide fuel on a straightforward commercial basis. In Federal Germany, however, the plutonium fuel programme did embody one distinctive feature, otherwise virtually unheard-of. The requisite subsidies involved in using plutonium as power plant fuel – in thermal reactors, at any rate – were provided not by the taxpayers, via the government, but by the electricity suppliers themselves. Whether they would continue this support indefinitely if the economic status of plutonium fuel did not show marked improvement was quite another matter.

Although the suppliers were picking up the tab for development of mixed-oxide fuel for conventional reactors, research on reprocessing was still being carried out mainly at the small WAK facility at the Karlsruhe research centre, and financed primarily by the Bonn government. The WAK unit had been shut down in May 1980, after the dissolver vessel sprang a leak. It was out of operation for more than two years, but came back into service in October 1982. The track record suggests that it is likely to remain the only reprocessing plant in Federal Germany for some years to come.

Belgium

In Belgium, in 1984, controversy continued to envelop the Eurochemic plant at Mol. Since the late 1970s, the Belgian government and Belgian nuclear interests had returned repeatedly to the theme of Mol. At one stage the plan had been for Belgium to take it over from its erstwhile international masters and reopen it to service the expanding Belgian nuclear programme – and of course foreign customers. As usual, however, the plan came up against a certain problem: no one wanted to put up the money, not even the Belgian government.

Belgian electrical suppliers were meanwhile growing disgruntled about their reprocessing contracts with the French. Quite apart from having to pay through the nose, and indeed to provide capital to finance the expansion of facilities at la Hague, the Belgians were finding it difficult to retrieve their separated plutonium from Cogema. Possibly prompted by the presence of Euratom in Brussels, they were determined to go through Euratom channels, as required by the Euratom Treaty, which stipulated that the European Supply Agency of Euratom should handle all transactions involving fissile material. But the French, although signatories to the Treaty, had long refused to cede their national control over fissile material, and extended this refusal to the contracts with the

168

Belgians. The Belgians were especially irritated that the Germans, who had made bilateral contracts with the French, bypassing the Supply Agency, were getting their plutonium back from la Hague with no apparent difficulty. The French airily attributed the delays to 'rigorous procedures' for export licences; but this did not soothe Belgian sensibilities.

In August 1982, the Belgian Parliament decided at last to restart the Eurochemic plant. That would at least give the Belgian suppliers something else to do with their spent fuel. The recommissioning was expected to take some six years, and the Parliamentary go-ahead was hedged with a stricture limiting throughput at Mol to its present capacity of about 60 tonnes per year. Belgian plants alone would be producing 150 tonnes per year by the mid-1980s. The suppliers would have preferred to see the plant expanded to 300 tonnes per year, to permit the involvement of suppliers from Sweden and Switzerland – who would presumably be invited to find capital for the privilege. In March 1983 the Senate finally gave approval to reopen the plant. But the source of the capital required – more than $340 million – was in 1984 still unclear.

Japan

In Japan, in 1984, the Tokai Mura reprocessing plant was shut down yet again with technical trouble, as it had been repeatedly since its start-up in September 1977. The plant had been plagued by leaks in highly active areas. Pinholes had been discovered in dissolver R–11 in April 1982 and in dissolver R–10 in February 1983. Making the best of a bad job, the owners formally changed the designation of this part of the plant: it was now a 'remote-control repair development facility'. A new dissolver, R–12, was to be designed and installed, but was not expected to be in service until 1985.

Reprocessing policy, like reprocessing technology, had also encountered yet another glitch. The advent of the Reagan administration in the United States, with its more amenable approach to the commercialization of plutonium, had encouraged Japanese nuclear policy-makers to look forward to unhindered progress with their plans for reprocessing and

169

plutonium fuel. They had not, however, reckoned on the durability of the legislative legacy of the Carter years: the Nuclear Non-Proliferation Act.

The Act laid down a battery of requirements that the Japanese had to meet, including full-scope safeguards, prior American approval of the transfer or alteration of all spent fuel regardless of origin – even fuel with no American connection – and Japanese acknowledgement that safeguards and plutonium-control provisions remain in force in perpetuity. Compliance with the Act would have to be approved by the Japanese Diet; and Japanese nuclear officials were unenthusiastic about going to it for fear of rekindling the domestic nuclear controversy.

The Japanese were aggrieved that the Act was at variance with the policy of President Reagan, stated as recently as June 1982 at the Versailles Summit. An American State Department official was reported in December 1982 as saying that the United States continued to require compliance with the Act, and that for the President to make an exception for the Japanese would be 'pretty significant' – and accordingly, presumably, unlikely. In the light of this disagreement, the long-standing Japanese plans to construct a second, much larger reprocessing plant remained at a standstill in all respects save the rhetorical.

At the Tokai Mura plant, the Act's strictures had still to be felt. Although the Carter administration had only given the Japanese permission to reprocess 99 tonnes of spent fuel, to which an extra 50 tonnes was added in February 1982, operating problems at the plant had kept the cumulative total actually reprocessed by June 1981 to only 106 tonnes. The Power Reactor and Nuclear Fuel Development Corporation, operators of the plant, conceded that its nominal 210–tonnes-per-year capacity could not be achieved in practice. Be that as it might, the operators contracted with seven Japanese suppliers to reprocess a further 200 tonnes of their spent fuel by October 1983 – at a price of some $587 000 per tonne, up from $348 000. The utilities did not protest about the price rise, since to have the fuel reprocessed in Europe would have cost from $783 000 to $870 000 per tonne, including transportation. At some stage, nevertheless, depending on the technical state of play at Tokai Mura, this contract was going to have to be reconciled with the American Non-Proliferation Act, in the light of negotiations about 'blanket approval' as suggested by President Reagan.

Argentina

In Argentina, in 1984, the entire context of the country's long-running nuclear programme was being fundamentally reappraised. The advent of a democratically elected civil government under President Raul Alfonsín was followed by the dismissal of Rear-Admiral Carlos Castro Madero from his post as head of the Argentine Atomic Energy Commission. President Alfonsín announced a comprehensive review of Argentine nuclear activities, and declared that they would henceforth be placed under civilian administration. What this might mean for the future of the Ezeiza reprocessing plant remained unclear. But the outlook for acceptance of comprehensive international safeguards, and possibly even accession to the Treaty of Tlatelolco (establishing a Latin American nuclear weapon-free zone) or even to the Non-Proliferation Treaty, was brighter than anyone would have been prepared to wager a year earlier.

India

In India, in 1984, the civil nuclear programme was marking time, if not indeed slipping back. But Indian nuclear rhetoric was as high-flown as ever. Despite the sporadic operation of the nuclear power plants at Tarapur and Rajasthan, and the fitful sluggishness of construction work at Narora and Kalpakkam, the Indian nuclear élite continued to make grandiose speeches painting an Indian nuclear future in which 10 000 megawatts would be in service by the year 2000 – a more than tenfold increase over current nominal capacity, to say nothing of the actual output currently achieved.

The first stage, they proclaimed, would bring the roster of conventional nuclear plants up to some 8000 megawatts; the second stage would add fast breeders to burn the plutonium from the conventional plants, and the third would be fuelled with plutonium and with uranium–233 bred from thorium in the second-generation plants. Accordingly, Indian nuclear

171

planners continued with their commitment to reprocessing. The original 50-tonnes-per-year reprocessing plant at Trombay had been shut down since 1974 – more or less since it had produced the plutonium for the Pokharan explosion. But the Tarapur reprocessing plant, with a nominal capacity of 100 tonnes of spent fuel per year, had started up in 1982, and continued in trial operation, to prepare for reprocessing the spent fuel from the Tarapur nuclear power plant in the event of a final schism with the United States.

Even within India, however, critics had begun to question the advisability of devoting such vast resources to a programme whose track record would have been an acute embarrassment and probably a national scandal were it not for the privileged position of what a leading Indian scholar, Dhirendra Sharma, called *India's Nuclear Estate.* His scathing study with this title, published in India in 1983, declared flatly:

> India's experience with nuclear power is also not a happy one. The performance of the D[epartment of] A[tomic] E[nergy] has been dismal, especially in the last decade and the future is equally uncertain. Power projects and breeder programmes have slipped by anything between eight to fifteen years with hardly any explanation. Costs have escalated prodigiously making a mockery of estimates and budgets. . . . But the nuclear estate commands an immeasurably powerful lobby and because of its power of patronage it has stifled healthy discussion, criticism and analysis of nuclear power in the country.

Strong words – and they were backed by ample historical evidence. Nevertheless, Indian Prime Minister Indira Gandhi continued to laud India's nuclear achievements, and to support them in the style to which they had long been accustomed. If Indian plutonium people wanted more reprocessing plants, more reprocessing plants they would have. It was an approach to plutonium policy which produced an echoing resonance throughout other leading nuclear nations in the Third World – including Brazil and Pakistan. The vibrations it produced beyond these countries were less sympathetic.

172

19   Plugging in plutonium

Given the lengthening catalogue of plutonium production facilities, what of the international market: the potential buyers and users of plutonium? Ignoring for a moment one all too important category of potential user – the bombmaker – what of plutonium as power plant fuel, and of the power plants that might burn it?

In 1984, the prospects for using mixed-oxide plutonium fuel in conventional nuclear power plants had receded perceptibly almost everywhere. The reason was quite straightforward: most conventional nuclear power plants were run by organizations with no emotional commitment to plutonium. They could see little advantage in paying a heavy premium for fuel just to be the first kid on the block to burn plutonium. Some private suppliers, to be sure – notably those in Federal Germany, Switzerland and Japan – are supporting experimental mixed-oxide fuel development programmes. However, the majority of the support for such programmes continues to come from government nuclear organizations. Mixed-oxide fuel still has to cross the threshold of commercial competition; and unless its immediately visible cost comes down substantially it is unlikely to make much headway against conventional low-enriched uranium fuel.

That leaves the fast breeder as the ultimate justification for wanting plutonium – at any rate the ultimate civil justification. In 1984 there were pilot-scale and prototype fast breeder power plants in operation in the United States, Britain, France, the Soviet Union and Japan. Others were under construction in Federal Germany, Italy and India. (See Table 2.) Countries that have proclaimed their intention of moving to fast breeders, but have yet to do anything unambiguously substantive, include Argentina, Brazil, Pakistan, South Korea and Taiwan. What will become of their aspirations is debatable.

Britain

In Britain, in 1984, the fast breeder was coming closer to reality than ever before – in the sense that its real costs and future prospects had at last reached the political agenda. It had taken an unconscionable time. The Royal Commission on Environmental Pollution (the Flowers Commission) was told by the Atomic Energy Authority in September 1975 that Britain might have 33 000 megawatts of fast breeder power stations in operation by the year 2000, as part of a total of 104 000 megawatts of nuclear power in all. At the time, the nuclear plant capacity in operation in Britain was less than 5000 megawatts; the second-generation advanced gas-cooled reactors were all at least four years behind schedule; and the nuclear industry was in disorder. The Authority's view of fast breeder prospects was a quintessential demonstration of the fantasyland in which they appeared to dwell.

Many in the British nuclear establishment had confidently expected in 1976 that the government would give the go-ahead – and the money – for the Authority to build its long-sought Commercial Fast Reactor, soon to be renamed – with more accuracy if less clarity – the Commercial Demonstration Fast Reactor. But these expectations were dimmed by the publication of the Flowers report, with its strictures about any premature move toward commercialization of plutonium as power plant fuel. The government, although dragging its feet on the 'commercial demonstration' plant, nevertheless continued to hand over fully £100 million every year for the fast breeder, as part of the Authority's financial grant voted by Parliament. It was by far the largest single item in the entire budget for government-funded energy research and development in Britain.

The fast breeder proponents did, however, have a serious administrative problem. The British nuclear programme was facing so many immediate troubles that the fast breeder had a very low priority – low, that is, for everybody but the Authority. For the Authority the fast breeder was of overriding importance, for one obvious reason: it was the only reactor the Authority had left. Thermal reactors were the responsibility of the nominally commercial National Nuclear Corporation. The high temperature reactor had been shut down. For the Authority it was the fast breeder or nothing. Even at that, the Authority somewhat perversely insisted that the 'commercial demonstration' plant would not be an experimental facility, but just another power station. All the technology was, they claimed, well understood and proven. Behind this assertion lay the Authority's desire to have the cost of the plant picked up not by itself but by the Central Electricity Generating Board. The Board, however, wanted nothing to do with the idea. It would provide a site for the plant, and accept the electricity it generated; but putting up the capital cost was out of the question. The Board was already building plants it did not need, and the excess capacity on the system was becoming embarrassing.

The Authority and British Nuclear Fuels had also incorporated the fast breeder into their case for the Thermal Oxide Reprocessing Plant, THORP, at Windscale, declaring that the long-term need for the fast breeder in turn made it necessary to ensure the provision of suitable plutonium-extraction facilities. The Parker report on the Windscale Inquiry into THORP had accepted this view, although objectors had demonstrated – using official figures – that no plausible fast breeder programme would require the low-quality plutonium from oxide fuel reprocessed in THORP.

The Authority continued to create its dream-world. It commissioned a 5-tonnes-per-year reprocessing line for fast breeder fuel at the Dounreay site. It fed spent fuel elements from the Prototype Fast Reactor into this line. It recovered the plutonium therefrom. It shipped this plutonium, in the form of nitrate solution, by sea around Cape Wrath to Windscale. It had the plutonium refabricated into fresh fuel, which was then shipped back to Dounreay and reloaded into the Prototype Fast Reactor. This, said the Authority in triumph, was the first time anyone had 'closed the fast breeder fuel cycle'. What precisely it was proving was less apparent, except that the Authority was prepared to ship hair-raising quantities of accessible fissile material through some of the most remote and inhospitable waters around

175

Britain, merely to score prestige points over fast breeder people elsewhere. Certainly the exercise was economically devoid of meaning. The government Health and Safety Executive examined the planned plutonium shipments before they took place, and gave them a clean bill of health. But the Executive disavowed any consideration of the security implications. It was not within their brief to ask whether and if so how the shipments were to be guarded against possible hijacking, nor whether such measures could be guaranteed effective off Cape Wrath. The sophistication and cold-blooded ferocity of terrorism in Britain in recent years requires no reminder. How would the government respond if a shipment of fresh plutonium fuel were to disappear en route to Dounreay? Officialdom as usual remained mute.

In November 1982 the British government at last made its long-awaited policy statement on the fast breeder. At any rate that was how it was billed. What the statement actually contained was something else again, as many commentators were quick to point out. The statement, as usual, applauded the achievements of the British fast breeder community, and reiterated the usual litany about the unique potential of the plutonium-fuelled fast breeder. The government remained totally behind the concept. Not until halfway down the second page did it become apparent how far behind. When stripped of its windy rhetoric, the statement bore little cheer for British plutonium people:

> In common with most other leading fast reactor nations, we now believe that the series ordering phase will begin in the earlier part of the next century, and thus on a longer timescale than we have previously envisaged. We shall therefore have more time in which to develop further the technology and before undertaking the construction of a first full-scale reactor in the UK: and the development programme will be geared to this timescale.

It was, for the first time, official acknowledgement that the fast breeder had no role to play in Britain's energy planning for at least a generation. Once this key point was made, the British fast breeder programme was exposed as never before to the harsh reality of everyday economics. As a corollary of its statement, the government announced that the Authority had been invited to prepare and submit a revised programme for British fast breeder research. To some commentators it appeared that in Britain the long plutonium honeymoon might at last be coming to an end. But the powerful fast breeder lobby was marshalling its forces for one final push. If it got its way, the fast breeder programme, however ill-advised and irrelevant, would thenceforth be invulnerable.

The United States

In the United States, on 26 October 1983, the Senate rejected by 56 votes to 40 a supplemental appropriations bill that would have kept the Clinch River fast breeder alive. 'I am very disappointed,' Energy Secretary Donald Hodel told the annual meeting of the Atomic Industrial Forum in San Francisco. The Department of Energy estimated that termination of Clinch River would cost from $150 million to $350 million, depending on how much of the hardware already ordered could be sold, transferred to other projects or sold for scrap. Some $380 million worth of major components had already been delivered; another $400 million worth was completed or on order. Some $1.6 billion had thus far been spent.

The demise of Clinch River did not, however, signal the end of the American fast breeder programme. Hodel told the Forum meeting that the task would now be to salvage the base breeder programme, and to seek ways of integrating it into an effective international effort. Gordon Chipman, deputy assistant secretary for breeder programmes, told the Forum meeting that the cancellation of Clinch River did not mean that the United States would 'fail to have a strong vital national breeder development programme':

> But the US government simply will not finance future breeder demonstration power plants. The challenge is to leap beyond what would have been the next incremental step and to develop a breeder that can be built by the private sector on an economic basis with the federal government providing the institutional framework that will allow such a development to take place.

Chipman added that work on conceptual design of the next demonstration fast breeder indicated a possible saving of

177

$1000 per kilowatt of capital cost, to be achieved by improved fuel cycle cost, systems and components, and safety design criteria:

> We need to demonstrate that major safety components can be confined to the primary system and perhaps even the pressure vessel itself.

In this way, said Chipman, a cost-competitive fast breeder acceptable to the American people could be available by the turn of the century. Although saddened by the loss of Clinch River, American plutonium people were clearly not preparing to leave the field. On the contrary, the Department of Energy announced that it would seek funds from Congress to 'close the fuel cycle' at the Fast Flux Test Facility at Hanford, by building a plutonium fuel fabrication facility, a 10-tonnes-per-year fast breeder reprocessing facility and a waste solidification plant.

Meanwhile, in March 1983, Allied General Nuclear Services, proprietors of the Barnwell reprocessing plant, sued the United States government for $500 million, charging that the government had induced private industry to get into the reprocessing business, and then – under the Carter administration – reversed its policy, effectively taking private property without just compensation. By autumn 1983 Allied General, while still trying to put together a rescue package for Barnwell, had begun laying off staff.

France
In France, in 1984, work on the Super-Phénix fast breeder was entering its final stages. It was expected to start up late in the year, about two years later than originally intended. By this time, however, the economic context of the longer-term plans for six replicas of Super-Phénix had altered drastically. In 1978 the cost of the plant had been estimated to be Fr6 billion, of which 30 per cent was to be contributed by the sharcholders of Nersa, and the rest to be raised by loans from Euratom, the European Investment Bank and financial institutions in the participating countries. By 1982, however, the estimated cost had reached Fr10 billion. The cost of electricity from the plant would therefore be about twice that of

electricity from conventional French nuclear plants. Following its loss of Fr8 billion in 1982, Electricité de France posted a further loss of Fr6 billion in 1983; and analyses pointed to a staggering surplus of generating capacity by the end of the decade.

On 14 October 1983 Nersa approved a new estimated cost of nearly Fr19 billion – $8.63 billion – for Super-Phénix. The prospect for fast breeders to follow Super-Phénix looked bleaker by the month.

Federal Germany

In Federal Germany, in 1984, the fast breeder programme continued to hang by a thread. Throughout 1982, the future of the SNR–300 fast breeder had been in the balance. In March 1982, the Bonn government, facing costs which by that time had risen from the original DM1500 million to some DM5 billion, agreed reluctantly to provide a further six-month increment while discussing ways to increase the share paid by the electricity suppliers. In September 1982, however, just as a formula had been found for the purpose, it was announced that the probable cost of the plant had escalated a further 20 per cent, and was now more like DM6 billion.

For the suppliers the sticking point was the Bonn parliament's veto, which could deny the plant an operating licence even after it had been completed. In November 1982 the official parliamentary 'Enquête Kommission' recommended by a split vote that the parliament withdraw its right of veto. But the suppliers remained unenthusiastic. The German Federal election brought about a change of government; and the incoming Christian Democrats were significantly more favourably inclined to nuclear energy. The new Minister for Research and Technology commissioned a lengthy report on the status of the project. In May 1983 he announced that although in the light of present-day knowledge the decisions on timing taken in the early 1970s might have been different, on both economic and industrial-political grounds it now made sense to finish the work – not least because a decision to cancel would mean writing off billions of DM. The suppliers agreed to increase to 28 per cent the share of the cost that they would contribute. The estimated cost of the Kalkar plant in 1984 had reached DM6.5 billion. The plant was expected to be in commercial operation in mid-1987 – 15 years after its inception.

The Soviet Union
In the Soviet Union, in 1984, the fast breeder was facing difficulties closely parallel to those arising in the West. The successor to the BN–350 at Shevchenko was the BN–600 at Beloyarsk, which had started up in 1980, some years behind schedule. In the mid-1970s Soviet planners had been intending to move directly to a huge 1500-megawatt plant, a BN–1500, for which design work was underway even before the start-up of the BN–600. By the beginning of the 1980s the Soviets had let it be known that their ambitions had moderated by almost half: that the next plant would be a BN–800. In 1984, so far as is known, the proposed BN–800 has proceeded no farther than Soviet drawing boards. The capital costs of the BN–600 were said to be 1.6 times those of the most recent Soviet light-water reactor.

Japan
In Japan, in 1984, the immediate intention of the planners was to use the anticipated inventory of separated plutonium to make mixed-oxide fuel for conventional nuclear plants. Such plans were still, however, in the conceptual stage; the first demonstration of this plutonium recycle was not expected to be accomplished until the mid-1990s. The long-delayed prototype fast reactor, Monju, finally received the government go-ahead in 1982, and site work commenced in January 1983. The financing of the plant, however, remains mainly governmental; commercialization of fast reactors is not now expected until 2010.

Italy
In Italy, in 1984, the future of the country's only fast breeder remained problematical. Construction of the Prova Elementi di Combustibile, a 120–megawatt (thermal) reactor known as PEC, had started in 1974. By 1982 its costs, originally estimated at about $600 million, had risen by between 30 and 60 per cent. The Interministerial Committee on Economic

Planning intervened. Work was suspended, and a scientific commission was set up to examine the plant's economic and technical validity. In 1983 it concluded that conventional light-water reactors would be a 'valid economic alternative', and recommended that the plant be finished only if the energy authorities provided precise guarantees on programme schedules, and on the financial involvement of foreign industries and other partners. In particular, the commission sought an explicit and binding indication of interest from the Italian electricity suppliers Enel. It was not immediately forthcoming.

Fast breeders international

By 1983 the vision of the plutonium-fuelled fast breeder as the wonder-source of energy for the infinite future was distinctly tarnished, even in the eyes of its most fervent apostles. One last possibility, however, remained. As the economic prospects for the fast breeder inexorably receded, the world's plutonium people began to proclaim the advantages of international collaboration. By 1984 such international collaboration was becoming the subject of increasingly urgent high-level discussions between the United States, Britain, France and Japan, with other interested parties egging them on from the sidelines.

Various ideas were floated. American fast breeder supporters proposed a Large Demonstration Plant, to be built and financed jointly by the United States and perhaps Europe – Britain and France in particular. Another possibility was a joint programme combining the talents of Britain and France. This latter proposal reminded some of an earlier joint British-French technical collaboration: the agreement to design, build and market the Concorde supersonic passenger aircraft. When 'technological turkeys' come home to roost, the Concorde must be a prime contender: stupefyingly over budget and impossible to sell. Not a single customer could be found, apart from the government-owned airlines of the two countries; and even they held out for lavish subsidies both of purchase and of operating costs.

Nevertheless, in 1984 the Concorde agreement was still in effect – each partner trying to outwait the other and force it to carry the cost of cancellation. The Concorde agreement would serve as an ideal model for the British and French fast breeder community. If it could just persuade the two governments to agree to a joint programme on the fast breeder, it could virtually guarantee the indefinite survival both of the technology and of its community of proponents.

Sceptics watched the proceedings with concern; and they included even the editor of the industry trade magazine *Nuclear Engineering International*. In a pungent editorial in February 1983, entitled 'Facing facts on fast reactors', he commented:

> The large amounts of money being spent world-wide by the nuclear industry on the development of fast breeder reactors is becoming increasingly difficult to justify. Is this continuing level of expenditure appropriate if one takes a rational view of future trends in energy demand and fuel supply? Will it ever be possible to recoup the vast sums that have been spent and the much greater sums that will need to be spent before the fast reactor can become a commercial option for electricity utilities?. . . . Uranium will not be suddenly exhausted or become excessively expensive in the early years of the next century. There will be plenty of time to identify the trend and decide when it is worth ordering FBRs instead of thermal reactors . . .
>
> But perhaps of greater significance to fast reactor economics than the availability of uranium is the fact that with advances in techniques for the storage of irradiated fuel from light water reactors utilities can avoid reprocessing. The uncertain and growing costs of reprocessing are then properly loaded on the fast reactor and with limited reprocessing there will be doubts about the availability of plutonium to fuel a large programme of fast reactors. In these circumstances fast reactors may never be economic.
>
> There still remains the strategic argument but the benefits must still be properly quantified and balanced against the premium it is worth paying for an insurance policy of fast reactors. At present it seems excessive. If the nuclear industry is to win support and acceptance for the fast reactor it will have to provide effective answers nationally and internationally. Evangelical fervour is not a substitute for sound technical argument.

In September 1983, Peter Walker, British Secretary of State for Energy, announced that:

> The government has decided to open formal negotiations to seek agreement on joint development of fast reactors with France, Germany, Italy, Belgium and the Netherlands. . . . However, we

are also conscious that countries outside Europe, particularly the USA and Japan, are also experienced in this field. We are therefore keen to keep open the possibility of extending this international collaboration outside Europe when the time is right.

On 10 January 1984 Walker and his opposite numbers in France, Federal Germany, Italy and Belgium signed just such an agreement; the Netherlands was expected to add its name soon thereafter. In February 1984 Britain's Central Electricity Generating Board, headed by Sir Walter Marshall, signed an agreement to collaborate with Electricité de France on the next fast breeder to follow Super-Phénix, to put up perhaps 15 per cent of the capital and to accept electricity from the station via the cross-Channel link. Within the following six weeks similar co-operation agreements were signed by the fuel cycle companies of the participating countries, and by their national nuclear research organizatons. True to nuclear form none of these agreements was preceded by any public discussion whatever.

In the light of its track record, the fast breeder seemed likely to leave Concorde far behind.

20   Bad business

After four decades of unparalleled support and advocacy, plutonium rolls on, with a momentum that has little to do with civil, commercial or diplomatic reality. Consider today's global energy scene. In the past ten years, the world's electricity suppliers have had to come to terms with a discomfiting realization. Until the early 1970s they had been able to plan with some confidence, on the basis of an anticipated growth in electricity use of seven per cent per year. By 1984, they have been forced to acknowledge that in the industrial countries demand has virtually ceased to grow. In the United States, in 1982, for the first time in thirty years, it decreased.

The more sanguine electricity planners attribute this standstill to the global recession. In their view, demand will begin to grow again as the global economy recovers. Others think differently. In their analysis, the fall-off in electricity use indicates a deeper trend, a shift in the balance of industrial activity away from energy-intensive heavy industry toward more elegant technologies like those based on microelectronics. These involve very low energy-use per unit of added value. Moreover, habits of energy use that took root when energy, including electricity, was cheap have begun to seem foolish and unnecessary now that the cost of energy is significant. Year by year the forecasts of future energy and electricity use have dwindled. The vast and rapid expansion of electricity use in industrial society foretold ten years ago has not happened, nor is it likely to. It is thus increasingly difficult to see any role for the plutonium-fuelled fast breeder.

If it were a genuinely competitive supply technology, its supporters might be able to advocate it as preferable. If it could produce cheaper electricity more reliably, they could press for the replacement of existing plants with fast breeders.

184

Such is far from the case. Consider the purely technical status of the 'commercial' plutonium business in 1984. Oxide fuel reprocessing, the essential plutonium-supply technology, has proved to be technically extremely difficult and punishingly expensive. In an exhaustive analysis published in the December 1982 issue of *Energy Policy*, French economist Dominique Finon declared that the cost of oxide fuel reprocessing was, and would remain, so high that fast breeder electricity would always be more expensive than that from light-water reactors. Using official figures, he calculated that the total cost of reprocessing light-water fuel in 1982 was at least Fr7 500 000 per tonne of uranium, and might be as high as Fr10 500 000. If a supplier compared this cost with that of long-term storage and eventual disposal of spent fuel, the latter option would obviously be more economic. The cost of plutonium must therefore be charged not to the light-water reactors but to the fast breeder, since reprocessing was essential only to supply its fuel. According to Finon:

... (I)nternational nuclear authorities always defend the inevitability aspect of reprocessing on the pretext that it represents the optimum method of managing nuclear waste. Indeed, it is crucial that plutonium should have the status of a by-product of this activity, in order that extraction costs should at no stage be attributed to it. In this way F[ast] B[reeder] R[eactors] can seem economically competitive in the eyes of electrical utilities.

If reprocessing is no longer obligatory ... the excess FBR cost would represent a long-term insurance premium to protect the economy against the risks of uranium depletion. The almost mythical appeal of breeder generation, enabling the replacement of all [light-water reactors] by FBRs, is thus presented in economic terms: such a replacement will progressively reduce the requirements for, and thus imports of, uranium.

It matters little if the characteristics of FBRs only allow a very slow decrease in uranium requirements. (Very simple technological adaptations, e.g. lowering the tails assay in the enrichment process or increasing [light-water reactor] burnup would enable this to be achieved much more quickly.) The important thing is to take a perspective 100 years hence, to ensure supplies of fissile fuels well into the next century. Who would not be swayed by this argument, when confronted by the uncertainties of the international energy market and when national chauvinism is encouraged by past technological successes? Economic rationality has become weakened in an evangelical fervour in which doubts and criticism no longer have any role.

And yet to exploit the miraculous process of 'reproducing fuel from its own ashes' is so costly that it would be economic folly to adopt this as an industrial process for at least the next 100 years. Indeed, the viability of the once-through cycle obliges the economist to attribute the entire cost differential between the two options to plutonium. This would effectively remove any chance of FBRs becoming competitive. . . . The economic problem with FBRs is not even one of economic uncertainty. It is a simple, insurmountable problem – that of reprocessing.

Fast breeder technology itself is far from proven, after more than thirty years of extravagantly costly government support. Basic design features are still being disputed, even among fast breeder engineers: for instance, which configuration of cooling pipes to use. Fast breeder steam generators are stubbornly prone to leak and allow sodium and water to mix, with destructive consequences. Apart from such problems with the reactor design itself, there also remain question-marks about the technical feasibility of reprocessing fast breeder fuel on an industrial scale, and indeed of fabricating plutonium fast breeder fuel commercially.

These technical uncertainties, awkward in themselves, bring in their train profound uncertainties about the economic status and prospects of plutonium-fuelled power plants. The slow, if not negligible, growth in electricity use has reduced the entire market for new power plants of any kind. The competition for orders among plant manufacturers with an embarrassing surplus of construction capacity is already cut-throat. A novel technology offering only a very speculative payoff, sometime in the next century if ever, is going to find it prohibitively difficult to win a significant piece of the shrinking market for new power plants. The commercial prospect for the plutonium-fuelled fast breeder is, in a word, nil.

The putative payoff from the plutonium-fuelled fast breeder has always been the possibility of extracting more energy from each kilogram of uranium. In the 1980s, however, uranium is no longer a rarity. In 1982 its price fell as low as $17 per pound. It continues to hover not much higher than $20 per pound, as more and more mines, in Canada, Australia and elsewhere, come into service. Electricity suppliers can now play the uranium suppliers off against each other and get more uranium than they can possibly use, at bargain prices. Long-term stockpiling of uranium is now much the cheapest form of insurance against any significant price rise, or any other undesirable influence on uranium supply. Compared to this option, reprocessing and the fast breeder are more like the kind of insurance deal offered in glossy brochures from companies with addresses in the Cayman Islands. The plutonium business, in purely business terms, is bad business.

In political and diplomatic terms it is very bad business indeed. The quasi-commercial activities of the 'civil' plutonium industry offer an ideal springboard to nuclear weapons. No pious allusions to 'safeguards' can ultimately disguise the fact that 'civil' activities involving separated plutonium are not now and may never be adequately safeguarded. A growing number of countries – following the lead of the nuclear exporting countries, even assisted by them – are pressing on into plutonium fuel cycles. In at least four countries – Argentina, Brazil, India and Pakistan – the claims of purely civil commercial intent are patently indefensible. They have, moreover, refused to ratify the Non-Proliferation Treaty, to put their plutonium facilities under international safeguards, or to take any diplomatic pledge against producing nuclear explosives.

The quasi-civil separation of plutonium is the most immediately available avenue to the acquisition of usable quantities of potential nuclear weapons material. The technology of weapons design is described in the open literature; the relevant physics of fission explosives is an intimate first cousin to the physics of a plutonium-fuelled fast breeder, and can be found on many a library shelf. The requisite hardware is all readily accessible. The one key requirement for production of a fission weapon is high-quality fissile material; and the separated plutonium from an ostensibly civil programme would do nicely – at less than 10 kilograms per bomb.

In the interim, its possession is politically unembarrassing, because it is designated as 'civil'. Plutonium people argue that any nation that wishes to acquire nuclear weapons can now do so, and that the more direct route is via small, secret facilities constructed for that purpose: so-called 'dedicated' facilities. This problem is real and worrying. Nevertheless, compare the alternatives. On one hand, a country could opt for a dedicated facility, designed, built and paid for by the government in secret, whose discovery would bring acute diplomatic embarrassment and conceivably direct intervention from alarmed foreign powers. On the other hand, a country could have legitimate 'civil' plutonium facilities – a reprocessing plant to recover plutonium for use in power plant fuel, a plutonium fabrication plant to make the fuel, and fast breeders to burn it – and of course breed more plutonium. At present, a government can openly equip itself with these 'civil' installations, and acquire prestige to boot. Moreover, the government choosing this approach may well find enthusiastic nuclear exporters queuing up to offer bargain rates on necessary hardware. It can also arrange to have the non-nuclear components for bombs designed and assembled and set quietly aside, for contingencies. Once equipped, the government can relax in the knowledge that, should circumstances warrant, it can have nuclear weapons ready to deliver and detonate within weeks, if not days.

Another aspect of the overlap between 'civil' plutonium activities and weapons surfaced in 1982. Even as the commercial future of the French fast breeder programme was looking distinctly less impressive, French nuclear critics drew attention to some startling official comments in obscure publications. In April 1982, in the official journal *Energies*, one L. Lammers acknowledged that the two remaining military plutonium-production reactors, G–2 and G–3 at Marcoule, were nearing the end of their serviceable lives. Fortunately, said Lammers, this would not lead to any shortage of weapons material for the French Force de Frappe:

> It is therefore necessary to find a replacement, and this is assured (after Phénix) with Super-Phénix, which will be able to produce in the blanket around its core a sufficient quantity of plutonium of ad hoc quality to manufacture some sixty tactical atomic bombs a year.

In a scorching and incisive article in the French monthly *Science et Vie*, in October 1982, two critics, Yves Lenoir and Michel

Genestout, explored the role of the fast breeder in the
weapons programme:

All things considered, the great serenity shown in nuclear circles
faced with an accumulation of delays in the field of fast breeders
has only one explanation: there is no real need for these machines
to ensure long-term electricity production. But why then is
France pursuing this direction? Why have its present leaders, who
were hostile to any industrial development of this branch before
taking office, changed their minds? What are the reasons for
accepting today what was condemned yesterday?
    The answer is succinct: the military needs breeders. Indeed, a
fast breeder produces plutonium of high isotopic quality particularly suited to modern nuclear weapons. Furthermore, a fast
breeder represents, for the military – but only for the military –
the most economical means of procuring the highly effective
plutonium it requires.

They explained the process thus. Spent fuel from a conventional nuclear plant contains plutonium. It is of comparatively
low quality, suitable only for comparatively crude bombs.
However, it can be burned in the core of a fast breeder
reactor. While the fast breeder is generating electricity it is
also producing, in the 'blanket' around the core, very high-
grade plutonium, suitable for use in the most sophisticated
nuclear weapons. The fast breeder is in effect a 'plutonium
enrichment' plant, whose net accomplishment is to convert
low-quality conventional power-plant fuel into high-quality
plutonium ideal for bombmaking. Such, it appears, has been
the unstated underlying purpose of the French 'civil' plutonium programme of reprocessing and fast breeders.
    This startling revelation has sparked bitter controversy in
Europe, especially in Federal Germany and the Netherlands.
Super-Phénix is an international project, of which the Federal German Company SBK – co-owned by Dutch, Belgian &
British electricity suppliers – owns 16 per cent and Enel of
Italy another 33. The German utility Rheinisches-Westfälis-
ches Elektrizitätswerke alone has a 10 per cent interest. The
obvious corollary is that German electricity users are helping
to finance French nuclear weapons – as are those in Italy,
Belgium, the Netherlands and Britain. It is far from clear how
these implications will evolve. But it is hard to see how even
the most fervent official supporters of international co-

operation on fast breeders and plutonium fuel cycles can contemplate further joint projects with the French. The indirect weapons link is already an embarrassment; the direct link demonstrated by France must surely scuttle any proposal for multinational projects involving the French. The French example shreds the credibility of any further attempts to insist that plutonium programmes anywhere can safely be regarded as 'civil'.

A situation remarkably similar to that in France is gradually arising in Britain. The dedicated military plutonium-production reactors at Calder Hall and Chapelcross are nearing the end of their functional lives, and there has been no mention of constructing any facilities to replace them. The Prototype Fast Reactor at Dounreay is under IAEA safeguards, and the British government has declared emphatically that it has 'no plans' to use civil plutonium for weapons. But the blanket plutonium from the reactor may be being stockpiled nevertheless, in the knowledge that it could be used for weapons if the need arose. The safeguards agreement between the International Atomic Energy Agency, Euratom and Britain – a weapons state – provides explicitly for just such a contingency. On 30 March 1984 the Department of Energy told Parliament that none of the blanket elements from the Prototype Fast Reactor had yet been reprocessed. In April 1984 France announced that it would be submitting Super-Phénix to Euratom safeguards. But France, as a weapons state, would expect to have a safeguards agreements equivalent to that applying to Britain – with the same contingency clause to allow the use of so-called 'civil' plutonium for weapons.

What other countries will make of the plutonium programmes in France and Britain can well be imagined. Nuclear weapons enthusiasts around the world must be praying that the 'civil' plutonium promoters in their countries will succeed in their advocacy of a plutonium future. It is increasingly difficult to believe that the plutonium people, lobbying for further support, do not make the occasional oblique allusion to the implicit weapons opportunities. Perhaps they no longer need to.

With a civil plutonium programme, a government does not

have to make any commitment to weapons development. It can keep its diplomatic nose clean until – should circumstances unhappily warrant – it suddenly decides that it needs a nuclear bomb more than it needs a clean bill of diplomatic health. By the time the international community comes to terms with the country's change of status, it will have achieved a nuclear fait accompli.

The use of nuclear explosive as fuel makes no economic sense, now or for the foreseeable future. It is costing taxpayers stupefying sums of money to support research and development and foster uneconomic exports. Electricity suppliers do not want to pay for it. Even its technical feasibility is in doubt. Worst of all, it is opening the floodgates to a worldwide spread of nuclear weapons. This is global insanity: and only a concerted international public outcry can put a stop to it before it brings about a global catastrophe.

The plutonium business:

What now?

The plutonium business is not a business. It is an obsession –
perhaps the most dangerous obsession to which anyone has
ever succumbed. But it is also a tragic obsession. The
plutonium people are the successors of Prometheus, dream-
ing of unlimited energy forever, only to find that the whole of
human society might in consequence pay a terrible price.
Even in purely economic terms, at the mundane level of
competing energy technologies, the plutonium dream has all
but collapsed. Yet its progenitors cling to their forlorn
conviction that, sooner or later, the world will welcome
plutonium, rely on it, thrive on it. What then is to become of
them, and of their obsession?

If they have their way, the plutonium people intend to press
on with the long-term pursuit of their ultimate objective – a
global plutonium economy. From their strongholds in the
national nuclear organizations, they expect to continue receiving open-ended financial support from governments and
taxpayers, apparently into the indefinite future. This is understandable. Many have devoted their entire careers to the
effort to turn plutonium into a commercial fuel. They are
unlikely to decide, of their own accord, this late in the day,
that their entire professional lives have been misguided and
futile. They face a grim quandary. It cannot be easy to
acknowledge that their life work, once apparently so lavish in
promise, now looms as part of the final threat to survival of
humanity. Their refusal to accept this distressing realization
is understandable. But the rest of humanity dare not share the
refusal, lest the threat become reality.

Those who do not share the plutonium dream must
therefore work, first of all, for a clearer and more immediate
understanding of the situation. This is patently beyond the

plutonium people themselves; it is not, however, beyond those who provide their organizational and financial support: governments and their taxpayers, and electricity suppliers and their ratepayers, all over the world. Governments and suppliers have always drawn their advice about plutonium policy primarily from the plutonium people themselves, behind the scenes. This self-interested advice must henceforth be matched and challenged by other advice, not from the plutonium people but from the rest of the people: the general public, and the taxpayers and the ratepayers who foot the bills. An early priority must be to lay bare the self-interest underlying decades of official policy advice.

Plutonium is expensive. For the foreseeable future, in the most favourable analysis, it cannot possibly pay its own way. The strongest lever available to those who wish to see the brakes applied is a cutback on the public money provided for plutonium. The annual government budgets for energy research and development in many industrial countries continue to allocate staggering sums to support plutonium work of various kinds. In Britain, for instance, the Atomic Energy Authority receives, by direct vote of Parliament, an annual grant which includes more than £100 million for the fast breeder alone – not for major capital investment, merely for research programmes. In the United States, the federal government was proposing to pay more than $3 billion for Clinch River alone, until Congress at last turned off the tap. Even after the demise of Clinch River the federal budget continues to earmark hundreds of millions of dollars annually for plutonium work. Similar grants from taxpayers support research on reprocessing and fast breeders in several other European countries and Japan – to say nothing of the Third World countries now embroiled in such activities. These budgets must be challenged by elected representatives, and they in turn must be spurred to such challenge by an informed electorate.

Creation of such an informed public must take urgent priority. The plutonium people are organized and powerful, with access to the innermost councils of government. The opposition must be likewise organized, to amplify the force of the rational arguments that support their viewpoint. Many existing organizations might well be prompted by their members to play an active part in the plutonium issue. Some, to be sure, are already doing so, notably peace groups and environmental organizations. But many others have a role to play: church groups, youth groups, women's groups, trades unions, service clubs, and above all political parties and their active subgroups. The print and broadcast media have an especially pivotal responsibility to create and foster an intelligent understanding of the ramifications and the gravity of the plans for commercialization of plutonium. Plutonium opponents should work to enlist the interest and involvement of media people, to be sure that they know what is happening on the issue and how important it is, and to help spread the message of concern.

The objectives of informed concern are manifold. Among them are the following:

– drastic cutbacks in government funding for plutonium work, leading to eventual cessation of such funding

– refusal of permission or support for any new plutonium facilities, be they research laboratories, pilot plants, reprocessing plants, mixed-oxide fuel plants, or fast breeders

– denial of involvement in the schemes for multinational fast breeder development now being concocted as a last resort, especially by fast breeder interests in Europe and Japan

– possibly a phased shutdown of existing fast breeders

– an end to reprocessing of civil spent fuel, coupled with provision of adequate long-term storage facilities for intact spent fuel

– more research on final disposal of post-reactor waste, but preferably not by those doctrinaire bodies hitherto determined that such final disposal must involve reprocessing

– a ban on plutonium-related exports of any kind, and on the international approval of the use of plutonium for 'civil' purposes anywhere.

There is a strong case for a detailed reappraisal, by an independent international group or commission, of 'safeguards' as they apply to separated plutonium and its use. At present such safeguards appear dangerously inadequate, and unable to provide a timely warning of diversion of separated plutonium to weapons use. A reappraisal might conclude that the possession of separated plutonium in any form by a non-weapons nation was ipso facto evidence of weapons-capability. Such a conclusion would bring in its train profound implications for the diplomatic and other treatment of the nation in question, as regards all forms of trade and aid. The reappraisal would also have to take a position as to the status of 'civil' plutonium programmes in existing weapons nations like the United States and Britain, and as to the validity and indeed the credibility of the safeguards now applied to these programmes.

Over a period of time, which might not be many years, all national nuclear organizations whose only substantial reason for continued existence is nominally 'civil' plutonium work should be phased out. That would apply, for instance, to the United Kingdom Atomic Energy Authority. Those national nuclear organizations involved with weapons, like the United States Department of Energy and the French Commissariat à l'Energie Atomique, should be considered to be military agencies, and their plutonium activities labelled accordingly.

One awkward question remains: what about the existing stocks of separated plutonium? For some years governments and international agencies have been discussing the concept of an international plutonium storage facility. They have made little progress, largely because of the reluctance of national governments to surrender control over their plutonium. No politically plausible solution to this problem is easy to envisage; but its existence must be recognized. Cessation of reprocessing will put an upper limit on global stocks of separated civilian plutonium; but the quantities already in existence are sizeable enough to be amply worrying. Indeed, a profound challenge for existing weapons states, especially the United States and the Soviet Union, is to find a way to freeze the production of further plutonium explicitly earmarked for weapons.

There is also a case for establishing one or more repositories for intact spent fuel, administered by an international agency. Countries could be encouraged to relieve themselves of the burden of managing spent fuel by delivering it to such a repository, pending agreement on a satisfactory mode of final disposal. Spent fuel thus stored under international supervision and safeguards would be proof against the possible temptation for a national government to reprocess it covertly for weapons purposes. It must be noted that any final disposal of spent fuel in any form would have to guard against subsequent attempts to recover it to obtain the plutonium it contained.

This last point is merely a particular instance of a general, grim truth already noted thirty years ago. The 'Candor report' prepared for American Secretary of State Dean Acheson in 1953 came to a dismaying conclusion: even by that time it had become impossible to be sure of the whereabouts of all the world's plutonium. In the ensuing decades this problem has increased ten-thousandfold. Even on the most optimistic assumption about progress toward nuclear disarmament, we can never henceforth be sure that there is not some separated plutonium in covert storage somewhere in the world. In a bleak sense this implies a sort of permanent deterrence, exercised even by countries with no acknowledged nuclear weapons. That leads on to another, yet more intractable problem: the irreducible problem of sharing a world with nuclear weapons. This problem now faces us forever. If we do not act soon to control the spread of plutonium, the problem will become rapidly and fatally insoluble.

Appendix I

ADDRESS BY PRESIDENT EISENHOWER BEFORE THE UNITED NATIONS GENERAL ASSEMBLY, DECEMBER 8, 1953

[From the Congressional Record, vol. 100, Jan. 7, 1954, pp. 61–63]

Atomic Power for Peace

When Secretary-General Hammarskjold's invitation to address this General Assembly reached me in Bermuda, I was just beginning a series of conferences with the Prime Ministers and Foreign Ministers of Great Britain and of France. Our subject was some of the problems that beset our world.

During the remainder of the Bermuda Conference, I had constantly in mind that ahead of me lay a great honor. That honor is mine today as I stand here, privileged to address the General Assembly of the United Nations.

At the same time that I appreciate the distinction of addressing you, I have a sense of exhilaration as I look upon this Assembly.

Never before in history has so much hope for so many people been gathered together in a single organization. Your deliberations and decisions during these somber years have already realized part of those hopes.

But the great tests and the great accomplishments still lie ahead. And in the confident expectation of those accomplishments, I would use the office which, for the time being, I hold, to assure you that the Government of the United States will remain steadfast in its support of this body. This we shall do in the conviction that you will provide a great share of the wisdom, the courage, and the faith which can bring to this world lasting peace for all nations, and happiness and well-being for all men.

Clearly, it would not be fitting for me to take this occasion to present to you a unilateral American report on Bermuda. Nevertheless, I assure you that in our deliberations on that lovely island we sought to invoke those same great concepts of universal peace and human dignity which are so cleanly etched in your charter.

Neither would it be a measure of this great opportunity merely to recite, however hopefully, pious platitudes.

A Danger Shared by All

I therefore decided that this occasion warranted my saying to you some of the things that have been on the minds and hearts of my legislative and executive associates and on mine for a great many months – thoughts I had originally planned to say primarily to the American people.

I know that the American people share my deep belief that if a danger exists in the world it is a danger shared by all, and, equally, that if hope exists in the mind of one nation that hope should be shared by all.

Finally, if there is to be advanced any proposal designed to ease even by the smallest measure the tensions of today's world, what more appropriate audience could there be than the members of the General Assembly of the United Nations?

I feel impelled to speak today in a language that in a sense is new – one which I, who have spent so much of my life in the military profession, would have preferred never to use.

That new language is the language of atomic warfare.

The atomic age has moved forward at such a pace that every citizen of the world should have some comprehension, at least, in comparative terms, of the extent of this development, of the utmost significance to every one of us. Clearly, if the peoples of the world are to conduct an intelligent search for peace, they must be armed with the significant facts of today's existence.

My recital of atomic danger and power is necessarily stated in United States terms, for these are the only incontrovertible facts that I know. I need hardly point out to this Assembly, however, that this subject is global, not merely national, in character.

On July 16, 1945, the United States set off the world's first atomic explosion.

Since that date in 1945 the United States of America has conducted 42 test explosions.

Atomic bombs today are more than 25 times as powerful as the weapons with which the atomic age dawned, while hydrogen weapons were in the ranges of millions of tons of TNT equivalent.

Today the United States stockpile of atomic weapons, which, of course, increases daily, exceeds by many times the explosive equivalent of the total of all bombs and all shells that came from every plane and every gun in every theater of war in all of the years of World War II.

A single air group, whether afloat or land-based, can now deliver to any reachable target a destructive cargo exceeding in power all the bombs that fell on Britain in all of World War II.

In size and variety, the development of atomic weapons has been no less remarkable. The development has been such that atomic weapons have virtually achieved conventional status within our armed services. In the United States, the Army, the Navy, the Air Force, and the Marine Corps are all capable of putting this weapon to military use.

But the dread secret, and the fearful engines of atomic might, are not ours alone.

In the first place, the secret is possessed by our friends and allies, Great Britain and Canada, whose scientific genius made a tremendous contribution to our original discoveries, and the designs of atomic bombs.

The secret is also known by the Soviet Union.

The Soviet Union has informed us that, over recent years, it has devoted extensive resources to atomic weapons. During this period, the Soviet Union has exploded a series of atomic devices, including at least one involving thermo-nuclear reactions.

No Monopoly of Atomic Power

If at one time the United States possessed what might have been called a monopoly of atomic power, that monopoly ceased to exist several years ago. Therefore, although our earlier start has permitted us to accumulate what is today a great quantitative advantage, the atomic realities of today comprehend two facts of even greater significance.

First, the knowledge now possessed by several nations will eventually be shared by others – possibly all others.

Second, even a vast superiority in numbers of weapons, and consequent capability of devastating retaliation, is no preventive, of itself, against the fearful material damage and toll of human lives that would be inflicted by surprise aggression.

The free world, at least dimly aware of these facts, has naturally embarked on a large program of warning and defense systems. That program will be accelerated and expanded.

But let no one think that the expenditure of vast sums for weapons and systems of defense can guarantee absolute safety for the cities and citizens of any nation. The awful arithmetic of the atomic bomb does not permit of any such easy solution. Even against the most powerful defense, an aggressor in possession of the effective minimum number of atomic bombs for a surprise attack could probably place a sufficient number of his bombs on the chosen targets to cause hideous damage.

Should such an atomic attack be launched against the United States, our reactions would be swift and resolute. But for me to say that the defense capabilities of the United States are such that they could inflict terrible losses upon an aggressor – for me to say that the retaliation capabilities of the United States are so great that such an aggressor's land would be laid waste – all this, while fact, is not the true expression of the purpose and the hope of the United States.

To pause there would be to confirm the hopeless finality of a belief that two atomic colossi are doomed malevolently to eye each other indefinitely across a trembling world. To stop there would be to accept helplessly the probability of civilization destroyed, the annihilation of the irreplaceable heritage of mankind handed down to us from generation to generation, and the condemnation of mankind to begin all over again the age-old struggle upward from savagery toward decency and right and justice.

Surely no sane member of the human race could discover

victory in such desolation. Could anyone wish his name to be coupled by history with such human degradation and destruction?

Occasional pages of history do record the faces of the 'great destroyers,' but the whole book of history reveals mankind's never-ending quest for peace and mankind's God-given capacity to build.

It is with the book of history and not with isolated pages that the United States will ever wish to be identified. My country wants to be constructive, not destructive. It wants agreements, not wars, among nations. It wants itself to live in freedom and in the confidence that the people of every other nation enjoy equally the right of choosing their own way of life.

No Idle Words or Shallow Visions

So my country's purpose is to help us move out of the dark chamber of horrors into the light – to find a way by which the minds of men, the hopes of men, the souls of men everywhere, can move forward toward peace and happiness and well-being.

In this quest I know that we must not lack patience.

I know that in a world divided such as ours today salvation cannot be attained by one dramatic act.

I know that many steps will have to be taken over many months before the world can look at itself one day and truly realize that a new climate of mutually peaceful confidence is abroad in the world.

But I know, above all else, that we must start to take these steps – now.

The United States and its allies, Great Britain and France, have over the past months tried to take some of these steps. Let no one say that we shun the conference table.

On the record has long stood the request of the United States, Great Britain, and France to negotiate with the Soviet Union the problems of a divided Germany.

On that record has long stood the request of the same three nations to negotiate an Austrian State Treaty.

On the same record still stands the request of the United Nations to negotiate the problems of Korea.

Most recently, we have received from the Soviet Union what

is in effect an expression of willingness to hold a Four Power meeting. Along with our allies, Great Britain and France, we were pleased to see that this note did not contain the unacceptable preconditions previously put forward.

As you already know from our joint Bermuda communique, the United States, Great Britain, and France have agreed promptly to meet with the Soviet Union.

The Government of the United States approaches this conference with hopeful sincerity. We will bend every effort of our minds to the single purpose of emerging from that conference with tangible results toward peace – the only true way of lessening international tension.

We never have, we never will, propose or suggest that the Soviet Union surrender what is rightfully theirs.

We will never say that the peoples of Russia are an enemy with whom we have no desire ever to deal or mingle in friendly and fruitful relationship.

On the contrary, we hope that this conference may initiate a relationship with the Soviet Union which will eventually bring about a free intermingling of the peoples of the East and of the West – the one sure, human way of developing the understanding required for confident and peaceful relations.

Instead of the discontent which is now settling upon Eastern Germany, occupied Austria, and the countries of Eastern Europe, we seek a harmonious family of free European nations, with none a threat to the other, and least of all a threat to the peoples of Russia.

Beyond the turmoil and strife and misery of Asia, we seek peaceful opportunity for these peoples to develop their natural resources and to elevate their lives.

These are not idle words or shallow visions. Behind them lies a story of nations lately come to independence, not as a result of war, but through free grant or peaceful negotiation. There is a record, already written, of assistance gladly given by nations of the West to needy peoples, and to those suffering the temporary effects of famine, drought, and natural disaster.

These are deeds of peace. They speak more loudly than promises or protestations of peaceful intent.

But I do not wish to rest either upon the reiteration of past proposals or the restatement of past deeds. The gravity of the time is such that every new avenue of peace, no matter how dimly discernible, should be explored.

There is at least one new avenue of peace which has not yet been well explored – an avenue now laid out by the General Assembly of the United Nations.

In its resolution of November 28, 1953, this General Assembly suggested – and I quote – 'that the Disarmament Commission study the desirability of establishing a subcommittee consisting of representatives of the Powers principally involved, which should seek in private an acceptable solution * * * and report on such a solution to the General Assembly and to the Security Council not later than September 1, 1954.'

The United States, heeding the suggestion of the General Assembly of the United Nations, is instantly prepared to meet privately with such other countries as may be principally involved, to seek an acceptable solution to the atomic armaments race which overshadows not only the peace, but the very life, of the world.

We shall carry into these private or diplomatic talks a new conception.

The United States would seek more than the mere reduction or elimination of atomic materials for military purposes.

It is not enough to take this weapon out of the hands of the soldiers. It must be put into the hands of those who will know how to strip its military casing and adapt it to the arts of peace.

The United States knows that if the fearful trend of atomic military buildup can be reversed, this greatest of destructive forces can be developed into a great boon, for the benefit of all mankind.

The United States knows that peaceful power from atomic energy is no dream of the future. That capability, already proved, is here – now – today. Who can doubt, if the entire body of the world's scientists and engineers had adequate amounts of fissionable material with which to test and develop

207

their ideas, that this capability would rapidly be transformed into universal, efficient, and economic usage.

To hasten the day when fear of the atom will begin to disappear from the minds of people, and the governments of the East and West, there are certain steps that can be taken now.

Proposal for Joint Atomic Contributions

I therefore make the following proposals:

The governments principally involved, to the extent permitted by elementary prudence, to begin now and continue to make joint contributions from their stockpiles of normal uranium and fissionable materials to an International Atomic Energy Agency. We would expect that such an agency would be set up under the aegis of the United Nations.

The ratios of contributions, the procedures and other details would properly be within the scope of the private conversations I have referred to earlier.

The United States is prepared to undertake these explorations in good faith. Any partner of the United States acting in the same good faith will find the United States a not unreasonable or ungenerous associate.

Undoubtedly initial and early contributions to this plan would be small in quantity. However, the proposal has the great virtue that it can be undertaken without the irritations and mutual suspicions incident to any attempt to set up a completely acceptable system of worldwide inspection and control.

The Atomic Energy Agency could be made responsible for the impounding, storage, and protection of the contributed fissionable and other materials. The ingenuity of our scientists will provide special safe conditions under which such a bank of fissionable material can be made essentially immune to surprise seizure.

The more important responsibility of this Atomic Energy Agency would be to devise methods whereby this fissionable material would be allocated to serve the peaceful pursuits of mankind. Experts would be mobilized to apply atomic energy to the needs of agriculture, medicine, and other peaceful

208

activities. A special purpose would be to provide abundant electrical energy in the power-starved areas of the world. Thus the contributing powers would be dedicating some of their strength to serve the needs rather than the fears of mankind.

The United States would be more than willing – it would be proud to take up with others principally involved the development of plans whereby such peaceful use of atomic energy would be expedited.

Of those principally involved the Soviet Union must, of course, be one.

Out of Fear and into Peace

I would be prepared to submit to the Congress of the United States, and with every expectation of approval, any such plan that would –

First, encourage worldwide investigation into the most effective peacetime uses of fissionable material, and with the certainty that they had all the material needed for the conduct of all experiments that were appropriate.

Second, begin to diminish the potential destructive power of the world's atomic stockpiles;

Third, allow all peoples of all nations to see that, in this enlightened age, the great powers of the earth, both of the East and of the West, are interested in human aspirations first, rather than in building up the armaments of war;

Fourth, open up a new channel for peaceful discussion and initiate at least a new approach to the many difficult problems that must be solved in both private and public conversations, if the world is to shake off the inertia imposed by fear; and is to make positive progress toward peace.

Against the dark background of the atomic bomb, the United States does not wish merely to present strength, but also the desire and the hope for peace.

The coming months will be fraught with fateful decisions. In this Assembly; in the capitals and military headquarters of the world; in the hearts of men everywhere, be they governors or governed, may they be the decisions which will lead this world out of fear and into peace.

To the making of these fateful decisions, the United States pledges before you – and therefore before the world – its determination to help solve the fearful atomic dilemma, to devote its entire heart and mind to find the way by which the miraculous inventiveness of man shall not be dedicated to his death, but consecrated to his life.

Appendix II

TREATY ON THE NON-PROLIFERATION OF NUCLEAR WEAPONS

The States concluding this Treaty, hereinafter referred to as the 'Parties to the Treaty',

Considering the devastation that would be visited upon all mankind by a nuclear war and the consequent need to make every effort to avert the danger of such a war and to take measures to safeguard the security of peoples,

Believing that the proliferation of nuclear weapons would seriously enhance the danger of nuclear war,

In conformity with resolutions of the United Nations General Assembly calling for the conclusion of an agreement on the prevention of wider dissemination of nuclear weapons,

Undertaking to co-operate in facilitating the application of International Atomic Energy Agency safeguards on peaceful nuclear activities,

Expressing their support for research, development and other efforts to further the application, within the framework of the International Atomic Energy Agency safeguards system, of the principle of safeguarding effectively the flow of source and special fissionable materials by use of instruments and other techniques at certain strategic points,

Affirming the principle that the benefits of peaceful applications of nuclear technology, including any technological by-products which may be derived by nuclear-weapon States from the development of nuclear explosive devices, should be available for peaceful purposes to all Parties to the Treaty, whether nuclear-weapon or non-nuclear-weapon States,

Convinced that, in furtherance of this principle, all Parties to the Treaty are entitled to participate in the fullest possible exchange of scientific information for, and to contribute alone or in co-operation with other States to, the further development of the applications of atomic energy for peaceful purposes,

Declaring their intention to achieve at the earliest possible date the cessation of the nuclear arms race and to undertake effective measures in the direction of nuclear disarmament,

Urging the co-operation of all States in the attainment of this objective,

Recalling the determination expressed by the Parties to the 1963 Treaty banning nuclear weapon tests in the atmosphere, in outer space and under water in its preamble to seek to achieve the discontinuance of all test explosions of nuclear weapons for all time and to continue negotiations to this end,

Desiring to further the easing of international tension and the strengthening of trust between States in order to facilitate the cessation of the manufacture of nuclear weapons, the liquidation of all their existing stockpiles, and the elimination from national arsenals of nuclear weapons and the means of their delivery pursuant to a Treaty on general and complete disarmament under strict and effective international control,

Recalling that, in accordance with the Charter of the United Nations, States must refrain in their international relations from the threat or use of force against the territorial integrity or political independence of any State, or in any other manner inconsistent with the purposes of the United Nations, and that the establishment and maintenance of international peace and security are to be promoted with the least diversion for armaments of the world's human and economic resources,

Have agreed as follows:

Article I

Each nuclear-weapon State Party to the Treaty undertakes not to transfer to any recipient whatsoever nuclear weapons or other nuclear explosive devices or control over such weapons or explosive devices directly, or indirectly; and not in any way to assist, encourage, or induce any non-nuclear-weapon State to manufacture or otherwise acquire nuclear weapons or other nuclear explosive devices, or control over such weapons or explosive devices.

Article II

Each non-nuclear-weapon State Party to the Treaty undertakes not to receive the transfer from any transferor whatsoever of nuclear weapons or other nuclear explosive devices or of control over such weapons or explosive devices directly, or indirectly; not to manufacture or otherwise acquire nuclear weapons or other nuclear explosive devices; and not to seek or receive any assistance in the manufacture of nuclear weapons or other nuclear explosive devices.

Article III

1 Each non-nuclear-weapon State Party to the Treaty undertakes to accept safeguards, as set forth in an agreement to be negotiated and concluded with the International Atomic Energy Agency in accordance with the Statute of the International Atomic Energy Agency and the Agency's safeguards system, for the exclusive purpose of verification of the fulfillment of its obligations assumed under this Treaty with a view to preventing diversion of nuclear energy from peaceful uses to nuclear weapons or other nuclear explosive devices. Procedures for the safeguards required by this article shall be followed with respect to source or special fissionable material whether it is being produced, processed or used in any principal nuclear facility or is outside any such facility. The safeguards required by this article shall be applied on all source or special fissionable material in all peaceful nuclear activities within the territory of such State, under its jurisdiction, or carried out under its control anywhere.
2 Each State Party to the Treaty undertakes not to provide: (a) source or special fissionable material, or (b) equipment or material especially designed or prepared for the processing, use or production of special fissionable material, to any non-nuclear-weapon State for peaceful purposes, unless the

source or special fissionable material shall be subject to the safeguards required by this article.

3 The safeguards required by this article shall be implemented in a manner designed to comply with article IV of this Treaty, and to avoid hampering the economic or technological development of the parties or international co-operation in the field of peaceful nuclear activities, including the international exchange of nuclear material and equipment for the processing, use or production of nuclear material for peaceful purposes in accordance with the provisions of this article and the principle of safeguarding set forth in the preamble.

4 Non-nuclear-weapon States Party to the Treaty shall conclude agreements with the International Atomic Energy Agency to meet the requirements of this article either individually or together with other States in accordance with the Statute of the International Atomic Energy Agency. Negotiation of such agreements shall commence within 180 days from the original entry into force of this Treaty. For States depositing their instruments of ratification or accession after the 180-day period, negotiation of such agreements shall commence not later than the date of such deposit. Such agreements shall enter into force not later than eighteen months after the date of initiation of negotiations.

Article IV

1 Nothing in this Treaty shall be interpreted as affecting the inalienable right of all the Parties to the Treaty to develop research, production and use of nuclear energy for peaceful purposes without discrimination and in conformity with articles I and II of this Treaty.

2 All the Parties to the Treaty undertake to facilitate, and have the right to participate in, the fullest possible exchange of equipment, materials and scientific and technological information for the peaceful uses of nuclear energy. Parties to the Treaty in a position to do so shall also co-operate in contributing alone or together with other States or international organizations to the further development of the applications of nuclear energy for peaceful purposes, especially in the territories of non-nuclear-weapon States Party to

the Treaty, with due consideration for the needs of the developing areas of the world.

Article V

Each Party to this Treaty undertakes to take appropriate measures to ensure that, in accordance with this Treaty, under appropriate international observation and through appropriate international procedures, potential benefits from any peaceful applications of nuclear explosions will be made available to non-nuclear-weapon States Party to this Treaty on a non-discriminatory basis and that the charge to such Parties for the explosive devices used will be as low as possible and exclude any charge for research and development. Non-nuclear-weapon States Party to the Treaty shall be able to obtain such benefits, pursuant to a special international agreement or agreements, through an appropriate international body with adequate representation of non-nuclear-weapon States. Negotiations on this subject shall commence as soon as possible after the Treaty enters into force. Non-nuclear-weapon States Party to the Treaty so desiring may also obtain such benefits pursuant to bilateral agreements.

Article VI

Each of the Parties to the Treaty undertakes to pursue negotiations in good faith on effective measures relating to cessation of the nuclear arms race at an early date and to nuclear disarmament, and on a Treaty on general and complete disarmament under strict and effective international control.

Article VII

Nothing in this Treaty affects the right of any group of States to conclude regional treaties in order to assure the total absence of nuclear weapons in their respective territories.

Article VIII

1 Any Party to the Treaty may propose amendments to this Treaty. The text of any proposed amendment shall be

215

submitted to the Depositary Governments which shall circulate it to all Parties to the Treaty. Thereupon, if requested to do so by one third or more of the Parties to the Treaty, the Depositary Governments shall convene a conference, to which they shall invite all the Parties to the Treaty, to consider such an amendment.

2 Any amendment to this Treaty must be approved by a majority of the votes of all the Parties to the Treaty, including the votes of all nuclear-weapon States Party to the Treaty and all other Parties which, on the date the amendment is circulated, are members of the Board of Governors of the International Atomic Energy Agency. The amendment shall enter into force for each Party that deposits its instrument of ratification of the amendment upon the deposit of such instruments of ratification by a majority of all the Parties, including the instruments of ratification of all nuclear-weapon States Party to the Treaty and all other Parties which, on the date the amendment is circulated, are members of the Board of Governors of the International Atomic Energy Agency. Thereafter, it shall enter into force for any other Party upon the deposit of its instrument of ratification of the amendment.

3 Five years after the entry into force of this Treaty, a conference of Parties to the Treaty shall be held in Geneva, Switzerland, in order to review the operation of this Treaty with a view to assuring that the purposes of the Preamble and the provisions of the Treaty are being realized. At intervals of five years thereafter, a majority of the Parties to the Treaty may obtain, by submitting a proposal to this effect to the Depositary Governments, the convening of further conferences with the same objective of reviewing the operation of the Treaty.

Article IX

1 This Treaty shall be open to all States for signature. Any State which does not sign the Treaty before its entry into force in accordance with paragraph 3 of this Article may accede to it at any time.

2 This Treaty shall be subject to ratification by signatory States. Instruments of ratification and instruments of acces-

216

sion shall be deposited with the Governments of the Union of Soviet Socialist Republics, the United Kingdom of Great Britain and Northern Ireland and the United States of America, which are hereby designated the Depositary Governments.

3 This Treaty shall enter into force after its ratification by the States, the Governments of which are designated Depositaries of the Treaty, and forty other States signatory to this Treaty and the deposit of their instruments of ratification. For the purposes of this Treaty, a nuclear-weapon State is one which has manufactured and exploded a nuclear weapon or other nuclear explosive device prior to 1 January 1967.

4 For States whose instruments of ratification or accession are deposited subsequent to the entry into force of this Treaty, it shall enter into force on the date of the deposit of their instruments of ratification or accession.

5 The Depositary Governments shall promptly inform all signatory and acceding States of the date of each signature, the date of deposit of each instrument of ratification or of accession, the date of the entry into force of this Treaty, and the date of receipt of any requests for convening a conference or other notices.

6 This Treaty shall be registered by the Depositary Governments pursuant to Article 102 of the Charter of the United Nations.

Article X

1 Each Party shall in exercising its national sovereignty have the right to withdraw from the Treaty if it decides that extraordinary events, related to the subject-matter of this Treaty, have jeopardized the supreme interests of its country. It shall give notice of such withdrawal to all other Parties to the Treaty and to the United Nations Security Council three months in advance. Such notice shall include a statement of the extraordinary events it regards as having jeopardized its supreme interests.

2 Twenty-five years after the entry into force of the Treaty, a Conference shall be convened to decide whether the Treaty shall continue in force indefinitely, or shall be extended for an

additional fixed period or periods. This decision shall be taken by a majority of the Parties to the Treaty.

Article XI

This Treaty, the English, Russian, French, Spanish and Chinese texts of which are equally authentic, shall be deposited in the archives of the Depositary Governments. Duly certified copies of this Treaty shall be transmitted by the Depositary Governments to the Governments of the signatory and acceding States.

In witness whereof the undersigned, duly authorized, have signed this Treaty.

Done in .... at .... this ....
.day of ....

Appendix III

NUCLEAR POLICY STATEMENT BY PRESIDENT GERALD R. FORD, OCTOBER 28, 1976

SOURCE: *Public Papers of the President,* 1976, document 987, pp. 2763–78

We have known since the age of nuclear energy began more than 30 years ago that this source of energy had the potential for tremendous benefits for mankind and the potential for unparalleled destruction.

On the one hand, there is no doubt that nuclear energy represents one of the best hopes for satisfying the rising world demand for energy with minimum environmental impact and with the potential for reducing dependence on uncertain and diminishing world supplies of oil.

On the other hand, nuclear fuel, as it produces power also produces plutonium, which can be chemically separated from the spent fuel. The plutonium can be recycled and used to generate additional nuclear power, thereby partially offsetting the need for additional energy resources. Unfortunately – and this is the root of the problem – the same plutonium produced in nuclear powerplants can, when chemically separated, also be used to make nuclear explosives.

The world community cannot afford to let potential nuclear weapons material or the technology to produce it proliferate uncontrolled over the globe. The world community must ensure that production and utilization of such material by any nation is carried out under the most stringent security conditions and arrangements.

Developing the enormous benefits of nuclear energy while simultaneously developing the means to prevent proliferation is one of the major challenges facing all nations of the world today.

The standards we apply in judging most domestic and international activities are not sufficiently rigorous to deal with this extraordinarily complex problem. Our answers cannot be partially successful. They will either work, in which case we shall stop proliferation, or they will fail and nuclear proliferation will accelerate as nations initially having no intention of acquiring nuclear weapons conclude that they are forced to do so by the actions of others. Should this happen, we would face a world in which the security of all is critically imperiled. Maintaining international stability in such an environment would be incalculably difficult and dangerous. In times of regional or global crisis, risks of nuclear devastation would be immeasurably increased – if not through direct attack, then through a process of ever-expanding escalation. The problem can be handled as long as we understand it clearly and act wisely in concert with other nations. But we are faced with a threat of tragedy if we fail to comprehend it or to take effective measures.

Thus the seriousness and complexity of the problem place a special burden on those who propose ways to control proliferation. They must avoid the temptation for rhetorical gestures, empty threats or righteous posturing. They must offer policies and programs which deal with the world as it is, not as we might wish it to be. The goal is to prevent proliferation, not simply to deplore it.

The first task in dealing with the problem of proliferation is to understand the world nuclear situation.

More than 30 nations have or plan to build nuclear powerplants to reap the benefits of nuclear energy. The 1973 energy crisis dramatically demonstrated to all nations not only the dangers of excessive reliance on oil imports but also the reality that the world's supply of fossil fuels is running out. As a result, nuclear energy is now properly seen by many nations as an indispensable way to satisfy rising energy demand without prematurely depleting finite fossil fuel resources. We must understand the motives which are leading these nations, developed and developing, to place even greater emphasis than we do on nuclear power development. For unless we comprehend their real needs, we cannot expect to find ways of working with them to ensure satisfaction of both our and their legitimate concerns. Moreover, several nations besides the United States have the technology needed to produce both the benefits and the destructive potential of nuclear energy. Nations with such capabilities are able to export their technology and facilities.

Thus, no single nation, not even the United States, can realistically hope – by itself – to control effectively the spread of reprocessing technology and the resulting availability of plutonium.

The United States once was the dominant world supplier of nuclear material equipment and technology. While we remain a leader in this field, other suppliers have come to share the international market – with the U.S. now supplying less than half of nuclear reactor exports. In short, for nearly a decade the U.S. has not had a monopoly on nuclear technology. Although our role is large, we are not able to control worldwide nuclear development.

For these reasons, action to control proliferation must be an international co-operative effort involving many nations, including both nuclear suppliers and customers. Common standards must be developed and accepted by all parties. If this is not done, unrestrained trade in sensitive nuclear technology and materials will develop – with no one in a position to stop it.

We in the United States must recognize that interests in nuclear energy vary widely among nations. We must recognize that some nations look to nuclear energy because they have no acceptable energy alternative. We must be sure that our efforts to control proliferation are not viewed by such nations as an act to prevent them from enjoying the benefits of nuclear energy. We must be sure that all nations recognize that the U.S. believes that nonproliferation objectives must take precedence over economic and energy benefits if a choice must be made.

Previous action

During the past 30 years, the U.S. has been the unquestioned leader in worldwide efforts to assure that the benefits of nuclear energy are made available widely while its destructive uses are prevented. I have given special attention to these objectives during the past 2 years, and we have made important new progress, particularly in efforts to control the proliferation of nuclear weapons capability among the nations of the world.

In 1974, soon after I assumed office, I became concerned that some nuclear supplier countries, in order to achieve competitive advantage, were prepared to offer nuclear exports under conditions less rigorous than we believe prudent. In the fall of that year, at the United Nations General Assembly, the United States proposed that nonproliferation measures be strengthened materially. I also expressed my concern directly to my counterparts in key supplier and recipient nations. I directed the Secretary of State to emphasize multilateral action to limit this dangerous form of competition.

At U.S. initiative, the first meeting of major nuclear suppliers was convened in London in April 1975. A series of meetings and intensive bilateral consultations followed. As a result of these meetings, we have significantly raised international standards through progressive new guidelines to govern nuclear exports. These involve both improved safeguards and controls to prevent diversion of nuclear materials and to guard against the misuse of nuclear technology and physical protection against theft and sabotage. The United States has adopted these guidelines as policy for nuclear exports.

In addition, we have acted to deal with the special dangers associated with plutonium.

– We have prohibited export of reprocessing and other nuclear technologies that could contribute to proliferation.

– We have firmly opposed reprocessing in Korea and Taiwan. We welcome the decisions of those nations to forego such activities. We will continue to discourage national reprocessing in other locations of particular concern.

– We negotiated agreements for cooperation with Egypt and Israel which contain the strictest reprocessing provisions and other nuclear controls ever included in the 20–year history of our nuclear cooperation program.

– In addition, the United States recently completed negotiations to place its civil nuclear facilities under the safeguards of the International Atomic Energy Agency – and the IAEA has approved a proposed agreement for this purpose.

New initiatives

Last summer, I directed that a thorough review be undertaken of all our nuclear policies and options to determine what further steps were needed. I have considered carefully the results of that review, held discussions with congressional leaders, and benefited from consultations with leaders of other nations. I have decided that new steps are needed, building upon the progress of the past 2 years. Today, I am announcing a number of actions and proposals aimed at:

– strengthening. the commitment of the nations of the world to the goal of nonproliferation and building an effective system of international controls to prevent proliferation;

– changing and strengthening U.S. domestic nuclear policies and programs to support our nonproliferation goals; and

– establishing, by these actions, a sound foundation for the continued and increased use of nuclear energy in the U.S. and in the world in a safe and economic manner.

The task we face calls for an international cooperative venture of unprecedented dimensions. The U.S. is prepared to work with all other nations.

Principal policy decisions

I have concluded that the reprocessing and recycling of plutonium should not proceed unless there is sound reason to conclude that the world community can effectively overcome the associated risks of proliferation. I believe that avoidance of proliferation must take precedence over economic interests. I have also concluded that the United States and other nations can and should increase their use of nuclear power for peaceful purposes even if reprocessing and recycling of plutonium are found to be unacceptable.

Vigorous action is required domestically and internationally to make these judgments effective.

– I have decided that the United States should greatly accelerate its diplomatic initiatives in conjunction with

223

nuclear supplier and consumer nations to control the spread of plutonium and technologies for separating plutonium.

Effective nonproliferation measures will require the participation and support of nuclear suppliers and consumers. There must be coordination in restraints so that an effective nonproliferation system is achieved, and there must be cooperation in assuring reliable fuel supplies so that peaceful energy needs are met.

– I have decided that the United States should no longer regard reprocessing of used nuclear fuel to produce plutonium as a necessary and inevitable step in the nuclear fuel cycle, and that we should pursue reprocessing and recycling in the future only if they are found to be consistent with our international objectives.

We must ensure that our domestic policies and programs are compatible with our international position on reprocessing and that we work closely with other nations in evaluating nuclear fuel reprocessing.

– The steps I am announcing today will assure that the necessity [sic] increase in our use of nuclear energy will be carried on with safety and without aggravating the danger of proliferation.

Even with strong efforts to conserve, we will have increasing demands for energy for a growing American economy. To satisfy these needs, we must rely on increased use of both nuclear energy and coal until more acceptable alternatives are developed. We will continue pushing ahead with work on all promising alternatives such as solar energy but now we must count on the technology that works. We cannot expect a major contribution to our energy supply from alternative technologies until late in this century.

To implement my overall policy decisions, I have decided on a number of policies that are necessary and appropriate to meet our nonproliferation and energy objectives.

– First, our domestic policies must be changed to conform to my decision on deferral of the commercialization of chemical reprocessing of nuclear fuel which results in the separation of plutonium.

– Second, I call upon all nations to join us in exercising maximum restraint in the transfer of reprocessing and enrich-

224

ment technology and facilities by avoiding such sensitive exports or commitments for a period of at least 3 years.

– Third, new cooperative steps are needed to help assure that all nations have an adequate and reliable supply of energy for their needs. I believe, most importantly, that nuclear supplier nations have a special obligation to assure that customer nations have an adequate supply of fuel for their nuclear powerplants, if those customer nations forego the acquisition of reprocessing and uranium enrichment capabilities and accept effective proliferation controls.

– Fourth, the U.S. must maintain its role as a major and reliable world supplier of nuclear reactors and fuel for peaceful purposes. Our strong position as a supplier has provided the principal basis for our influence and leadership in worldwide nonproliferation efforts. A strong position will be equally important in the future. While reaffirming this Nation's intent to be a reliable supplier, the U.S. seeks no competitive advantage by virtue of the worldwide system of effective nonproliferation controls that I am calling for today.

– Fifth, new efforts must be made to urge all nations to join in a full-scale international cooperative effort – which I shall outline in detail – to develop a system of effective controls to prevent proliferation.

– Sixth, the U.S. must take new steps with respect to its own exports to control proliferation, while seeking to improve multilateral guidelines.

– Seventh, the U.S. must undertake a program to evaluate reprocessing in support of the international policies I have adopted.

– Finally, I have concluded that new steps are needed to assure that we have in place when needed, both in the U.S. and around the world, the facilities for the long-term storage or disposal of nuclear wastes.

Actions to implement our nuclear policies

In order to implement the nuclear policies that I have outlined, major efforts will be required within the United States and by the many nations around the world with an interest in nuclear energy. To move forward with these efforts, I am today taking a number of actions and making a number of proposals to other nations.

I Change in U.S. policy on nuclear fuel reprocessing

With respect to nuclear fuel reprocessing, I am directing agencies of the executive branch to implement my decision to delay commercialization of reprocessing activities in the United States until uncertainties are resolved. Specifically, I am:

– Directing the Administrator of the Energy Research and Development Administration (ERDA) to:

● change ERDA policies and programs which heretofore have been based on the assumption that reprocessing would proceed;

● encourage prompt action to expand spent fuel storage facilities, thus assuring utilities that they need not be concerned about shutdown of nuclear reactors because of delays; and

● identify the research and development efforts needed to investigate the feasibility of recovering the energy value from used nuclear fuel without separating plutonium.

II Restraint in the transfer of sensitive nuclear technology and facilities

Despite the gains in controlling proliferation that have been made, the dangers posed by reprocessing and the prospect of uncontrolled availability of plutonium require further, decisive international action. Effective control of the parallel risk of spreading uranium enrichment technology is also necessary. To meet these dangers:

– I call upon all nations to join with us in exercising maximum restraint in the transfer of reprocessing and enrichment technology and facilities by avoiding such sensitive exports or commitments for a period of at least 3 years.

This will allow suppliers and consumers to work together to establish reliable means for meeting nuclear needs with minimum risk, as we assess carefully the wisdom of plutonium use. As we proceed in these efforts, we must not be influenced by pressures to approve the export of these sensitive facilities.

III Assuring an adequate energy supply for customer nations

– I urge nuclear suppliers to provide nuclear consumers with fuel services, instead of sensitive technology or facilities.

Nations accepting effective nonproliferation restraints have a right to expect reliable and economic supply of nuclear reactors and associated, nonsensitive fuel. All such nations would share in the benefits of an assured supply of nuclear fuel, even though the number and location of sensitive facilities to generate this fuel is limited to meet nonproliferation goals. The availability of fuel-cycle services in several different nations can provide ample assurance to consumers of a continuing and stable source of supply.

It is also desirable to continue studying the idea of a few suitably-sited multinational fuel-cycle centers to serve regional needs, when effectively safeguarded and economically warranted. Through these and related means, we can minimize incentives for the spread of dangerous fuel-cycle capabilities.

The United States stands ready to take action, in cooperation with other concerned nations, to assure reliable supplies of nuclear fuel at equitable prices to any country accepting responsible restraints on its nuclear power program with regard to reprocessing, plutonium disposition, and enrichment technology.

– I am directing the Secretary of State to initiate consultations to explore with other nations arrangements for coordinating fuel services and for developing other means of ensuring that suppliers will be able to offer, and consumers will be able to receive, an uninterrupted and economical supply of low-enriched uranium fuel and fuel services.

These discussions will address ways to ensure against economic disadvantage to cooperating nations and to remove any sources of competition which could undermine our common nonproliferation efforts.

To contribute to this initiative, the United States will offer binding letters of intent for the supply of nuclear fuel to current and prospective customers willing to accept such responsible restraints.

– In addition, I am directing the Secretary of State to enter into negotiations or arrangements for mutual agreement on disposition of spent fuel with consumer nations that adopt responsible restraints.

Where appropriate, the United States will provide consumer nations with either fresh, low-enriched uranium fuel or make other equitable arrangements in return for mutual agreement on the disposition of spent fuel where such disposition demonstrably fosters our common and cooperative nonproliferation objectives. The United States seeks no commercial advantage in pursuing options for fuel disposition and assured fuel supplies.

Finally, the United States will continue to expand cooperative efforts with other countries in developing their indigenous nonnuclear energy resources.

The United States has proposed and continues to advocate the establishment of an International Energy Institute, specifically designed to help developing countries match the most economic and readily available sources of energy to their power needs. Through this Institute and other appropriate means, we will offer technological assistance in the development of indigenous energy resources.

IV Strengthening the U.S. role as a reliable supplier

If the United States is to continue its leadership role in worldwide nonproliferation efforts, it must be a reliable supplier of nuclear reactors and fuel for peaceful purposes. There are two principal actions we can take to contribute to this objective:

– I will submit to the new Congress proposed legislation that will permit the expansion of capacity in the United States to produce enriched uranium, including the authority needed for expansion of the Government-owned plant at Portsmouth, Ohio. I will also work with Congress to establish a framework for a private, competitive industry to finance, build, own, and operate enrichment plants.

U.S. capacity has been fully committed since mid-1974

with the result that no new orders could be signed. The Congress did not act on my full proposal and provided only limited and temporary authority for proceeding with the Portsmouth plant. We must have additional authority to proceed with the expansion of capacity without further delay.

– I will work closely with the Congress to ensure that legislation for improving our export controls results in a system that provides maximum assurance that the United States will be a reliable supplier to other nations for the full period of agreements.

One of the principal concerns with export legislation proposed in the last Congress was the fear that foreign customers could be subjected to arbitrary new controls imposed well after a long-term agreement and specific contracts for nuclear powerplants and fuel had been signed. In the case of nuclear plants and fuel, reliable long-term agreements are essential, and we must adopt export controls that provide reliability while meeting nonproliferation objectives.

V International controls against proliferation

To reinforce the foregoing policies, we must develop means to establish international restraints over the accumulation of plutonium itself, whether in separated form or in unprocessed spent fuel. The accumulation of plutonium under national control, especially in a separated form, is a primary proliferation risk.

– I am directing the Secretary of State to pursue vigorously discussions aimed at the establishment of a new international regime to provide for storage of civil plutonium and spent reactor fuel.

The United States made this proposal to the International Atomic Energy Agency and other interested nations last spring.

Creation of such a regime will greatly strengthen world confidence that the growing accumulation of excess plutonium and spent fuel can be stored safely, pending reentry into the nuclear fuel cycle or other safe disposition. I urge the IAEA, which is empowered to establish plutonium depositories to give prompt implementation to this concept.

Once a broadly representative IAEA storage regime is in operation, we are prepared to place our own excess civil plutonium and spent fuel under its control. Moreover, we are prepared to consider providing a site for international storage under IAEA auspices.

The inspection system of the IAEA remains a key element in our entire nonproliferation strategy. The world community must make sure that the Agency has the technical and human resources needed to keep pace with its expanding responsibilities. At my direction, we have recently committed substantial additional resources to help upgrade the IAEA's technical safeguards capabilities, and I believe we must strengthen further the safeguard functions of the IAEA.

– I am directing the Secretary of State and Administrator of ERDA to undertake a major international effort to ensure that adequate resources for this purpose are made available, and that we mobilize our best scientific talent to support that Agency. Our principal national laboratories with expertise in this area have been directed to provide assistance, on a continuing basis, to the IAEA Secretariat.

The terrible increase in violence and terrorism throughout the world has sharpened our awareness of the need to assure rigorous protection for sensitive nuclear materials and equipment. Fortunately, the need to cope with this problem is now broadly recognized. Many nations have responded to the initiatives which I have taken in this area by materially strengthening their physical security and by cooperating in the development of international guidelines by the IAEA. As a result of consultations among the major suppliers, provision for adequate physical security is becoming a normal condition of supply.

We have an effective physical security system in the United States. But steps are needed to upgrade physical security systems and to assure timely international collaboration in the recovery of lost or stolen materials.

– I have directed the Secretary of State to address vigorously the problem of physical security at both bilateral and multilateral levels, including exploration of a possible international convention.

The United States is committed to the development of the

system of international controls that I have here outlined. Even when complete, however, no system of controls is likely to be effective if a potential violator judges that his acquisition of a nuclear explosive will be received with indifference by the international community.

Any material violation of a nuclear safeguards agreement – especially the diversion of nuclear material for use in making explosives – must be universally judged to be an extremely serious affront to the world community, calling for the immediate imposition of drastic sanctions.

– I serve notice today that the United States will, at a minimum, respond to violation by any nation of any safeguards agreement to which we are a party with an immediate cutoff of our supply of nuclear fuel and cooperation to that nation.

We would consider further steps, not necessarily confined to the area of nuclear cooperation, against the violator nation. Nor will our actions be limited to violations of agreements in which we are directly involved. In the event of material violation of any safeguards agreement, particularly agreements with the IAEA, we will initiate immediate consultations with all interested nations to determine appropriate action.

Universal recognition of the total unacceptability of the abrogation or violation of any nonproliferation agreements is one of the most important steps which can be taken to prevent further proliferation. We invite all concerned governments to affirm publicly that they will regard nuclear wrongdoing as an intolerable violation of acceptable norms of international behavior, which would set in motion strong and immediate countermeasures.

VI U.S. nuclear export policies

During the past 2 years, the United States has strengthened its own national nuclear export policies. Our interests, however, are not limited to controls alone. The United States has a special responsibility to share the benefits of peaceful nuclear energy with other countries. We have sought to serve other nations as a reliable supplier of nuclear fuel and equipment. Given the choice between economic benefits and progress toward our nonproliferation goals, we have given, and will continue to give priority to nonproliferation. But there should be no incompatibility between nonproliferation and assisting other nations in enjoying the benefits of peaceful nuclear power if all supplier countries pursue common nuclear export policies. There is need, however, for even more rigorous controls than those now commonly employed, and for policies that favor nations accepting responsible nonproliferation limitations.

– I have decided that we will henceforth apply new criteria in judging whether to enter into a new or expanded nuclear cooperation:

• Adherence to the nonproliferation treaty will be a strong positive factor favoring cooperation with a nonnuclear weapon state.

• Nonnuclear weapons states that have not yet adhered to the nonproliferation treaty will receive positive recognition if they are prepared to submit to full fuel cycle safeguards, pending adherence.

• We will favor recipient nations that are prepared to forego, or postpone for a substantial period, the establishment of national reprocessing or enrichment activities or, in certain cases, prepared to shape and schedule their reprocessing and enriching facilities to foster nonproliferation needs.

• Positive recognition will also be given to nations prepared to participate in an international storage regime, under which spent fuel and any separated plutonium would be placed pending use.

Exceptional cases may occur in which nonproliferation will be served best by cooperating with nations not yet meeting these tests. However, I pledge that the Congress will not be asked to approve any new or amended agreement not meeting these new criteria unless I personally determine that the agreement is fully supportive of our nonproliferation goals. In case of such a determination, my reasons will be fully presented to the Congress.

– With respect to countries that are current recipients of U.S. nuclear supply, I am directing the Secretary of State to enter into negotiations with the objective of conforming these agreements to established international guidelines, and to seek through diplomatic initiatives and fuel supply incentives to obtain their acceptance of our new criteria.

We must recognize the need for effective multilateral approaches to nonproliferation and prevent nuclear export controls from becoming an element of commercial competition.

– I am directing the Secretary of State to intensify discussions with other nuclear suppliers aimed at expanding common guidelines for peaceful cooperative agreements so that they conform with these criteria.

In this regard, the United States would discuss ways of developing incentives that can lead to acceptance of these criteria, such as assuring reliable fuel supplies for nations accepting new restraints.

The reliability of American assurances to other nations is an asset that few, if any, nations of the world can match. It must not be eroded. Indeed, nothing could more prejudice our efforts to strengthen our existing nonproliferation understandings than arbitrary suspension or unwarranted delays in meeting supply commitments to countries which are dealing with us in good faith regarding effective safeguards and restraints.

Despite my personal efforts, the 94th Congress adjourned without passing nuclear export legislation which would have strengthened our effectiveness in dealing with other nations on nuclear matters.

– In the absence of such legislation, I am directing the Secretary of State to work closely with the Nuclear Regulatory Commission to ensure proper emphasis on nonproliferation concerns in the nuclear export licensing process.

I will continue to work to develop bipartisan support in Congress for improvements in our nuclear export laws.

VII Reprocessing evaluation program

The world community requires an aggressive program to build the international controls and cooperative regimes I have just outlined. I am prepared to mount such a program in the United States.

– I am directing the Administrator of ERDA to:

• Begin immediately to define a reprocessing and recycle evaluation program consistent with meeting our international objectives outlined earlier in this statement. This program should complement the Nuclear Regulatory Commission's (NRC) ongoing considerations of safety, safeguards and environmental requirements for reprocessing and recycling activities, particularly its Generic Environmental Statement on Mixed Oxide Fuels.

• Investigate the feasibility of recovering the energy value from used nuclear fuel without separating out plutonium.

– I am directing the Secretary of State to invite other nations to participate in designing and carrying out ERDA's reprocessing and recycle evaluation program, consistent with our international energy cooperation and nonproliferation objectives. I will direct that activities carried out in the U.S. in connection with this program be subjected to full IAEA safeguards and inspections.

VIII Nuclear waste management

The area of our domestic nuclear program dealing with long-term management of nuclear wastes from our commercial nuclear powerplants has not in the past received sufficient attention. In my 1977 Budget, I proposed a fourfold increase in funding for this program, which involves the activities of several Federal agencies. We recently completed a review to determine what additional actions are needed to assure availability in the mid–1980's of a federally-owned and managed repository for long-term nuclear wastes, well before significant quantities of wastes begin to accumulate.

I have been assured that the technology for long-term management or disposal of nuclear wastes is available but demonstrations are needed.

– I have directed the Administrator of ERDA to take the necessary action to speed up this program so as to demonstrate all components of waste management technology by 1978 and to demonstrate a complete repository for such wastes by 1985.

– I have further directed that the first demonstration depository for high-level wastes which will be owned by the

Government be submitted for licensing by the independent NRC to assure its safety and acceptability to the public.

In view of the decisions announced today, I have also directed the Administrator of ERDA to assure that the waste repository will be able to handle spent fuel elements as well as the separated and solidified waste that would result if we proceed with nuclear fuel reprocessing.

The United States continues to provide world leadership in nuclear waste management. I am inviting other nations to participate in and learn from our programs.

– I am directing the Secretary of State to discuss with other nations and the IAEA the possibility of establishing centrally located, multinationally controlled nuclear waste repositories so that the number of sites that are needed can be limited.

Increased use of nuclear energy in the United States

Even with strong conservation efforts, energy demands in the United States will continue to increase in response to the needs of a growing economy. The only alternative over the next 15 to 20 years to increased use of both nuclear energy and coal is greater reliance on imported oil which will jeopardize our Nation's strength and welfare.

We now have in the United States 62 licensed nuclear plants, providing about 9 percent of our electrical energy. By 1985, we will have from 145 to 160 plants, supplying 20 percent or more of the Nation's electricity.

In many cases, electricity from nuclear plants is markedly cheaper than that produced from either oil or coal-fired plants. Nuclear energy is environmentally preferable in a number of respects to other principal ways of generating electricity.

Commercial nuclear power has an excellent safety record, with nearly 200 plant-years of experience (compiled over 18 chronological years) without a single death from a nuclear accident. I have acted to assure that this record is maintained in the years ahead. For example, I have increased funds for the independent Nuclear Regulatory Commission and for the Energy Research and Development Administration for reactor safety and research and development.

The decisions and actions I am announcing today will help overcome the uncertainties that have served to delay the expanded use of nuclear energy in the United States. While the decision to delay reprocessing is significant, it will not prevent us from increasing our use of nuclear energy. We are on the right course with our nuclear power program in America. The changes I am announcing today will ensure that we continue.

My decisions today do not affect the U.S. program of research and development on the breeder reactor. That program assumes that no decision on the commercial operations of breeder reactors, which require plutonium fuel, will be made before 1986.

Conclusion

I do not underestimate the challenge represented in the creation of a worldwide program that will permit capturing the benefits of nuclear energy while maintaining needed protection against nuclear proliferation. The challenge is one that can be managed only partially and temporarily by technical measures.

It can be managed fully if the task is faced realistically by nations prepared to forego perceived short-term advantages in favor of fundamental long-term gains. We call upon all nations to recognize that their individual and collective interests are best served by internationally assured and safeguarded nuclear fuel supply, services, and storage. We ask them to turn aside from pursuing nuclear capabilities which are of doubtful economic value and have ominous implications for nuclear proliferation and instability in the world.

The growing international consensus against the proliferation of nuclear weapons is a source of encouragement. But it is certainly not a basis for complacency.

Success in meeting the challenge now before us depends on an extraordinary coordination of the policies of all nations toward the common good. The United States is prepared to lead, but we cannot succeed alone. If nations can work together constructively and cooperatively to manage our common nuclear problems, we will enhance our collective security. And we will be better able to concentrate our energies and our resources on the great tasks of construction rather than consume them in increasingly dangerous rivalrv.

Appendix IV

REMARKS BY PRESIDENT JIMMY CARTER ON NUCLEAR POWER POLICY, APRIL 7, 1977

SOURCE: Presidential Documents – Jimmy Carter, 1977, vol. 13, no. 15, Apr. 18, 1977

The President's Remarks Announcing His Decisions Following a Review of US Policy and a Question-and-Answer Session With Reporters. April 7, 1977

THE PRESIDENT. Good morning, everybody . . .

Nuclear power policy

The second point I'd like to make before I answer questions is concerning our Nation's efforts to control the spread of nuclear explosive capability. As far back as 30 years ago, our Government made a proposal to the United Nations that there be tight international controls over nuclear fuels and particularly those that might be made into explosives.

Last year during the Presidential campaign, both I and President Ford called for strict controls over fuels to prevent the proliferation – further proliferation of nuclear explosive capability.

There is no dilemma today more difficult to address than that connected with the use of atomic power. Many countries see atomic power as their only real opportunity to deal with the dwindling supplies of oil, the increasing price of oil, and the ultimate exhaustion of both oil and natural gas.

Our country is in a little better position. We have oil supplies of our own, and we have very large reserves of coal. But even coal has its limitations. So, we will ourselves

238

continue to use atomic power as a share of our total energy production.

The benefits of nuclear power, particularly to some foreign countries that don't have oil and coal of their own, are very practical and critical. But a serious risk is involved in the handling of nuclear fuels – the risk that component parts of this power process will be turned to providing explosives or atomic weapons.

We took an important step in reducing this risk a number of years ago by the implementation of the nonproliferation treaty which has now been signed by approximately a hundred nations. But we must go further.

We have seen recently India evolve an explosive device derived from a peaceful nuclear powerplant, and we now feel that several other nations are on the verge of becoming nuclear explosive powers.

The United States is deeply concerned about the consequences of the uncontrolled spread of this nuclear weapon capability. We can't arrest it immediately and unilaterally. We have no authority over other countries. But we believe that these risks would be vastly increased by the further spread of reprocessing capabilities of the spent nuclear fuel from which explosives can be derived.

Plutonium is especially poisonous, and, of course, enriched uranium, thorium and other chemicals or metals can be used as well.

We are now completing an extremely thorough review of our own nuclear power program. We have concluded that serious consequences can be derived from our own laxity in the handling of these materials and the spread of their use by other countries. And we believe that there is strong scientific and economic evidence that a time for a change has come.

Therefore, we will make a major change in the United States domestic nuclear energy policies and programs which I am announcing today.

We will make a concerted effort among all other countries to find better answers to the problems and risks of nuclear proliferation. And I would like to outline a few things now that we will do specifically.

First of all, we will defer indefinitely the commercial

reprocessing and recycling of the plutonium produced in US nuclear power programs.

From my own experience, we have concluded that a viable and adequate economic nuclear program can be maintained without such reprocessing and recycling of plutonium. The plant at Barnwell, South Carolina, for instance, will receive neither Federal encouragement nor funding from us for its completion as a reprocessing facility.

Second, we will restructure our own U.S. breeder program to give greater priority to alternative designs of the breeder other than plutonium, and to defer the date when breeder reactors would be put into commercial use.

We will continue research and development, try to shift away from plutonium, defer dependence on the breeder reactor for commercial use.

Third, we will direct funding of U.S. nuclear research and development programs to accelerate our research into alternative nuclear fuel cycles which do not involve direct access to materials that can be used for nuclear weapons.

Fourth, we will increase the U.S. capacity to produce nuclear fuels, enriched uranium in particular, to provide adequate and timely supplies of nuclear fuels to countries that need them so that they will not be required or encouraged to reprocess their own materials.

Fifth, we will propose to the Congress the necessary legislative steps to permit us to sign these supply contracts and remove the pressure for the reprocessing of nuclear fuels by other countries that do not now have this capability.

Sixth, we will continue to embargo the export of either equipment or technology that could permit uranium enrichment and chemical reprocessing.

And seventh, we will continue discussions with supplying countries and recipient countries, as well, of a wide range of international approaches and frameworks that will permit all countries to achieve their own energy needs while at the same time reducing the spread of the capability for nuclear explosive development.

Among other things – and we have discussed this with 15 or 20 national leaders already – we will explore the establishment of an international fuel cycle evaluation program so that

240

we can share with countries that have to reprocess nuclear fuel the responsibility for curtailing the ability for the development of explosives.

One other point that ought to be made in the international negotiation field is that we have to help provide some means for the storage of spent nuclear fuel materials which are highly explosive, highly radioactive in nature.

I have been working very closely with and personally with some of the foreign leaders who are quite deeply involved in the decisions that we make. We are not trying to impose our will on those nations like Japan and France and Britain and Germany which already have reprocessing plants in operation. They have a special need that we don't have in that their supplies of petroleum products are not available.

But we hope that they will join with us – and I believe that they will – in trying to have some worldwide understanding of the extreme threat of the further proliferation of nuclear explosive capability.

I'd be glad to answer a few questions.

Questions

Q Mr President, in the last administration there was some proposal to have regional reprocessing centers which seem, to some people, to put the emphasis on the wrong thing. Does this mean that you are going to not favor regional reprocessing centers? And, secondly, would you be prepared to cut off supplies of any kind of nuclear material to countries that go nuclear?

THE PRESIDENT Well, I can't answer either one of those questions yet. I have had detailed discussions with Prime Minister Fukuda, with Chancellor Schmidt, and also with Prime Minister Callaghan, for instance, just in recent days about a joint approach to these kinds of problems.

Obviously, the smaller nations, the ones that now have established atomic powerplants, have to have someplace either to store their spent fuel or to have it reprocessed. And I think that we would very likely see a continuation of reprocessing capabilities within those nations that I have named and perhaps others.

241

We in our own country don't have this requirement. It's an option that we might have to explore many, many years in the future.

But I hope that by this unilateral action we can set a standard and that those countries that don't now have reprocessing capability will not acquire that capability in the future. Regional plants under tight international control obviously is one option that we would explore. No decision has been made about that.

If we felt that the provision of atomic fuel was being delivered to a nation that did not share with us our commitment to nonproliferation, we would not supply that fuel.

Q Mr President, this carries an assurance, which you had said earlier, for an assured and adequate supply of enriched uranium to replace the need for plutonium. Do you foresee any kind of price guarantees also for underdeveloped and poorer countries so that the supply would not only be assured but at a reasonable price in case lack of reprocessing drove prices up?

THE PRESIDENT I don't know what the future prices of uranium might be. At the present time, of the enriched uranium that we produce, about roughly a third of it is exported, roughly a third of it is used for our domestic needs, and about a third of it is put in storage.

There has been an attenuation in recent years of the projected atomic powerplant construction in our own country. Other nations, though, are moving more and more toward atomic powerplants. But I can't tell you at this point that we will guarantee a price for uranium fuel that's less than our own cost of production, and that would be a matter of negotiation, perhaps even on an individual national basis.

I think that a standard price would probably be preferable, but then we might very well give a particular nation that was destitute or a very close friend of ours or who cooperated with us in this matter some sort of financial aid to help them with the purchase.

Q You also said last year a couple of times that you hoped to call a world energy conference to discuss this as well as a lot of other things. Do you foresee that happening any time in the near future?

THE PRESIDENT The item of nuclear powerplants and the handling of spent nuclear fuels and the curtailment of the possibility of new nations joining us in their capability for explosives will be on the agenda in the discussion in London early in May. And this will be a continuing process for us.

I might add that Secretary Vance also discussed this question with the Soviet authorities on his recent visit to Moscow and asked them to join in with us in enhancing the nonproliferation concept. Their response was favorable. But it will entail a great deal of negotiation, and I can't anticipate what the results of those negotiations might be. We obviously hope for it to apply to all the nations in the world.

Q Mr President, does your change in the domestic program mean that you will not authorize building the Clinch River breeder reactor in Tennessee?

THE PRESIDENT The Clinch River breeder reactor will not be terminated as such. In my own budget recommendations to the Congress, we cut back – I can't remember the exact figure – about $250 million out of the plutonium breeder reactor – the liquid metal fast breeder reactor program.

I think that we would continue with the breeder reactor program on an experimental basis, research and development, but not move nearly so rapidly toward any sort of commercial use.

We also, obviously, are concerned about the adverse economic impact of these changes. And in the areas that would lose employment that was presently extant, as we increase our capacity for producing nuclear fuels, even using new techniques, other than gaseous diffusion, like centrifuge and laser beam use, then we would try to locate those facilities over a period of time – it's a very slow-moving process – in areas like Clinch River where they might be adversely affected.

Q Mr President, does this mean that Canada selling nuclear power equipment to France and others, and France selling to others – does this mean that we will supply those other countries so that they won't make more power?

THE PRESIDENT Well, I might say that the two countries that most nearly share our commitment and even moved ahead of us in this field have been Canada – perhaps because

243

of their unfortunate experience with India – and Australia. Both those countries, along with us, have substantial supplies of nuclear fuel themselves.

I would hope that we could develop an interrelationship with other countries to remove the competitive aspect of reprocessing itself. There is obviously going to be continued competition among our own Nation, Canada, France, Germany, England, in the selling of atomic powerplants themselves. It ought to be a clearly drawn distinction between the legitimate and necessary use of uranium and other enriched fuels to produce electricity, on the one hand, and a prohibition against the use of those fuels for explosives.

It would be impossible, counterproductive, and ill-advised for us to try to prevent other countries that need it from having the capability to produce electricity from atomic power. But I would hope that we and the other countries could form an alliance that might be fairly uniform in this respect. I know that all the other countries share with us this hope.

The one difference that has been very sensitive, as it relates to, say, Germany, Japan, and others, is that they fear that our unilateral action in renouncing the reprocessing of spent fuels to produce plutonium might imply that we prohibit them or criticize them severely because of their own need for reprocessing. This is not the case. They have a perfect right to go ahead and continue with their own reprocessing efforts. But we hope they'll join with us in eliminating in the future additional countries that might have had this capability evolve.

Q Mr President, is it your assessment, sir, that some of the smaller nations that are now seeking reprocessing technology are doing so in order to attain nuclear weapon capability as well as or in addition to meeting their legitimate energy needs?

THE PRESIDENT Well, without going into specifics – I wouldn't want to start naming names – I think it's obvious that some of the countries about whom we are concerned have used their domestic nuclear powerplants to develop explosive capability. There is no doubt about it.

India, which is basically a peaceful nation, at least as far as worldwide connotations are concerned, did evolve an explosive capability from supplies that were given to them by the Canadians and by us.

And we feel that there are other nations that have potential capacity already for the evolution of explosives. But we are trying to make sure that from this point on that the increasing number of nations that might have joined the nuclear nations is attenuated drastically.

We can't undo immediately the mistakes that have been made in the past. But I believe that this is a step in the right direction.

Bibliography

For those who wish to pursue the plutonium issue in more detail, the following books and periodicals are important sources of information; many in turn cite further sources. *See also* the Notes, page 251.

BOOKS

1. *The Atomic Complex*, by Bertrand Goldschmidt (American Nuclear Society, La Grange Park, Ill., 1980)
2. *Atomic Shield, 1947–52*, by R. G. Hewlett and F. Duncan (Pennsylvania State University Press, Philadelphia, 1969)
3. *Atoms for the World*, by Laura Fermi (University of Chicago Press, Chicago, 1957)
4. *Bericht Wiederaufarbeitung*, by the Naturwissenschaftlergruppe NG 350 Marburg, and the Gruppe Oekologie Hannover (Gruppe Oekologie, Hannover, 1982)
5. *Britain and Atomic Energy 1939–1945*, by Margaret Gowing (Macmillan, London, 1964)
6. *The Curve of Binding Energy*, by John McPhee (Ballantine, New York, 1974)
7. *Decision-Making for Energy Futures*, by David Pearce *et al.* (Macmillan, London, 1979)
8. *Defended to Death*, edited by Gwyn Prins (Penguin, London, 1983)
9. *Energy and the European Communities*, by N. J. D. Lucas (Europa, London, 1977)
10. *Energy and War*, by A. B. and L. H. Lovins (Friends of the Earth, San Francisco, 1980)
11. *Energy in France*, by N. J. D. Lucas (Europa, London, 1979)
12. *Facts on Nuclear Proliferation* (Congressional Research Service, Library of Congress, Washington D.C., April 1975)

13. *Fast Breeder Reactors*, edited by P. V. Evans (Pergamon, Oxford, 1965)
14. *Global Fission*, by Jim Falk (Oxford University Press, Oxford, 1983)
15. *Independence and Deterrence*, by Margaret Gowing (Macmillan, London, 1974)
16. *India's Nuclear Estate*, by D. Sharma (Lancers, New Delhi, 1983)
17. *International Nuclear Fuel Cycle Evaluation* (International Atomic Energy Agency, Vienna, 1980)
18. *International Safeguards and Nuclear Industry*, edited by Mason Willrich (Johns Hopkins University Press, Baltimore, 1973)
19. *The Last Chance*, by William Epstein (Free Press, New York, 1976)
20. *Light Water: How the Nuclear Dream Dissolved*, by I. C. Bupp and J.-C. Derian (Basic Books, New York, 1978)
21. *The Liquid Metal Fast Breeder Reactor*, by T. B. Cochran (Resources for the Future, Baltimore, 1974)
22. *The Management of Radioactive Wastes from Fuel Reprocessing* (OECD Nuclear Energy Agency/International Atomic Energy Agency, Paris, 1972)
23. *Moving Toward Life in a Nuclear-Armed Crowd?*, by Albert Wohlstetter *et al.* (Pan Heuristics, Los Angeles, 1976)
24. *The New World, 1939–1945*, by R. G. Hewlett and O. E. Anderson (Pennsylvania State University Press, Philadelphia, 1962)
25. *The Nuclear Barons*, by Peter Pringle and James Spigelman (Michael Joseph, London, 1982)
26. *The Nuclear Fix*, by Thijs de la Court *et al.* (World Information Service on Energy, Amsterdam, 1982)
27. *Nuclear India*, by J. P. Jain (Radiant, New Delhi)
28. *Nuclear Power*, by Walter C. Patterson (Penguin, revised edition, London, 1983)
29. *Nuclear Power and the Environment:* Sixth Report from the Royal Commission on Environmental Pollution (Her Majesty's Stationery Office, London, 1976)
30. *Nuclear Power and Non-Proliferation*, by Michael J. Brenner (Cambridge University Press, Cambridge, 1981)

31. *The Nuclear Power Decisions*, by Roger Williams (Croom Helm, London, 1980)
32. *Nuclear Power Issues and Choices*, by the Nuclear Energy Policy Study Group (Ballinger, Cambridge, Mass., 1977)
33. *Nuclear Power: its Development in the United Kingdom*, by R. F. Pocock (Unwin/Inst. Nuc. Eng., London, 1977)
34. *Nuclear Power Struggles*, by William Walker and Måns Lönnroth (Allen & Unwin, London, 1983)
35. *Nuclear Proliferation Factbook* (Congressional Research Service, Library of Congress, Washington D.C., September 1980)
36. *Nuclear Theft: Risks and Safeguards*, by Mason Willrich and Theodore Taylor (Ballinger, Cambridge, Mass., 1974)
37. *Peaceful Nuclear Power and Weapons Proliferation* (Congressional Research Service, Library of Congress, Washington D.C., April 1975)
38. *The Plumbat Affair*, by Elaine Davenport *et al.* (André Deutsch, London, 1978)
39. *Plutonium, Power and Politics*, by Gene I. Rochlin (University of California Press, Berkeley, 1979)
40. *Policymaking in a Nuclear Program*, by Otto Keck (Lexington, Lexington, Mass., 1981)
41. *The Politics of Uranium*, by Norman Moss (André Deutsch, London, 1981)
42. *Preventing Nuclear Theft*, edited by R. B. Leachman and Philip Althoff (Praeger, New York, 1972)
43. *Rapport du Group du Travail sur la Gestion des Combustibles Irradiés*, by the Conseil Supérieur de la Sûreté Nucléaire (Ministère de la Recherche et de l'Industrie, Paris, 1983)
44. *Report on the Atom*, by Gordon Dean (Knopf, New York, 1953)
45. *Sourcebook on Atomic Energy*, by Samuel Glasstone (Van Nostrand Reinhold, third edition, New York, 1968)
46. *The Technology of Nuclear Reactor Safety*, by Theos Thompson and J. G. Beckerley (MIT Press, Cambridge, Mass., 1965 and 1973)
47. *Windscale Fallout*, by Ian Breach (Penguin, London, 1978)
48. *The Windscale Inquiry:* Report by the Hon. Mr Justice Parker (Her Majesty's Stationery Office, London, 1978)
49. *World Armaments and Disarmament: SIPRI Yearbook 1983:*

Stockholm International Peace Research Institute
(Taylor & Francis, London, 1983)

PERIODICALS

50. *Atom*, United Kingdom Atomic Energy Authority, 11 Charles II St, London SW1, UK.
51. *Bulletin of the Atomic Scientists*, 5801 S. Kenwood, Chicago 60637, Ill, USA.
52. *European Energy Report, Bracken House, Cannon St, London EC4P 4BY, UK.*
53. *Nuclear Engineering International*, Quadrant House, The Quadrant, Sutton, Surrey SM2 5AS, UK.
54. *Nuclear Europe*, PO Box 2613, CH–3001 Berne, Switzerland.
55. *Nuclear Fuel*, 1221 Avenue of the Americas, New York, NY 10021, USA.
56. *Nuclear News*, American Nuclear Society, 555 N. Kensington Ave, La Grange Park, Ill 60525, USA.
57. *Nucleonics Week*, 1221 Avenue of the Americas, New York, NY 10021, USA.

Notes

(Numbers in parentheses refer to titles in the Bibliography – see pages 247–250.)

Chapter 1

For basic history see (2), (5), (15) and (24), the official histories of the American and British nuclear programmes. See also (25), a recent critical history of these and other nuclear programmes, thoroughly indexed and massively annotated as to primary sources.

Page 5: The Acheson-Lilienthal report is reprinted in (37), pp. 127–202

6: ibid., pp. 142–3 and p. 159 and p. 167

Chapter 2

For basic science and engineering see (28), Chapters 1–3, in particular pp. 23–32, 66–74, and 86–9. See also (45), prepared for the United States Atomic Energy Commission.

Page 11: 'The Savannah River plant . . .': see *Nuclear Weapons Databook*, by Thomas B. Cochran et al., Ballinger, Cambridge, Mass., 1984.

'less satisfactory': but see Taylor comment, note p. 279ff

12: Britain: see (5) and (15)

13: 'B204': see (15), Volume 2 pp. 402–23

'Calder Hall': see (33), pp. 22ff and 124ff

'Low Separation Plant': see (15), pp. 423ff, in particular p. 424 and p. 441

'Soviet Union': see (25) pp. 57ff; 'France': see (25) pp. 125ff, (1) and (11)

251

Chapter 3

Page 15: See (28), pp. 66–9

16ff: 'Dream Machine', by William Lanouette, *Atlantic Monthly*, April 1983, gives a recent and detailed account of the thinking of American fast breeder people through the years

17ff: See (28), first edition, Macmillan, London, 1952, pp. 408–9

18ff: EBR–1, see (45), p. 599. Dean quotation, see (44), pp. 180–1

20: Gowing quotation, see (15), Volume 2, p. 266

'The Development and Future of Nuclear Energy', The Romanes Lecture by Sir John Cockcroft, 2 June 1950; Oxford University Press, 1950. Harwell, see (15), pp. 266ff. Note especially the quotation from a report by Risley engineers in 1953 (p. 269): 'At first sight this fast reactor scheme appears unrealistic. On closer examination it appears fantastic. It might well be argued that it could never become a serious engineering proposition.' The engineers at Risley took a view that frequently clashed with that of the physicists at Harwell

Atomic Energy Authority, see (31) and (33). Dounreay, see (33), pp. 75ff

21: BR–5: see *The Soviet Energy System*, by L. Dienes and T. Shabad, Winston/Wiley, Washington, D.C., 1979, pp. 161–2

Chapter 4

Page 23ff: See (25), pp. 111–3 and pp. 121–4

Eisenhower speech: reprinted in (37), pp. 214–20

24ff: Geneva conference: see (25), pp. 165–8. See also (3), a memoir by the official historian for the United States delegation

26: 'Atoms for the World': see previous note. National nuclear organizations: see, for instance, (25) and (41), in particular (25) pp. 210–6

Sweden: personal communication to author

27: India: see (16), (27) and (19) pp. 221ff. Power Reactor Demonstration Program: see (20) p. 33. British programme: see (33) pp. 48ff. 'Lucrative future': see (20)

29: 'Propaganda': see for instance *Nukespeak*, by S. Hilgartner *et al.*, Sierra Club, San Francisco, 1982; the style established by the United States Atomic Energy Commission served as a

model for other nuclear promoters elsewhere. 'Power plants':
see *Power Reactors in Member States*, published by the International Atomic Energy Agency, and the annual *Power Reactors*
supplement from (53). 'Fuel cycle': see (28) Chapter 3

30: 'Encouraging the others': see (20) for the classic example of
how American nuclear promoters fostered European nuclear
programmes in the 1950s, in order to persuade American
industry to support American nuclear programmes. 'Canada':
see 'The Management of Spent CANDU Fuel', W. W.
Morgan, *Nuclear Technology* vol. 24, 1974 p. 409

31ff: The classic study on the history and philosophy of the
international control of nuclear technology is *Atomic Safeguards*
by Allan McKnight, the first Inspector-General of the International Atomic Energy Agency, published by UNITAR, New
York, in 1971. See also *Nuclear Weapons Proliferation and the
International Atomic Energy Agency*, by the Congressional Research Service, Library of Congress, March 1976; (18), Chapters 1, 2, and 4; and (19)

34: France: see (1), pp. 130–9, and (25), pp. 125–36

China: see (25), pp. 204–10. Non-Proliferation Treaty: see
Atomic Safeguards (note p. 53) Chapter 4. The Treaty is also
reprinted in many other documents, for instance (18) pp. 255ff,
(30), pp. 259ff and (37) pp. 287ff

Chapter 5

Page 37: United States, see (20); Britain, see (31) and (33). Other
countries, see (1), (11), (25) and (41)

38: For those who read German, a remarkable recent study of
reprocessing technology, its history and status, is to be found in
(4), some 360 pages of minute detail compiled from a vast array
of primary sources – many of them, however, likewise in
German. The commentary on the following pages has been
greatly assisted by reference to (4), although supported by
other sources as cited below. For the history of Mol, see the
annual *Activity Reports* of the European Nuclear Energy Agency
until 1971, and thereafter the *Activity Reports* of the renamed
OECD Nuclear Energy Agency until the closedown in 1974.
See also (22), pp. 314ff, for data about plant processes. Note
that data about the total amount of fuel handled appears to be
inconsistent from source to source. This inconsistency of
official data recurs also in the context of other plants to be
discussed

44ff: United Reprocessors: see 'Reprocessing in Europe', by
G. Rossney, (53), April/May 1976, pp. 20–1, and 'The

European Reprocessing Cooperation in URG', by P. Zuehlke, (54), June 1982, pp. 14–6. West Valley: see 'Hot Wastes from Nuclear Power', by George G. Berg, *Environment*, May 1973, pp. 36–44, and 'West Valley: Remnant of the AEC', by Gene I. Rochlin *et al.*, (51), January 1978, pp. 17–26

46ff: Morris: see 'Nuclear Fuel Reprocessing: GE's Balky Plant Poses Shortage', by Robert Gillette, *Science*, 30 August 1974, pp. 770–1

48ff: B205: see 'BNFL's Reprocessing Work and Experience: Past, Present and Future', by C. Allday, (54), June 1982, pp. 11–13; 'Design and Development of the Windscale reprocessing plant', by B. F. Warner, Risley: UKAEA Production Group, 1967; (28) pp. 86–9; (39) pp. 72–3. Calder Hall: see (33) pp. 28ff; 'military . . .' see p. 30

'plutonium recovered . . .': see (8), p. 331.

B204: see 'Reprocessing of oxide fuel at Windscale', by T. G. Hughes and E. F. Kemp, (50), October 1970, pp. 206–11; 'Reprocessing – what went wrong?', by Simon Rippon, (53), February 1976, pp. 21–7; and *Report by the Chief Inspector of Nuclear Installations on the incident in building B204 at the Windscale works of British Nuclear Fuels Limited on 26 September 1973* (Cmnd 5703); Her Majesty's Stationery Office, London 1974

50: 'restored to service . . .'; see for instance Rippon, note p. 75, pp. 24 and 26. 'Write-off': see for instance *New Scientist*, 1 September 1977, p. 518

See 'Reprocessing spent fuel in France', by J. Megy, (53), March 1983, pp. 40–2. 'Strategic military material . . .': personal communication to author

51: 'French government decreed . . .': see (1), and (11), pp. 139ff. HAO: see 'Reprocessing of LWR Spent Fuel at la Hague 1976–82', by Maurice Delange, (54), January 1983, pp. 33–7

Chapter 6

Page 53ff: see Lanouette, note p. 29

60: see (46); (28), pp. 127–8 and 134–7; and *The Cult of the Atom*, by Daniel Ford, Simon and Schuster, New York, 1982, pp. 54–7

61: see UKAEA *Annual Reports* 1966 onwards

62: for conference see (53), April 1974, p. 251, and May 1974, pp. 419–22. See also *Fast Reactor Power Stations*, British

Nuclear Energy Society, London, 1975. France: see (53) as above, and 'Super-Phénix and Beyond', by Remy Carle, (54), January 1983, pp. 18–20

63: Soviet Union: see *The Soviet Energy System*, note p. 40; the conference references on p. 86; and 'Prototype fast breeder reactors operating in Europe and the USSR', by Simon Rippon, (53), June/July 1975, pp. 545–50. (The 'no explosion' answer was given in response to a question from the floor by the present author.)

63ff: SNR–300: see (4)), which also gives the history of earlier German activities, including the insertion of a fast-neutron core in the KNK research reactor at the Karlsruhe Nuclear Research Centre. See also (53), July 1976, for a series of articles on the Kalkar plant; and 'The Benelux-German fast reactor programme', by K. Traube, *Journal of the British Nuclear Energy Society*, July 1976, pp. 215–24

64ff: Japan: see 'Japan's Nuclear Industry at a Turning Point', *Japanese Finance and Industry*, Quarterly Survey by the Industrial Bank of Japan, No. 50, January–June 1982, and No. 51, July–September 1982. See also Lanouette, note p. 29

66: Seaborg report: see Lanouette, note p. 29

Shaw: see (13), pp. 35–65. Nixon Message: quoted in document cited

67: Clinch River: see (53), October 1974, pp. 835–65. See also Lanouette, note p. 29

Chapter 7

Page 68: Barnwell: see *Construction and operation of Barnwell Nuclear Fuel Plant, Allied Gulf Nuclear Services*, Docket No. 50–332, Directorate of Licensing (AEC), Washington, D.C.

69: WAK: see (39), p. 78

69ff: see *Zur Friedlichen Nutzung der Kernenergie*, published by the Federal Ministry for Research and Technology, 1977; *Bericht ueber das in der Bundesrepublik Deutschland geplante Entsorgungszentrum fuer ausgediente Brennelemente aus Kernkraftwerken*, published by the Deutsche Gesellschaft fuer Wiederaufarbeitung von Kernbrennstoffen mbH, Hannover, 1977; Chapter 1 of the Report by the Gorleben International Review, published by the State Government of Lower Saxony, Hannover, 1979; and *Der Gorleben-Report*, by H. Hatzfeldt *et al.*, Fischer, Frankfurt, 1979

70· Saluggia: see (39), pp. 75 and p. 78

70: see (26), p. 22, and 'Argentina is very close to producing its own nuclear bomb – with German help', by R. Denselow and D. C. Taylor, *The Listener*, 22 April 1982, pp. 2–4. See also (54), July–August 1983, pp. 31–3

71ff: see (16) and (27) for contrasting views

Chapter 8

Page 73: see, for instance, (28), pp. 140ff, and (14)

West Valley: see Berg, note p. 67. Hanford: see *Report on the Investigation of the 106T Tank Leak at the Hanford Reservation, Richland, Washington*, by the USAEC, Washington, D.C., July 1973. Fast breeder: see (21), pp. 9–22.

74: see *Proposed Final Environmental Statement, Liquid Metal Fast Breeder Program*, WASH–1535, USAEC, Washington D.C., December 1974

75: 'conferences': see for instance (42). Taylor: see (6). Willrich and Taylor: see (36)

76: Rosenbaum: see *Congressional Record*, 30 April 1974. Report reprinted, in slightly revised text, in (37), pp. 467–83. GAO: as cited

77: see Rosenbaum, note p. 106, in particular pp. 467–8 and 475–8; and (36), pp. 83–7

78: 'challenge': see for instance (36), p. 150. Concern was to mount rapidly in the following months; see for instance *The Plutonium Decision* by J.G. Speth *et al.*, Natural Resources Defense Council, Washington, D.C., September 1974

78ff: see 'Present State and Future Trends in Nuclear Fuel Reprocessing with a View to Economic Power Generation and Reliable Waste Disposal', by J. Couture *et al.*, *World Energy Conference*, Paper No. 4.2–24, September 1974

Chapter 9

Page 83ff: see *Newsweek*, 3 June 1974, pp. 36–8. See also (27), pp. 128–47; *India's Nuclear Option*, by A. Kapur, Praeger, 1976, pp. 213ff; and (25), pp. 374ff

84: quotation: see (27), Vol. II, pp. 369–70. American attacks: see for instance (25), p. 375, and (30), pp. 69–70

85: CIRUS: see (25), p. 379

86: France: see (19), pp. 226–7

'within fourteen months': see (25), pp 379–80 See also (53) June/July 1975, p. 497

87ff: see (30), pp. 94ff; and (25), pp. 380–1. The authors of (25) assert (pp. 203–4) that the London Suppliers' Group was a successor to another, even more secret, cartel, the Western Suppliers' Group. They say that the 1975 initiative came from Canada; Brenner (33) says that it came from Henry Kissinger

see (30), p. 96

Chapter 10

Page 89: Britain: see for instance (31) and (33). France: see for instance (11). United States: see for instance (20)

enrichment: see (30), Chapter 2, pp. 14ff; see (53), September 1973, pp. 673–4, for comments on capital costs – $1.5 billion per plant, plus dedicated power plants to supply the electricity required. The $8 billion estimate was offered orally at the November 1973 joint conference of the American Nuclear Society and Atomic Industrial Forum, attended by the present author

91: hearings: see Congressional Record, 21 March 1974, pp. S4178–4183. See also (36)

data books: see (37). ERDA and OTA: see documents cited. Symington Amendment: see (30), p. 91

92: see *Export Reorganization Act of 1976: Hearings before the Committee on Government Operations, United States Senate, on S. 1439, January 19, 20, 29, 30, and March 9, 1976.* Gilinsky: ibid., p. 404

93: Barnwell: see note p. 95

GESMO: see document cited; see also (30), pp. 102–3

Wohlstetter: see (23). Seamans: see (30), pp. 101–2

Chapter 11

Page 95: United Reprocessors: see Rossney, note p. 67, and British Nuclear Fuels Annual Report, 1972–73, p. 24

96ff: THORP: see *Financial Times*, 31 January 1975; (28), pp. 160–2; (48); (31), pp. 261–311; (7); and (10)

see *Daily Mirror*, 21 October 1975. Approval: see statement by Tony Benn, Secretary of State for Energy, Hansard, 12 March 1976. Friends of the Earth: see for instance *Nuclear Times*, Vol. 1 No. 1, FOE, London, May 1975, p. 1. Italy and

Japan: each had a Magnox power station supplied by Britain, whose fuel was returned to Windscale for reprocessing under the terms of the original contract

96: see (29)

98: quotation: see (29) as cited. Fast reactor: see (53), July 1976, p. 14

leak: see *Daily Telegraph*, 10 December 1976, and *Report on the silo leak at Windscale*, by the Chief Inspector of Nuclear Installations, Health and Safety Executive, London, 1980. Magnox: see Windscale Inquiry, transcript, 4 July 1977, pp. 4–8

99: finance: see (53), October 1976, p. 7

100: fast breeder: see *Energy Research and Development in the United Kingdom*, Energy Paper No. 11, Her Majesty's Stationery Office, London, 1976. Expenditure: see UKAEA *Annual Reports*

The present author participated in trip cited. Steam generators: see (53), February 1984, pp. 26–30

101ff: see (11), pp. 80–5, and *Le Dossier Electronucléaire*, by the Syndicat CFDT de l'Energie Atomique, Editions du Seuil, Paris, new edition 1980

102: Japan: see (53), April/May 1976, p. 9

103ff: fast breeders: see (53), August 1977, p. 10; 'Super-Phénix and Beyond', by R. Carle, (54), January 1983, pp. 18–20; (11), pp. 195–207

Chapter 12

Page 105: Kissinger: see (30), pp. 103–4. Carter: see (51), October 1976, pp. 8–14

106ff: Fri: see (30), pp. 104ff

107: Carter: see (30), p. 113

Chapter 13

Page 109: report: see (32)

110: quotation: see (32), p. 29. Carter: see (30), Chapter 4, pp. 116ff

111: commitments: see for example report, note p. 142; (11) on French policy; Japanese contracts with Britain and France, and domestic reprocessing plans; and Gorleben proposal in Federal Germany.

Carter: see (30), Chapter 4; statement, pp. 140ff

112ff: see Appendix for full text and transcript

113: see also (30), pp. 142–3

Chapter 14

Page 115: Soviet Union: see for instance (39), p. 22: the Soviet Union has always required that its foreign clients return their spent fuel to the Soviet Union. Ford: see (30), pp. 93–7; (53), March 1976, p. 5; and (25), pp. 380–2

French and West Germans: see (25), p. 381. Carter: see (30), pp. 130–2

116: conference: see (57), 5 May 1977. Document: see (53), May 1977, p. 14

117: 'drafted': see (30), p. 154. Salzburg: see (30), pp. 154–60; present author attended conference

118: see (38)

see for instance *Financial Times*, 9 May 1977, which reprinted the text of the 'Downing Street Declaration'; and (30), pp. 163–5 and 172ff

119ff: see (30), pp. 186ff

Chapter 15

Page 122: France: see (11). Federal Germany: see (40). Japan: see report, note p. 90

see (7); (47); (48); *The Windscale Inquiry* by Ian Breach, *New Scientist* publication, 1978; and 'The Windscale Report: A Nuclear Apologia', by W. C. Patterson, (51), June 1978, pp. 44–9

123: see also *What Choice Windscale?*, by Czech Conroy, Friends of the Earth, London, 1978

see (48), paragraph 9.5

125: 'extraordinary performance': author was present at inquiry

see British national dailies 7 March 1978, and *New Scientist*, 9 March 1978. Rebuttals: see for instance *The Parker Inquiry*, by W. C. Patterson and C. Conroy, Friends of the Earth, London, April 1978

¹26: Fawcett: see *The Guardian*, 20 April 1978

see Hansard, 22 March and 15 May 1978

127ff: see references, note p. 97. See also *Der Spiegel*, 28 February 1977, p. 66, and 14 March 1977, pp. 35–6

128: see 'Harrisburg ist Uberall', by Walter C. Patterson, (51), June 1979, pp. 9–11, and *Der Spiegel*, 26 March 1979, pp. 32ff, 2 April 1979, pp. 116–7, and 9 April 1979, pp. 19ff

129: see (53), June 1979, p. 4, and *Der Spiegel*, 25 June 1979, p. 99

Chapter 16

Page 131: uranium: see for instance (53), November 1978, pp. 35ff

132: contract: see Windscale Inquiry, BNFL document no. 179, 23 June 1977

Plutonium: see *Financial Times*, 26 April 1977

133ff: for background see 'Survey of Japan', (53), July 1973, pp. 541ff, and reference, note p. 90. See also 'Survey of Japan', (53), December 1979, in particular pp. 72–3

see for instance (30), pp. 146–7

134: 'rebuff': see for instance *Financial Times*, 10 February 1978. 'Coprocessing': see for instance (30), p. 313 note 8, and pp. 195–9

135ff: India: see (16) and (27)

Tarapur: see also (30), in particular pp. 109–204

136: Soviet heavy water: see (53), July 1979, p. 9

137ff: see 'Pakistan and the bomb', by Zalmay Khalilzad, (51), January 1980, pp. 11–16; *Der Spiegel*, 12 November 1979, 202–9; *The Guardian*, 22 June and 26 June 1979. Attacks: see *Financial Times*, 28 and 30 June 1979, and *The Guardian*, 28 and 30 June 1979. See also (30), pp. 201–2

see (30), pp. 203–4

138: Argentina: see (26), pp. 21–7, and references, note p. 99

139: South Korea and Taiwan: see (30), p. 100, and (25), pp. 380–1

Vela: see (51), April 1980, pp. 9–11

140ff: Salzburg: comment made to present author. CIVEX: see 'Proceedings of the Energy Technology Conference', Session 27, February 1978, Washington, DC; *Nuclear Power and the*

Proliferation Issue, by Walter Marshall, (50), April 1978, pp. 78–102; and (53), March 1978, p. 5

141ff: see *International Nuclear Fuel Cycle Evaluation*, INFCE/PC/2/1–9, published by the International Atomic Energy Agency, Vienna, February 1980; (30), pp. 136–7 and pp. 204–12; (53), April 1980, pp. 21–6; and *European Reactions to the International Nuclear Fuel Cycle Evaluation*, Congressional Research Service, Library of Congress, August 1982

142: quotations: see INFCE Summary Volume, pp. 23–4

143: see press summary cited in text

Chapter 17

Page 147: see for instance (28), pp. 140ff, and (14)

148: see 'Weekly Compilation of Presidential Documents', Vol. 17, No. 29, 20 July 1981, pp. 768–70

149: ibid.

quotation: see (53), November 1981, p. 9. Japan: see 'Confirmation of an unannounced change in the US policy on reprocessing and plutonium', State Department, 9 June 1982; see also *Washington Post*, 9 June 1982.

150: see (53), December 1981, pp. 7–9, and August 1982, pp. 30–3

costs: see *Analysis of the Department of Energy's Clinch River Breeder Reactor Cost Estimate*, US General Accounting Office, Washington, D.C., December 1982. Coalition: see 'Clinch River Breeder Project Draws Opposition of Strange Bedfellows', by William Lanouette, *National Journal*, 2 October 1982, pp. 1678–9

152: spent fuel: see *New York Times*, 22 September 1982. Bradford: see 'Emerging Federal Policy and its Effect on Safety in the States', speech delivered 19 October 1981, reprinted in *News Releases*, US Nuclear Regulatory Commission, Washington, D.C., week ending 28 October 1981

153: see *The Guardian*, 12 October 1981. 'Five tonnes': comment by Sir Walter Marshall to present author after 'Woman's Hour' broadcast, BBC Radio 4, October 1981. Comment: letter from R. V. Hesketh, Berkeley Nuclear Laboratories, CEGB, *The Times*, 30 October 1981

154ff: conference: see *Nuclear News*, September 1982, pp. 98ff. Super-Phénix: ibid., pp. 73–9, and 'Europe's Fast Breeders

Move to a Slow Track', by David Dickson, *Science*, 10 December 1982, pp. 1094–7. EdF: see *Financial Times*, 2 July 1982

154: catchphrases: see for instance 'Are Russia and France ahead in developing breeders?', published in the late 1970s by the Advanced Reactors Division, Westinghouse Electric Corporation

155: Kalkar: see (53), November 1982, pp. 6–7

Chapter 18

Page 158: see *World Inventories of Civilian Plutonium and the Spread of Nuclear Weapons*, Nuclear Control Institute, 1983. Britain: see (8), Appendix D, pp. 330–43

159: 'weapons-grade': see *Proof of evidence of Albert Wohlstetter on behalf of Friends of the Earth Ltd*, Windscale Inquiry, 6–7 September 1977, in particular paragraph 38.'riskier': because it emits more penetrating radiation. Some commentators have suggested a problem of 'pre-ignition' caused by spontaneous neutrons, producing a nuclear 'fizzle' instead of a major yield of fission energy; but Ted Taylor (q.v.) says this can be overcome by careful design.

see BNFL/P/1(Add 2), Sizewell Inquiry, pp. 2–3 and p. 8; see also BNFL *Annual Report*, 1983

161: costs: see (55), December 1983, quoted in *Financial Times*, 5 December 1983. Storage: see (53) August 1981, pp. 32–6

162: storage: see 'Nuclear giants fight over reprocessing contract', *New Scientist*, 10 February 1983, p. 355

Dounreay: see UK Atomic Energy Authority *Annual Report*, 1983. Cap la Hague: 'poorly matched': personal communication from Castaing commission member; see for instance letter in *New York Times*, 15 October 1982, from F. de l'Estang, president of Cogema, which says that the head end was 'designed to handle 250 tons a year'. All official data in the 1970s gave the design capacity as 400 tons a year; but the practical capacity of the design proved to be 250 tons a year. See also Megy, note p. 78, and Delange, note p. 79; and (55), 8 November 1982, pp. 3–4

163ff: 'next two instalments': see Megy and Delange, note p. 236, and (11), pp. 80–5. Contract: see WISE News Communiqué No. 158, 7 October 1982

164ff: see (43); (55), 3 January 1983; (57), 3 January and 20 January 1983; and (53), February 1983, p. 6

165: quotation: see (48), pp. 46–7

166: see (53), January 1983, p. 9; (56), February 1983, p. 101; WISE News Communiqué No. 166, 3 December 1982; (57), 11 November 1982; and (54), April 1983, pp. 35–9

167: plutonium fuel: see (55), 22 November 1982

168: WAK: see (53), December 1982, and (54), April 1983, pp. 35–9

utilities: see (55), 22 November 1982

169: Eurochemic: see (53), August 1982, p. 3, and (57), 17 February and 31 March 1983

Tokai Mura: see (53), December 1983, p. 14

170: State Department: see (55), 6 December 1982

Japan: see (55), 23 November 1981. India: see (16); *The Times of India*, Bombay, 21 October 1982; *The Hindu*, Madras, 23 October 1982; and (53), February 1983, p. 12

172: reprocessing: see (55), 14 February 1983

quotation: (16), p. 171

Chapter 19

Page 174: AEA: see Royal Commission on Environmental Pollution, *Supplementary Memorandum by the United Kingdom Atomic Energy Authority*, September 1975

'disorder': see (31). Fast breeder: see UK Atomic Energy Authority *Annual Reports*

175: THORP: see (48), and *What Choice Windscale?* by Czech Conroy, Friends of the Earth, London, 1978. Dounreay: see UK Atomic Energy Authority *Annual Reports; The transport of plutonium in the form of nitrate solution between Dounreay and Windscale*, Health and Safety Executive, 1979

176: statement: see Hansard, 29 November 1982; (50), February 1983, pp. 37–8

178: Clinch River: see (53), December 1983, pp. 3–4

Super-Phénix: see (53), June 1978, pp. 43ff

France: Electricité de France: see annual reports. Federal Germany: see (56), March 1982, pp. 60–1; (57), 11 March 1982; (53), November 1982, pp. 6–7; 'Advanced Reactor Development in the FRG', by H. H. Hennies, (54), April 1983, pp. 22–4; (53), June 1983, pp. 14–15

180: Soviet Union: see *Energy Daily*, 7 May 1982, and (56), November 1982, pp. 136–9

Japan: see *Nuclear Energy Committee, Energy Research Commission, Report III, on Plutonium Utilization in the Future*, 27 September 1982, translated from the Japanese by the Congressional Research Service, Library of Congress. Italy: see (53), October 1973; (57), 5 August 1982; (53), February 1983, p. 11

181: Large Demonstration Plant: see (56), September 1982, pp. 83–4

182: quotation: see (53), February 1983, p. 16

quotation: see Department of Energy press notice No. 106, 5 September 1983. British-French agreement: see *The Guardian*, 8 February 1984

Chapter 20

Page 184: US electricity: see *Washington Post*, 11 September 1982

185: Finon: see *Energy Policy*, December 1982, pp. 305–21

quotation: ibid., pp. 318–9

186: competition: see (49)

uranium: see *Wall Street Journal*, 14 September 1982, and *Uranium Resources, Production and Demand*, OECD, Paris, November 1983

187: weapons: see for instance (36), and (10), in particular Chapter 2 and its notes

exporters: see 'The wages of renouncing sin', by Ian Smart, (53), May 1983, pp. 40–2

188: Lammers: see *Energies*, 23 April 1982, pp. 3–7. Lenoir and Genestout: see *Science et Vie*, October 1982. For further information contact the Groupe Energie et Développement, rue du Chateau 72, 75010 Paris, tel. 770 02 32

189: Federal Germany: see *Der Spiegel*, Nr. 47/1982, pp. 71–6. See also 'Breeders and Bombs', *Science*, 10 December 1982, p. 1095

190: Dounreay: see also 'Pay your electricity bill and buy a bomb', by W. C. Patterson, *The Guardian*, 16 December 1982; level of CEGB participation should be 1 per cent of SBK, not of Super-Phénix as a whole, but point of article remains unaffected

Index

269

271

272